Taylor University

THE FIRST 150 YEARS

Taylor University

THE FIRST 150 YEARS

BY

WILLIAM C. RINGENBERG

WILLIAM B. EERDMANS PUBLISHING COMPANY
GRAND RAPIDS, MICHIGAN
AND
THE TAYLOR UNIVERSITY PRESS
UPLAND, INDIANA

Dedicated To

Those thousands of Taylor University faculty and staff members, trustees, students, and friends—both from the past and the present—whose names do not appear in the narrative of this history.

Recorded history tends to chronicle the deeds of the most visible individuals, especially those who leave written records behind them. Hopefully, this emphasis is more a statement of the limitations with which historians work than of their belief in what and who are important historically. It is basic Christian doctrine, as I understand it, that ultimate significance for each of us is determined less by human recognition or even by human achievement than by faithfulness in serving in one's divinely appointed corner of the world, regardless of the nature of that corner.

The sweetest lives are those to duty wed,
Whose deeds both great and small
Are close-knit strands of an unbroken thread,
Where love ennobles all.
The world may sound no trumpets, ring no bells (but)
The Book of Life the faithful record tells.

Elizabeth Barrett Browning

Portions of this manuscript appeared first in *Christianity Today,* the *Taylor Magazine,*

Old Fort News, and the *Mennonite Quarterly Review.*

Used by permission.

CONTENTS

The Taylor Towers: Past and Present

Up beyond the village border,
Pointing in the air,
Stand her towers seen far distant
When the day is fair.

When Melvin Hill wrote the Taylor song, he focused in his beginning lines upon the tower of the original administration building on the Upland campus. This building was known as the H. Maria Wright Hall. It was constructed in 1894 as the first major building on the new campus following the relocation of the school from Fort Wayne in 1893. Wright Hall burned to the ground in January of 1960; however, the Taylor school song referring to its celebrated tower continued to exist.

Now once again, after a lapse of a generation, Taylor students and alumni have a currently existing tower to think about when they sing the school song. The Rice Bell Tower is located at the center of campus and is double or twin in structure. Thus its location and architectural pattern are meant to communicate to all who see its form by day and its lights by night the central institutional conviction that the search for knowledge and truth in the universe is essentially a search for God and is dual in nature. This quest for God is both a rational one with our minds and an emotive one with our hearts. It is precisely this double-faceted quest that is symbolized by the twin spires reaching as it were from earth to heaven in this, the most important and most basic of all human quests. This quest finds ultimate fulfillment, of course, partly in this life and altogether in the next one. For to seek is to find and to find is to realize the deepest longings of the heart and mind.

H. Maria Wright Hall

Rice Bell Tower

Melvin Hill

FOREWORD

*I*t is of interest that when the respected historian Bernard DeVoto chose a topic for his opus on the history of the United States, he passed over the Civil War epic partly because the subject was already well worn but also because he felt that the year 1846 was "the year of decision." James K. Polk was an unashamed expansionist whose dream was fulfilled when Texas, New Mexico, and California territories were ceded by Mexico and the 49th parallel was negotiated from the slogan "54.40 or fight." This was the year the Mormon trek to the Great Salt Lake began, the winter of the Donner party, and the year that seamstresses gave up the needle and thimble for the new sewing machine of Elias Howe.

During that same "year of decision" a group of frontier citizens in Fort Wayne, Indiana, was planning the establishment of a college for young women. The very idea of educating women was novel in itself and all the more so by people busy carving out a civilization at the jumping-off part of the settled west. Through unusual foresight Fort Wayne Female College, the antecedent of Taylor University, was born in the wake of frontier revivalism and in the spirit of optimism that typified manifest destiny.

Dr. Ringenberg has done a great service in documenting the people and events that shaped the foundations that now constitute Taylor University. To have simply survived the century and a half since the Mexican War is an accomplishment, but to have done so within the dream and vision of being a Christian institution is truly remarkable. The temptations and seductions of modernity, the theological gyrations of the religious culture, the inevitable economic cycles of recession, depression, recovery and prosperity, and the vicissitudes of leadership all tend to warp, even destroy, institutions. Few survive these influences intact; most do not survive at all.

This history is a tribute to the faith, foresight, sacrifice, tenacity, resourcefulness, and talent of the scores of men and women in large and smaller positions whose contributions provide the prologue. Some are named; far more are forgotten except by God Himself. All would quickly add that the real forging influence behind their labors and whatever successes are documented has been the favor of the heavenly Father on the enterprise. Indeed they would warn those of us who steward the present that if we forget to glorify God "the house will be built in vain." All of these contributors would understand that their significance as mortals and their contribution to history finds its meaning somewhere in the Pauline phrase, "Paul planted, Apollos watered, but God gave the increase."

This volume is the abiding project of the Taylor University sesquicentennial celebration. It is a careful work, a balanced work and a reverent and loving work carried out by a scholar who to a large degree personifies the core of the college, its faculty. It is, after all, the work of scholars that is unique to higher education, and it is the faith commitment and character of these teachers that provide the integrity of the word *Christian* when used to describe an institution. It is not the financial stability, the buildings, the governance or, as they arrive as freshmen, even the students. It is the preserved learned culture deeply committed to God in its basic assumptions and lived out in fidelity to the gospel and model of Jesus Christ that provides the reason and uniqueness of the institution. Dr. Ringenberg has given us a framework of understanding and remembrance.

It is of necessity compressed history, but the theme is alive and inspiring, often mundane but heroic in the sense that the story of our civilization and the story of redemptive history has its significance in the lives of human beings created in the divine image and working together to the glory of God. Histories are dependent on the memories and records of ordinary people; time clouds memories and most go with us to the grave. We are indebted to Dr. Ringenberg for his careful research and his work of love in preserving the Taylor memory for this sesquicentennial celebration.

Jay Kesler
1996

PREFACE TO THE FIRST EDITION

This volume is an effort to trace the history of Taylor University from its beginnings as Fort Wayne Female College in 1846 through the 1970-71 school year in Upland, Indiana. Except for periodic historical sketches, little has been done in the past to record the history of the institution. The only major effect was a manuscript by Burt W. Ayres, which he titled "History of Taylor University." Ayres served as a Taylor professor and administrator during most of the school's first fifty years in Upland. His work is a personal account of the administrative history of the school between 1897 and 1942, and it is a prime source for the material of chapters five and six of this work.

Admittedly, this book is a "house organ." I have written it for the occasion of the college's 125th anniversary, and the institution itself has underwritten the project. Some of the facts discussed here will be of little interest to those who are not members of the Taylor "in group." Yet I trust that this volume will be more than just a work of parochial interest. Hopefully, it will also be a chapter in the religious and educational history of Indiana and the nation.

While I view the history of the college from a sympathetic perspective, I would not argue that its record is above criticism. As with most schools, it has had some serious weaknesses and faults, and those college historians who write in an excessively laudatory tone contribute little to a balanced sense of history. My purpose, therefore, has been to re-create the story as I see it, including the unattractive as well as the attractive parts. To do otherwise would serve neither the cause of historical scholarship nor Christian higher education.

The major sources of information for this study were the primary source materials in the Taylor archives. Especially helpful were the catalogs, the minutes of the trustees' meetings, the minutes of the yearly meetings of the North Indiana Conference of the Methodist Episcopal Church, the memoirs of Burt Ayres, the school newspapers, and the many miscellaneous items contained in the archival vertical file.

The materials for the Upland period of the school's history were adequate, but only a very limited amount of information was available on the Fort Wayne years. There are almost no catalogs before the 1880s, no school newspapers before the twentieth century, and very little information in the vertical file pertaining to the pre-Upland years. Efforts to locate source materials in Fort Wayne were largely fruitless. Fortunately, the school officials brought the trustees' minutes of the Fort Wayne period to Upland with them when they moved the school. Without these trustees' records, writing this history of the school's entire past would have been almost impossible; yet even with them there remain major gaps in the record of the early years.

Many people contributed to the making of this book. Special thanks go to History Department Chairman Dwight L. Mikkelson, Dean Gordon G. Zimmerman, and President Milo A. Rediger, who had the vision to believe in the value of a history of the school. Librarians Alice K. Holcombe and Lois A. Weed gave cheerfully of their time and knowledge in locating resource materials. I am very appreciative of the valuable stylistic help rendered by Professor Hazel Butz Carruth. Credit for help in locating and preparing the illustrative material belongs to Wilbur Cleveland, University Editor, and David Drury, Director of the Allen County-Fort Wayne Historical Museum. President Rediger, former President Evan H. Bergwall, former Professor and Dean George E. Fenstermacher, former Professor Frances Phillips, and many other faculty members and Upland residents gave helpful insights on the Upland years of the school. I also profited from the research on the late Fort Wayne period by former Dean and University Historian E. Sterl Phinney. Taylor University secretaries Mattie Sellers, Betty Ann Atkins, and Freda Heath typed and proofread the final draft of the manuscript. Two students gave special assistance: Thomas G. Jones served as a research assistant, and Gwendolyn Potter Tetrick compiled the index. Finally, I am indebted to my parents, Loyal R. and Rhoda R. Ringenberg; they not only carefully proofread the entire manuscript, but they also gave me my original interest in Christian higher education.

WCR
1973

PREFACE TO THE SECOND EDITION

his is a good time to publish a new edition of the Taylor history. The institution's sesquicentennial year amidst the approaching end of the current century and millennium suggest the appropriateness of retrospection. Furthermore the university's record in the recent past makes this a pleasant time to update its story, for by many criteria Taylor at the present is as prosperous as it has ever been.

In the preparation of this volume it has been a delight to work with both the William B. Eerdmans Publishing Company, the publisher of the first edition, and the university's still quite new—or newly resurrected—Taylor University Press, directed by Daniel Jordan. The current edition contains a new cover design, a new internal format, new preliminary material including an introduction by President Jay Kesler, an updated epilogue, appendices including faculty and trustee listings, and many new photographs. The seven chapters of the first edition continue largely intact with the few changes including 1) new material in chapter four on Sammy Morris, William Taylor, and the Fort Wayne College of Medicine—including prominent medical school alumnus, Alice Hamilton; and 2) a new ending—including an enlarged evaluation of Milo Rediger—to chapter seven. The major change, of course, is the addition of three chapters to summarize the major developments of the most recent twenty-five years. These developments include the growth in both the quality of the faculty and the role of the faculty in institutional governance, the development of an unusually effective psychological support environment for students as a part of the institutional commitment to "whole person education," the continually improving state of the physical plant to the point that for the first time it has become one of the most attractive features of the university, the ability of Jay Kesler and others to represent the Taylor experience in a way to attract an unprecedented number of students and capital campaign contributions, an institutional mind-set that increasingly thinks in global as opposed to insular terms, and the return to Fort Wayne to acquire a campus there during the 100th year since the move to Upland from that city.

The primary research materials for this project included the minutes of the meetings of the board of trustees, the issues of the *Taylor Magazine,* and oral interviews. Also significant were the college catalogs, presidential papers, correspondence with former officials, and the minutes of faculty meetings. The trustee minutes were essential; no college history can be told adequately without a careful reading of the records of the immediate deliberations and actions of the institution's ultimate governing group. Nicely completing these minutes were the news reports in the *Taylor Magazine*, the single best-written aid that I had in translating the primary documents into this secondary record. The major difference between the research for this edition and that for the original one is that this time the oral interviews have been so valuable. Many members of the Taylor community have served through much or all of the twenty-five year period recorded in these three chapters. Usually a story is more credible if it develops from a combination of oral and written sources than if it relies upon only one of these. Those sharing helpful insights included Stephen Bedi, Thomas Beers, David Biberstein, Leland and LaRita Boren, Joseph Brain, David Brewer, Stanley Burden, Walter Campbell, David Dickey, Richard Dugan, Betty Freese, William Fry, Herbert Frye, William Gerig, Donald Gerig, Jared Gerig, Wesley Gerig, Robert Gilkison, George Glass, Robert Gortner, Dale Heath, Timothy Herrmann, Robert Hodge, Charles Jaggers, Roger Jenkinson, Thomas Jones, Jay Kesler, Jack King, Charles (Tim) Kirkpatrick, Wynn Lembright, Connie Lightfoot, Philip Loy, Joe Lund, Stephen Messer, Timothy Nace, David Neuhouser, Robert Nienhuis, Herbert Nygren, Don Odle, Robert Pitts, Walter Randall, Jeff Raymond, Nelson Rediger, Loyal Ringenberg, Roger Ringenberg, Wesley Robinson, Joe Romine, Wally Roth, Jessica Rousselow, James Saddington, Dale Sloat, Al Smith, Richard Squiers, Richard Stanislaw, Kenneth Swan, and Daryl Yost.

Many people contributed in other ways to the making of this history. Daryl Yost, Charles Jaggers and Gene Rupp provided the same overall guidance, support, and freedom that had been given by Milo Rediger and Gordon Zimmerman on the original edition. Archivists Dwight Mikkelson and Bonnie Houser, Librarian David Dickey, Institutional Researcher Jack Letarte, and student assistants Heidi Oakley, Trudy Williams, and Betsy Boush provided generous assistance in locating materials. Several Taylor faculty and staff contributed important new material from their recent research: Alan Winquist and Heidi Clark on William Taylor, Tim Kirkpatrick on Sammy Morris and William Taylor, and Douglas Marlow on the Fort Wayne College of Medicine. Mildred Chapman provided very valuable service as the copy editor for the project. Donna Downs, Rebecca Ringenberg and William Stevenson served as proof readers. Brenda Mantha, Linda Mealy, Barbara Davenport, Lagatha Adkison, Gaylene Smith, and Marian Kendall supplied information from their administrative offices for the charts and appendices. Lavonna Shockey, Nancy Gillespie, and Darlene Jordan typed the manuscript. Roger Judd served as the desktop publisher. June Corduan, Dawn McIlvain and William Stevenson compiled the index. Angela Angelovska, James Garringer, Herbert K. Harjes, and Randal Dillinger with the assistance of Mary Ann McDaniels and Shelly Shrieve served as layout designers and major contributors to the sidebar features that are interspersed throughout the text. James Garringer designed and organized the photographic material.

Parts of the book appeared previously in article form in *Christianity Today,* the *Taylor Magazine, Old Fort News,* and the *Mennonite Quarterly Review* and are reprinted here by permission.

WCR
1996

Chapter One

BEFORE THE FEMALE COLLEGE

*F*ort Wayne Female College began in 1846 as a Methodist, female, Indiana institution; and in a sense its history dates from the year of its birth. Yet just as the life story of an individual is incomplete without a consideration of one's family background, so also the history of a college is not complete without a discussion of the larger cultural environment to which it belonged. Thus the purpose of this opening chapter is to present the general religious and educational context of which the school was a part.

1. THE SECOND GREAT AWAKENING AND COLLEGE FOUNDING

Fort Wayne Female College had its beginning during one of the most prolific periods of college founding in American history. While only nine colleges came into existence during the colonial period and less than thirty permanent schools had their origin before 1830, the second generation of the nineteenth century gave birth to over one hundred permanent institutions of higher education, and almost all of these began under the leadership of religious interests.[1]

One cannot fully appreciate the origin of the mid-nineteenth-century schools apart from the inspiration stemming from the second great national revival of religion. The Second Great Awakening (approximately 1795-1835) witnessed the intellectual conversion of American Protestantism from Calvinism to Arminianism. The early nineteenth-century revivals differed considerably in nature from those of the colonial period. The earlier revivalists had believed that they could do no more than wait for God to initiate a spirit of renewal, and when it came they keenly marveled at the "surprising" work of God. Not so with Charles G. Finney, the leading evangelist of the Second Great Awakening, and many of his contemporaries who believed that God and the revivalist worked as partners, with the latter responsible for assuming a very large role in leading

Charles Finney

Revivalist

The Second Great Awakening is arguably the defining experience in American religious history. Charles G. Finney (see the facing photo) was the most important revivalist of the awakening and its most representative figure. In the words of intellectual historian, Perry Miller, "for the mass of American democracy, the decades after 1800 were a continuing, even though intermittent, revival, [and promoting revival was] the dominant theme in America from 1800 to 1860. [Because revival was so important,] not Jefferson or Madison or Monroe led America out of the eighteenth century, but Charles G. Finney." Of the major evangelists in American history, none was more rational in approach and no other so set in motion a religious impulse that resulted in the establishment of scores of Christian liberal arts colleges.

1

men to seek God's forgiveness.

The new thought suggested not only that man was a free moral agent who could choose for or against Christian salvation, but also that he had the responsibility to work for the reformation of society. Revivalists like Finney taught that social concern should follow personal regeneration. Thus the pre-Civil War generation was one aflame with movements for social reform. Two of these reform movements were home missions and college founding. In a sense, the second of these developed to make the first unnecessary. Religious leaders from the East thought of the missionary movement to the frontier regions as a temporary enterprise. One of the major reasons for establishing colleges was to allow the new areas to train their own religious leaders.[2]

The missionary impetus resulting from the Second Great Awakening explains the origin of most of the mid-nineteenth-century colleges. This generalization applies more to those schools affiliated with traditionally Calvinistic denominations—Congregationalist, Presbyterian, and Baptist—than it does to the Methodist schools. The development of the "New Theology" in Calvinism led its proponents to assume a responsibility for converting the West; the Arminian theology of the Methodist Church and the fact that it had never been a state church made it a missionary church from its inception. The Methodists certainly participated in the Second Great Awakening, but they did not need it to arouse them to a sense of missionary responsibility. This they already possessed. That they were slow to found colleges before 1830 was due less to disbelief in the importance of missionary activity than to lack of belief in the need for educated missionaries and preachers.[3]

2. EARLY METHODISM AND HIGHER EDUCATION

Early nineteenth-century Methodism in this country enlisted its greatest support among the lower classes, especially those living in frontier areas. Because of the primitive nature of their life style, these people usually did not possess the time, money, or energy to devote to learning. What they could not obtain, many of them decried as inherently evil. Thus the Methodists of this period talked much of the dangers of "book learning"—especially about how it made ministers "less spiritual." They often confused being "less spiritual" with being less emotional than the average Methodist in one's approach to religion. From the days of John Wesley the Methodists had emphasized the experiential aspects of religion, yet one should note that the founders of the Church in England did not oppose education. In fact, Methodism had its origin and took its name in a collegiate setting (Oxford University).[4]

The anti-intellectual attitude in early Methodism had at least one advantage. It allowed the denomination to use enthusiastic but uneducated—and sometimes illiterate—circuit riders to carry the Gospel to the interior regions of America. Because in the early nineteenth century there always existed a greater supply of these zealots than of educated clergy, the Methodists (along with the Baptists, who used uneducated farmers as their preachers) increased much more rapidly in the Midwest than did the more intellectually sophisticated denominations, such as the Congregationalists and Presbyterians.

The change in the Methodist view toward education came in about 1830. With the rise in wealth and social status of the denomination, its members desired to have educational institutions like those of the higher-class denominations. Not to do so, they recognized, would likely mean a loss of many of the most able Methodist youths from the denomination. The Church also gradually accepted the idea that formal learning could be an asset rather than a liability to a minister.[5]

Changing attitudes led to action. In the early years of the nineteenth century the meetings of the Church's General Conference (the quadrennial meetings of all of American Methodism) gave scant attention to education. In 1820 the General Conference suggested that the annual conferences (the regional organizations that met yearly) make plans to establish literary institutions within their boundaries. Succeeding General Conferences continued to promote the cause of education. Before 1831 only nineteen Methodist institutions of secondary and college level existed. The Church established twenty-one more by 1835, and an additional nineteen by 1845. Thus a total of fifty-nine Methodist educational institutions had their origin before the beginning of Fort Wayne Female College. Most of these, however, either failed to develop into collegiate institutions or else failed to survive at all beyond a few years.[6]

One school that did survive and whose degree of success in survival explains much about the history of Fort Wayne College and Taylor University was Indiana Asbury College (renamed DePauw University in 1884). Asbury obtained its charter from the Indiana legislature on January 10, 1837, but planning for the institution had begun several years earlier. Five years before the beginning of Asbury, the Methodist General Conference of 1832 had created the Indiana Conference from all of the state of Indiana and a small section of Michigan. At that time the Indiana Conference could not claim one college graduate among its sixty circuit riders; however, the state leaders recognized the need to change

The first Methodist circuit riders came to Indiana from Kentucky and Ohio as early as 1801. Elmer Clark in his *Album of Methodist History* identifies the above structure as "the First Methodist Church in Indiana." It was located three miles from Charleston in Clark County.

Source: Elmer Clark, *An Album of Methodist History* (1952).

this situation. Consequently, the first session of the Indiana Conference, meeting at New Albany in October, 1832, appointed a committee to investigate the possibility of establishing a conference seminary.[7] The Methodists delayed serious planning for the new school for several years while they sought to gain some control of the Presbyterian-dominated state college at Bloomington. When they became certain that the Presbyterians—numerically a much smaller denomination in the state—were not going to give them an "equitable share" of influence in governing Indiana Asbury, they made serious plans to found their own school. In response to the invitation of Conference officials, five cities submitted bids to be the site of the new school. The officials accepted Greencastle's offer of $25,000 in 1836, and the next year the school opened a preparatory department with four barefoot boys in attendance. A regular college curriculum began in 1839.[8]

The first major building of Indiana Asbury College.

Source: Elmer Clark, *An Album of Methodist History* (1952).

But Indiana Asbury was a school for boys. It admitted no women until after the Civil War.[9] Coeducation was still a novel and controversial idea. Yet many of the state Methodists desired to have a denominational school to educate their young ladies. This, then, explains the reason for founding Fort Wayne Female College so soon after the beginning of the state's first Methodist institution. The Fort Wayne school remained a college exclusively for women for only a brief period, yet its early identification as a girls' institution probably led many Indiana Methodists to see it as "the other Methodist school." The "real" school (i.e., the one for the boys) was Indiana Asbury.

Other reasons help to explain Asbury's early ascendancy over Fort Wayne Female College. The most obvious one is that it began first. Its earlier beginning provided it with a lead in the competition for the general favor, including economic support, of Indiana Methodism, and the Fort Wayne school never overcame this original disadvantage.

The one Indiana Methodist school other than Indiana Asbury College and Fort Wayne Female College that did survive its mid-nineteenth-century period of infancy and that continues to the present is Moore's Hill College (now the University of Evansville). The Dearborn County institution began as Moore's

Hill Male and Female Collegiate Institute in 1854, when John L. Moore and other sponsors asked the Southeast Indiana Conference to assume control. The institution took its name from Moore's father, Adam, a Methodist local preacher who came from Maryland to southeastern Indiana in 1818. The school moved to its present Evansville site in 1919, when it was nearly defunct because of inadequate financing.[10]

3. COLLEGE FOR WOMEN

While the Methodists only slowly accepted the idea of an advanced education for their young men, they preceded much of the rest of society in their willingness to found schools (secondary and college) for young women. Until the last third of the nineteenth century, much of society sincerely feared the results of women pursuing a college education. Many of his contemporaries would have agreed with the opinion of President Henry P. Tappan of the University of Michigan, who as late as 1867 proclaimed that to allow women to compete in education and other areas of life on the same level as men was to "disturb God's order"; such a practice, he argued, would result in "defeminated women and demasculated men." Other critics feared that the rigorous demands of educational study would undermine the health of female scholars. One clergyman who held this view asked, "Must we crowd education upon our daughters, and for the sake of having them 'intellectual' make them puny, nervous, and their whole earthly existence a struggle between life and death?"[11]

> *To allow women to compete in education and other areas of life on the same level as men was to "disturb God's order"; such a practice, would result in "defeminated women and demasculated men."*
> — *A common view in the mid-1800s*

Few people accepted the idea of higher education for females before the post-Civil War period when colleges for women (e.g. Vassar, Wellesley, Smith) began to appear in the East and the Midwestern state universities began to accept coeds. Oberlin College became the first coeducational college when it opened its doors to women in 1837, and during the next quarter of a century most of the schools that followed the Oberlin precedent were small church-related institutions. Meanwhile, many small female colleges came into existence. The best of these included Georgia Female College, Macon, Georgia (1836); Mary Sharp College, Winchester, Tennessee (1850); and Elmira College, Elmira, New

York (1855).[12]

Preceding the women's college was the female seminary or academy. Secondary schools for girls began at least as early as 1727; however, few such institutions appeared before the Revolutionary War period. Some of these secondary schools were quite good (e.g. Troy Female Academy, Troy, New York; and Mount Holyoke Seminary, South Hadley, Massachusetts), but most of them offered only limited intellectual challenge. Gradually, the more able female students, realizing that they could not proceed to any higher level of education, began to criticize the superficiality of the curriculum and the incompetence of the teachers. Such dissatisfaction was a major factor leading to the growth of the female college.[13]

Taylor University was the first Protestant College to develop in northern Indiana.

Once the Methodists accepted the value of secondary and college education in general, they did not hesitate to promote female education. Methodist female education in America began a generation before the founding of Fort Wayne Female College in 1846. Perhaps the first Methodist female secondary school was the Elizabeth Female Academy, founded at Washington, Mississippi, in 1818. Of the forty-four Methodist secondary schools in existence by the Civil War, six were for women only and many of the others enrolled many female students. Meanwhile, in the 1840s and 1850s there began to appear in the Midwest such colleges for women as Albion College, Albion, Michigan (founded in 1849 as a school for girls only), and Ohio Wesleyan Female College (1853).[14]

Among the newly established female colleges were several in Indiana. In the decade after 1845, Indiana Methodists began no less than seven such schools. Colleges in addition to the Fort Wayne institution included Whitewater Female College, Centerville; Indiana Asbury Female College, New Albany; Bloomington Female College; Greencastle Female Collegiate Institute; Indianapolis Female College; and Indianapolis Female Collegiate Institute. Of the above institutions only Fort Wayne Female College became a permanent school.[15]

4. EDUCATION IN EARLY INDIANA

Pre-college education in Indiana before the Civil War was largely under private control. Churches or private individuals sponsored the earliest educational institutions. A few public schools appeared in northern Indiana after the beginning of statehood in 1816, but many of these charged tuition and operated much like private institutions. The average elementary teacher usually could claim no education other than his or her own primary-school learning and limited study in a secondary school. Secondary schools before 1850 were usually private seminaries or academies. Only a few public county seminaries existed before 1850, when high schools first began to appear. Not until 1900 did the public primary and secondary institutions become dominant in the state.[16]

This system of public education before the Civil War was grossly inadequate. Its inadequacy explains why many nineteenth-century "colleges" (including the Methodist school in Fort Wayne and Upland) often trained more secondary pupils than college students. They had to do this until the state assumed its full responsibility to educate secondary students. Otherwise, many of the pupils would have been unprepared to do college-level work. Indiana's poor record in public education before the Civil War was partly due to the fact that many sections of the state were still in a post-frontier stage of development. This situation characterized other states as well, yet few of them—none in the North—possessed as low an adult literacy rate as did Indiana. By the eve of the Civil War, the state was beginning to improve the quality of public education. The 1852 School Law provided for a state-supported system of free common schools, and by 1856 half of the state's incorporated towns and cities operated public school systems.[17]

Public higher education developed as slowly as did the state system of learning on the lower levels. Technically, the college begun at Bloomington in the 1820s was a public institution, but it received no financial allotment from the state before the Civil War. In this early period it operated more as a Presbyterian college than as a state institution, and it was a much less influential factor in the state's educational system than were the private colleges. In the last third of the nineteenth century in Indiana—as in the other Midwestern states—the public university began to overcome the early superiority of the private colleges and rise to a position of preeminence among the state's institutions of higher education.[18]

Eight private colleges that began in Indiana before the Civil War continue to the present. They are (in order of the year in which they received their state charters and with their present names) Hanover College (1833), Wabash College (1834), Franklin College (1836), DePauw University (1837), the University of

Methodist schools for women established in Indiana 1845-1855

Fort Wayne Female College

★ Whitewater Female College, Centerville

✩ Indiana Asbury Female College, New Albany

★ Bloomington Female College

✯ Greencastle Female Collegiate Institute

✩ Indianapolis Female College

✩ Indianapolis Female Collegiate Institute

Of the above institutions only Fort Wayne Female College became a permanent school.

Notre Dame (1844), Taylor University (1847), Earlham College (1850), Butler University (1850), and the University of Evansville (1854). The earliest of the schools began in the southern and central parts of the state because most of the early Indiana settlers lived in these regions. Of the educational institutions to develop in northern Indiana, Taylor University (Fort Wayne Female College) was the first Protestant college.[19]

Such was the cultural milieu of which Fort Wayne College became a part in 1846. The school began in an era when the Methodists and other denominations, rather than the state governments, dominated the efforts to found and maintain colleges and universities. This dominance existed in the founding of female colleges (as the Fort Wayne school was initially) and coeducational schools (as the college became in the early 1850s) as well as in the establishing of the traditional male schools.

Calhoun Street in old Fort Wayne.

[1] Donald G. Tewksbury, *The Founding of American Colleges and Universities before the Civil War* (New York, 1932), pp. 55, 70-72.

[2] William G. McLoughlin, Jr., *Modern Revivalism: Charles Finney to Billy Graham* (New York, 1959), p. 11.

[3] Wade Crawford Barclay, *History of Methodist Missions*, 6 vols. (New York, 1949-57), I, vii, 124-25.

[4] Francis I. Moats, "The Educational Policy of the Methodist Episcopal Church Prior to 1860" (unpublished Ph.D. dissertation, University of Iowa, 1926), pp. 154-55.

[5] Frederick Rudolph, *The American College and University: A History* (New York, 1962), pp. 55-57.

[6] Sylvanus Milne Duvall, *The Methodist Episcopal Church and Education Up to 1869* (New York, 1928), pp. 63-66.

[7] The term "seminary" in this early period usually referred to a secondary institution.

[8] H. N. Herrick and William W. Sweet, *History of the North Indiana Conference* (Indianapolis, 1917), pp. 25-41.

[9] *Ibid.*, p. 115.

[10] John W. Winkley, *Moore's Hill College* (Evansville, 1954), pp. 7-14, 65-68.

[11] Charles M. Perry, *Henry Philip Tappan, Philosopher and University President* (Ann Arbor, 1933), p. 362; Thomas Woody, *A History of Women's Education in the United States* (New York, 1929), II, 154.

[12] Woody, *Women's Education*, II, 139-47; George P. Schmidt, *The Liberal Arts College* (New Brunswick, 1957), pp. 129-31.

[13] Woody, *Women's Education*, I, 329, 441 and II, 138.

[14] Duvall, *Methodist Education*, pp. 65, 73,75; Michigan Conference of the Methodist Episcopal Church, *Minutes of the 1849 Annual Meeting* (Detroit, 1849), p. 23.

[15] Herrick and Sweet, *North Indiana Conference*, pp. 170, 180-82; Moats, "Methodist Educational Policy," pp. 252-53.

[16] John D. Barnhart and Donald F. Carmony, *Indiana: From Frontier to Industrial Commonwealth* (New York, 1954), I, 261-75 and II, 327, 329.

[17] *Ibid.,* II, 105-06.

[18] *Ibid.,* I, 271-72 and II, 327.

[19] Tewksbury, *Founding of American Colleges*, p. 213.

Chapter Two

BEGINNINGS IN FORT WAYNE

T he year 1846 was an exciting one in American history. Pioneers in record numbers were moving westward along the Oregon and California trails to establish homes in the American West. Those with "Oregon fever" were going to the Willamette River Valley in the Northwest; the Mormons—forced out of their most recent home in Nauvoo, Illinois—were moving to the valley of the Great Salt Lake; and already a few hardy souls were trekking to California in this period just before the discovery of gold. American troops also were moving westward—southwestward—to fight against Mexico in the war that continued into 1848.

Meanwhile, farther to the east, some Indiana Methodists and Fort Wayne citizens were experiencing an exciting year also. They were planning to open a college for women in the small city in the northern part of the state. While it was in 1846 that the North Indiana Conference of the Methodist Episcopal Church officially approved the decision to establish the school, it is more accurate to say that the college began in 1847 because in this latter year the institution obtained its charter from the state and held its first classes. Yet perhaps one can justify the use of the earlier date as the beginning year; most American colleges and universities place their founding date as early as possible. Apparently antiquity adds prestige to an educational institution.

As was the case with most nineteenth-century colleges, the school experienced much difficulty in its beginning years. The school leaders began construction on the college building early, but they delayed its completion for many years. The constant change of presidents also prevented needed stability in this beginning period; five presidents served in the first eight years. Especially disappointing was the failure of prominent Fort Wayne residents to support the institution adequately. The original board of trustees included many of the first citizens—

financially and otherwise—of the city, and it is difficult to imagine the school's not becoming a prosperous one (both in the initial years and later) if it had obtained their enthusiastic support. Perhaps many people were reluctant to support the college because they viewed it as "just" a girls' school. If this was the case, it may explain the early decision of the board first to add an affiliate college for boys and shortly thereafter to make the school coeducational.

1. The Making of the College

The northern Indiana Methodists at their annual Conference at LaPorte on September 16-22, 1846, officially voted to establish a female college in Fort Wayne; however, considerable planning and negotiating must have preceded the conference. Mention of the proposed Fort Wayne Female Seminary first appears in the *Fort Wayne Sentinel* on July 18, 1846, and the article reports that a meeting was held in the Hedekin House (a local inn) to discuss the formation of the school. Apparently, the North Indiana Conference had decided to establish a female college to complement the college for men at Greencastle and had solicited bids from Indiana towns wishing to have the school in their community. Perhaps the purpose of the July meeting at the Hedekin House was to decide the nature of the bid that the Fort Wayne officials would make to the Conference. The Fort Wayne leaders offered $13,000 in cash and three acres of land for the building site; apparently no other community submitted a better proposal. The contribution of three acres came from William Rockhill, one of the leading Fort Wayne citizens in the middle part of the nineteenth century. Rockhill later served for years as chairman of the school's board of trustees. Another active participant in the early planning for the college was Samuel Bigger, Whig governor of Indiana from 1840 to 1843. Bigger had moved to Fort Wayne to practice law after he had lost his bid for reelection in 1843. He died just one week before the Methodist leaders officially accepted Fort Wayne as the site of the school, but his law partner, Joseph K. Edgerton, became one of the original trustees.[1]

After the Conference at LaPorte accepted the Fort Wayne offer, it proceeded to pass several additional resolutions relative to the school. The Conference delegates decided to erect a building immediately, to appoint a financial agent—Rev. John S. Bayless, and to select fifteen trustees. These original trustees were William Rockhill, Joseph K. Edgerton, Asa Fairfield, Samuel Edsall, Henry Williams, John Walpole, Benjamin Mason, William G. Ewing, Lemual G. Jones, Samuel Shryock, Wesley Parks, James A. Whitcomb, G. S. Beswick, Thomas Sale, and R. W. Thompson. The first nine lived in Fort Wayne, and only the last four did not reside either in or near the city. The conference chose a diverse group of trustees; their criteria for selection apparently emphasized civic prominence at least as much as Methodist piety.[2]

The Board of Trustees began its work promptly. It held its first meeting on September 28, 1846. Only seven of the fifteen trustees attended the initial meeting, but these seven voted to establish five as the necessary quorum for transacting business and they then selected as temporary officers William Rockhill, chairman, and Joseph Edgerton, secretary. The board continued to meet frequently throughout the fall. In November it decided to open the school on May 1, 1847, and to announce this decision in the local newspapers. Meanwhile, the Fort Wayne public already had learned of the general nature and the proposed curriculum of the school from a statement appearing in a front-page advertisement in the *Fort Wayne Sentinel* as early as October 10, 1846. This same advertisement continued to reappear periodically in the *Sentinel* during the months prior to the beginning of classes.[3]

Another important item of business at the early trustees' meetings was the preparation of the application for a charter. The Indiana State Legislature approved the Articles of Incorporation of the female college on January 18, 1847, and specified that the incorporation would become effective on June 19, 1847. The charter gave the institution the right to grant "such Literary...degrees as are usually conferred by the best female colleges...." This statement probably meant that these degrees nearly (but not completely) equaled the standing of the Bachelor of Arts degrees conferred by the male colleges. The charter granted the North Indiana Conference—or such other conference or conferences that might develop from it—the right to fill all vacancies on the board. An interesting provision in the act limited to $50,000 the amount of real estate (apart from the college buildings) the school could own. The Michigan legislature placed a similar limitation on the Methodist school (Albion College) in its state in this early period. Apparently, some of the Midwestern state governments wanted to prevent the church colleges from becoming too well-endowed before the state universities established themselves as solid institutions.[4]

On the date designated for the charter to become effective, Smallwood Noel, a Fort Wayne justice of the peace, formally installed into office nine of the trustees. The remaining six trustees took the oath of office later. Now meeting officially, the board made permanent its selection of William Rockhill as president and Joseph K. Edgerton as secretary. It also selected Samuel Edsall as vice-president and Asa Fairfield as treasurer.[5]

Meanwhile, construction had been proceeding on the college building. Early

Samuel Bigger

Samuel Bigger, a Fort Wayne lawyer and former governor of Indiana (1840-43), was among the planners of the school. Though as a state legislator in the 1830s, the Presbyterian Bigger had opposed legislation that led to the establishment of the Methodist Indiana Asbury College, Bigger gave his support to the founding of the Fort Wayne Methodist school. He died shortly before the opening of the college.

Source: William W. Woollen, *Biographical and Historical Sketches of Early Indiana* (1883).

in the fall of 1846 Board Member Henry Williams drew the plans for the building, and in November the trustees solicited bids from contractors. They chose George E. Ross as the builder, and he agreed to complete the structure by June 25, 1847. In March the trustees anticipated that the building might not be ready for use by May, the month in which they originally had hoped to begin classes; consequently they arranged to rent temporarily another building. When the school officials laid the cornerstone on June 23, 1847, the building was not yet finished. Lack of funds delayed the completion of the building as originally designed. In March of 1849 the first two floors were only partially finished, and at least as late as 1858 the trustees still had not obtained the finances necessary to complete the building.[6]

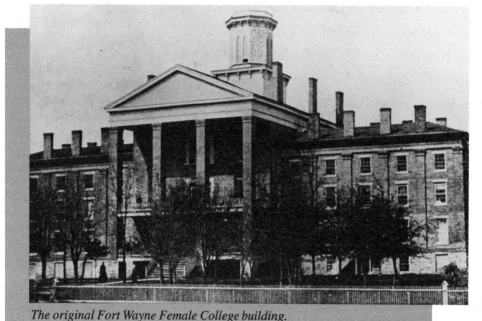

The original Fort Wayne Female College building.

The building when completed was a four-story structure of brick with stone trimmings. Its dimensions measured 160' x 80', and it had three sections. The central part (80' x 50') housed the recitation rooms, offices, and chapel. The two wings provided accommodations for eighty to one hundred boarders. The three-acre campus site (approximately equivalent to a city block of twelve lots) on which the building rested included five hundred feet of frontage on the St. Mary's River at the west end of Wayne Street, approximately one mile from the center of the city.[7]

While the building remained partially unfinished for several years, work on it was sufficiently complete by late summer, 1847, to permit the first school year to begin in the fall of 1847. It is probable that classes commenced in the summer of 1847. While the trustees originally had hoped to begin classes in May, they decided in that month to delay the opening date to June 14. I found no record explicitly stating that classes actually began in the summer, but a September 3 entry in the trustees' minutes allocates funds to Miss Elizabeth Irving and Miss Jane Irving for their "services" from July 15 to October 1. Since the Irving ladies taught at the school during the 1847-48 year, it is likely that the "services" they rendered were teaching services.[8]

Regardless of whether a summer term preceded it or not, the year 1847-48 was the first full school year in the institution's history. Approximately one hundred girls pursued studies in departments ranging from primary to college. The curriculum included courses in grammar, arithmetic, geography, Latin, Greek, French, Spanish, music, drawing, logic, algebra, chemistry, literary criticism, and history. The school charged a tuition rate of $22.50 per year for a student doing college-level work; it reduced the fee charge for the preparatory and primary pupils. Boarding students paid an additional $1.25 per week.[9]

The school charged a tuition rate of $22.50 per year for a student doing college-level work.

2. THE FORT WAYNE SETTING

At some point in recounting the history of the school, it is necessary to depart from the strictly institutional record to discuss the larger community in which the college existed. The history of Fort Wayne dates from the eighteenth century. The city's geography explains its origin. Like many other American inland cities, it developed at a terminal or connecting point on the early water transportation systems. Many Indians, explorers, and traders traveling from the Great Lakes to the Mississippi River followed the Maumee and Wabash Rivers. The Fort Wayne site was at the western terminal of the Maumee River and thus on the eastern end of the portage between the two river systems. The city took its name from General Anthony Wayne, who built a fort on the site in 1794, the same year in which he defeated the Indians in the decisive Battle of Fallen Timbers. Earlier in the century, however, French traders and soldiers had established a fort in the area. During the administration of Thomas Jefferson, Fort Wayne served as an Indian agency and trading house (national officials did not completely remove the Miami Indians to the trans-Mississippi reservations until the year the college began). In the 1820s the federal government established a land office in Fort Wayne, and the town became the seat of the newly created Allen County—a political division that then included much of northeastern Indiana. The population of the frontier county grew from 200 in 1825 to 1,000 in 1830 to 6,000 in 1840. In the latter year about 1,500 of the residents lived in Fort Wayne.[10]

The rapid growth of population in the decade of the 1830s resulted from the construction and beginning of operation in Fort Wayne of the Wabash and Erie Canal. This canal was one of the longest of the many such waterways that appeared in the Eastern and Midwestern states in the decades before the growth of railroad transportation; when completed it linked Lake Erie with the Ohio River. Construction of the canal in Fort Wayne began in 1832, and during the next few years 1000 to 2000 men worked on the project between Fort Wayne and Huntington.

By 1837 the canal reached Logansport, and six years later it was carrying boats from Lake Erie to Lafayette. In 1853, when the canal finally operated from Toledo to the Ohio River, its economic significance to Fort Wayne was declining because railroad lines by then linked the city with the East. The man responsible for building the section of the canal that went through the town was William Rockhill, one of the early leaders in the establishment of the college. In addition to collecting payment for the construction of the waterway, Rockhill profited by the increased value of his land which bordered the canal.[11]

Because of the canal Fort Wayne at mid-century had a disproportionately high percentage of foreign-born in its population. Opportunities to work on the construction of the canal attracted Irish immigrants, many of whom established permanent residence in the town. Many others came primarily because the canal made Fort Wayne unusually accessible. European immigrants could reach the town by an all-water route: north from New York City on the Hudson River, east through New York State on the Erie Canal, across Lake Erie to Toledo, and from Toledo to Fort Wayne via the Wabash and Erie Canal. In this period the Germans moved to the town in larger numbers than did any other foreign group. Allen County (to which Fort Wayne belonged) contained a higher percentage of foreign-born residents among its population in 1850 than did ninety of the other ninety-one Indiana counties. Even as late as 1870 the percentage of immigrants was two to three times as great in Fort Wayne as in the nation as a whole.[12]

While Fort Wayne at the time of the founding of the college was changing from a town to a city, it had not yet lost its status as a frontier settlement. Hogs still roamed freely through the streets. No public school existed in the city. Technically, one could describe the county "seminary" on Bar Street as public in nature, but the only public funds it received were the negligible sums collected as fines from lawbreakers and men seeking exemption from military service. Two of the city's private schools operated as pre-college women's institutions, namely Fort Wayne Female Seminary (founded in 1844 by a Presbyterian lady, Lydia Sykes) and St. Augustine's Academy (founded about 1846 by the Roman Catholics).[13]

The prominent religious groups in the city at mid-century were the Roman Catholics, the Lutherans, the Presbyterians, and the Methodists. The Catholics had come first. Since the early days of French settlement, Catholic missionaries had visited the region and maintained a Catholic influence. The Roman Church became a more significant force in the area, however, with the coming of the Irish and Germans during the canal period. Only part of the Germans professed Catholicism, however. Many of them were conservative Lutherans. The earliest

Protestant church in the town was the one established by the Presbyterians in 1831. During the 1830s most of the Protestants in the city worshipped in this church on the corner of Harrison and Berry Streets. In the 1840s the congregation became involved in the theological struggle that then was sweeping the Calvinistic denominations. The liberal, or "New Light," faction led by the theologian Nathaniel Taylor, the evangelist Charles Finney, and the popular preacher Lyman Beecher had been calling for a modification of the old Calvinism to allow for acceptance of the idea that God has given man an element of free will.[14] The most prominent of Beecher's many prominent children, Henry Ward, came to Fort Wayne in 1844, led a faction of the church in organizing the Second Presbyterian Church along "New Light" principles, and installed his younger brother Charles in its pulpit. Charles Beecher remained in Fort Wayne until 1851.[15]

Methodist preaching services in the Fort Wayne area began as early as the 1820s; but not until the 1830s did the Methodists become an official organization in the town, and not until the 1840s did they own their own church buildings. Perhaps the first to conduct Methodist meetings was James Holman, a local preacher from Boston who delivered sermons "without command of conference or bishop." Holman often preached in homes and small shops. In 1830 the Ohio Conference[16] established a mission station in Fort Wayne, and shortly thereafter the Methodists of the town received their first resident minister. The local congregation first worshipped in their own sanctuary in 1840, and seven years later they were able to organize a second congregation (the Wayne Street Methodist Church).[17]

> *Methodist preaching services in the Fort Wayne area began as early as the 1820s; but not until the 1830s did the Methodists become an official organization in the town, and not until the 1840s did they own their own church buildings.*

3. THE FIRST TRUSTEES

A number of the leading citizens of Fort Wayne served on the first college board of trustees. Some of them (e.g. William Rockhill, Samuel Edsall, Asa Fairfield, George Boyd—and later Samuel Brenton) worked very hard to promote the interests of the school. The contribution of others (e.g. William G. Ewing, Joseph K. Edgerton, and non-Fort Wayne citizen James Whitcomb) probably amounted to little more than allowing their well-known names to appear on the list of trustees.

Easily the most important of the first trustees was William Rockhill. With William G. Ewing he was one of the two leading citizens of Fort Wayne, and for

William Rockhill

William Rockhill was:
1) one of the two leading citizens in Fort Wayne at mid-century,
2) the single most significant individual in the pre-Civil War period of the college, and
3) to this day, the holder of one of the longest tenures as a board member of the college.

years the college trustees reelected him as president of the board. He came to Fort Wayne from New Jersey shortly after the federal government began selling land in the area in the 1820s. He soon became a county commissioner, a justice of the peace, a member of the first city council, and a representative to the state legislature. He also served as a city assessor, a director of the first bank in Fort Wayne, and an officer in the first gas company in the city; and he actively participated in the early efforts to found the public school system in the city. He held church membership with the local Presbyterian congregation. In 1846 the Democrat Rockhill defeated fellow college trustee and Whig William Ewing in the election for the congressional house seat from the Fort Wayne area. It is amazing that he found time to participate so actively and regularly in the early organization and administration of the college while he was serving in Congress from 1847 to 1849. Except for a brief interval in 1849, he presided over the college board from its inception through the 1850s.[18]

William Ewing became one of the first citizens of the city primarily because of his success in the fur-trading business. He and his brother George W. acquired a fortune from their trading endeavors, which extended as far west as the Missouri River. Ewing also participated actively in local affairs. He was the first man admitted to the bar in Allen County, the first judge of the probate court, and a treasurer of the county. He also held the office of state senator during the two years prior to his unsuccessful candidacy for a congressional seat. While no doubt existed about Ewing's prominence, there was some question about his integrity. At least one major historian of the early Midwest suggests that he used unscrupulous business practices in his intense competition with the American Fur Company. Like Rockhill, he attended the Presbyterian Church, but not as a member.[19]

The only man other than Rockhill to serve as board president in the early years was Samuel Edsall. He was the original vice-president of the trustees and one of the group's most regular participants. Edsall operated a flour mill and two sawmills along the canal, and he used the water from the canal to provide the power for them. He was one of the most prominent and active participants in the Methodist Church, and he also helped to organize the city fire company. He held many positions, including county sheriff, director of the Fort Wayne branch of the State Bank of Indiana, and member of the city school board.[20]

The original secretary of the board was Joseph K. Edgerton. He was a prominent Fort Wayne lawyer and one of the leading railroad promoters in the Midwest. Originally from Vermont, he began practicing law in New York City in 1839 and then moved to Fort Wayne (as did a number of other Easterners) when the canal brought increased economic opportunity to the city. As a lawyer he became the attorney for the city council, but he gained his greatest fame as a railroad promoter. He served as president of the Fort Wayne and Chicago Railroad Company, president of the Grand Rapids and Indiana Railroad Company, and director of the Ohio and Indiana Railroad Company. Later he helped to lead the effort to consolidate many of the smaller Midwestern lines into a larger system known as the Pennsylvania Railroad Company. Edgerton became the vice-president for its branches west of Pittsburgh. In 1862 he won election as a Democrat to represent the Fort Wayne area congressional district in Washington; his reelection bid in 1864 failed.[21]

The most prestigious member of the first board was James A. Whitcomb, governor of Indiana. The governor (he served in this position from 1843 to 1848) belonged to the Methodist Church, and at the time of his death (1852) he was vice-president of the American Bible Society. His administration gave major emphasis to education. He created the office of superintendent of common schools in 1843; a state school for the deaf and the Indiana Institute for the Education of the Blind also began during his administration. When he died he gave his personal library to DePauw University. The last three years of his life he spent as a United States Senator.[22]

Wayne Street Methodist Church.

Two of the remaining original trustees were George M. Boyd and Asa Fairfield; both participated actively on the board. Boyd was one of the ministers of the First Methodist Church. Fairfield, a veteran sailor, came to Fort Wayne in 1834 and operated the first boat—*The Indiana*—to pass through the Fort Wayne section of the Wabash and Erie Canal. He served as a director of the local bank, and reportedly he was a moderately wealthy man.[23]

Technically, Samuel Brenton was not an original trustee, but none of those on the first board did more to promote the institution than did he. As early as 1846 he served on various committees to organize the school; and in June, 1847, the board voted him a two-year tuition scholarship (to give to whom he wished) in

21

appreciation for his efforts for the school. Later the same summer he became a trustee, and promptly the board members elected him as its secretary. The trustees' minutes show him performing endless duties (e.g., obtaining equipment, recruiting teachers).[24]

Brenton was a native of Kentucky and an anti-slavery Methodist minister who expressed his views by political participation as well as by pulpit preaching. Born in Kentucky's Gallatin County, he served in the legislature of that state from 1838 to 1841. After a period of poor health he moved to Indiana, where he gained appointment as registrar of the land office in Fort Wayne. While in Fort Wayne during the 1850s, he three times won election to Congress, serving from 1851 to 1853 and from 1855 to his death in 1857. After he lost a reelection bid in 1852, he accepted the presidency of the Fort Wayne college. Thus Brenton was the third early trustee who—at one time or another—represented the Fort Wayne district in Congress.[25]

Given the high degree of public prominence, influence, and wealth of the early trustees of the college, it is difficult to understand why the school could not establish a solid economic base in Fort Wayne. Chapter one has already shown how the college received only minimal support from the Indiana Methodists because of the competition of Indiana Asbury College; equally crippling to the school was its inability to attract adequate support from the city from which it took its name and whose leaders were its leaders. Part of the explanation for this situation may be that some of the trustees failed to show the same degree of interest in promoting the college that they did in promoting the business and civic endeavors that gave them their personal prestige. If one can equate interest in the college with faithfulness in attending board meetings, then several of the best-known trustees possessed very little enthusiasm. Whitcomb attended none of the early board meetings, and Edgerton and Ewing went to very few of them.[26]

> *Samuel Brenton was the third early trustee who—at one time or another—represented the Fort Wayne district in Congress.*

4. THE LEADERSHIP OF THE COLLEGE

Tenures were very short for the early presidents of the college. In the period before 1855 no one remained in the position longer than two years. In fact, while the school remained in Fort Wayne only two men continued in office beyond a three-year term. This incontinuous leadership retarded the early development of the institution.

Alexander C. Huestis was the first president of the college and one of only two men to lead the Fort Wayne school on two different occasions. Huestis had come to Indiana from New York State where he had been both an educator and a wholesale grocer. Between his two terms as president, he taught in the school as professor of mathematics and natural science. There is evidence that the trustees considered both of his appointments as president to be temporary ones. Their first choice for the position in 1847 had been George M. Round of Georgia. While Round had declined the offer then, he stated that he would be willing to accept the position at some future date. The trustees hoped that that "future date" would be the next year (Round did accept the presidency a year later). Accordingly, the board named Huestis as president for one year only. During the first year of Huestis' second administration (1850-52), the trustees were actively looking for his replacement. After his years with the college, he reentered the wholesale grocery business and later became president of the Fort Wayne Savings Bank.[27]

Figure I

Presidents of Fort Wayne Female College and
Fort Wayne College

1.	Alexander C. Huestis	1847-1848
2.	George M. Round	1848-1849
3.	Cyrus Nutt	1849-1850
4.	Alexander C. Huestis	1850-1852
5.	Samuel T. Gillett	1852-1853
6.	Samuel Brenton	1853-1855
7.	Reuben D. Robinson	1855-1865
8.	W. F. Hemenway	1865-1868
9.	C. P. Hodge	1868-1869
10.	Reuben D. Robinson	1869-1870
11.	J. B. Robinson	1870-1871
	Levi Beers[a]	1871-1872
12.	Reuben D. Robinson	1872-1877
13.	William F. Yocum	1877-1888
14.	H. N. Herrick	1888-1890

[a] *Acting president.*

The trustees experienced as much difficulty in retaining Round in the presidency as they had had in hiring him in the first place. At the end of his one year as president (1848-49), he informed the board that "the interests of himself and family

Samuel Brenton

Samuel Brenton served as the president of the college during the two year interim between his tenure as a Whig congressman and his period as a congressional member of the new Republican party which had been founded in 1854. Like Abraham Lincoln, who also was a member of both parties, he strongly opposed slavery.

In 1850, Brenton was instrumental in establishing the Collegiate Institute for Men, the male division of Fort Wayne Female College. The two institutions became Fort Wayne College at the end of Brenton's tenure as president (1853-55.)

Following his 1855 congressional election, Brenton came under attack in print from the prominent publisher Horace Greeley, whose *New York Tribune* was the most widely-read newspaper in the country. Greeley later apologized to Brenton, but did so in typical Greeley fashion: ". . . [I am apologizing] not because it [the statement] was unjust, or that the effect was to injure the gentleman, but because it had resulted in exciting a sympathy for Mr. Brenton to which he is not entitled."

Source: B.J. Griswold, *The Pictorial History of Fort Wayne, Indiana,* vol. 1. (1917).

[would] require his absence from the state during the greater part of next year...." Therefore, he sought release from his responsibilities in July, 1849. The board at first granted him a leave of absence, but shortly thereafter—when the trustees found that they could hire Cyrus Nutt as president—they made Round's resignation permanent.[28]

Cyrus Nutt was in the early part of an impressive career as a Methodist minister and educator at the time of his appointment to the presidency of the female college. After he had graduated from Allegheny College in 1836, he had served as the first teacher in the new Indiana Asbury school. In the decade before coming to Fort Wayne, he had combined ministerial work with his teaching, but he invested his mature years mostly in educational endeavors. Following his year at Fort Wayne (1849-50), he became president of Whitewater College (near Richmond, Indiana) for five years, acting president of Indiana Asbury College for two years, and president of Indiana University for fifteen years (1860-75). Early in his career he had resided near the state university when he was the minister of the Bloomington Methodist Episcopal Church. One nineteenth-century historian of Indiana University described the young preacher as "earnest, diligent, and faithful and courteous."[29]

In many respects the state university under his leadership was little different from Fort Wayne College during the same period. Both schools operated from a Christian perspective with ministers providing most of the leadership, both governed student conduct with a rigid set of rules, and both required attendance at weekday chapel services and Sunday worship services.

Little is known of Nutt's presidency of the Fort Wayne school other than that he remained for only a brief period. Reportedly, he left after one year because the climate of northern Indiana "did not agree with Mrs. Nutt," a native of Kentucky.[30]

The record of Samuel T. Gillett (1852-53) further illustrates the tenuous nature of the presidency in the early years. Elected to the office in April of 1852, Gillett had scarcely entered his first full school year when in September, 1852, he submitted his resignation. However, he did complete the remainder of the school year.[31]

Perhaps from a desire to find a president who could give the college a much needed sense of stability or perhaps because the institution now likely could acquire a qualified man who had served the school well as a trustee, and perhaps for both reasons, the school invited Samuel Brenton to become president in April, 1853. The previous fall he had lost in a bid for reelection to his seat in the United States House of Representatives, and his term there had ended in March. During Brenton's two years as president, no issue created as much interest as the question of whether the institution should become coeducational. Brenton not only led the female school (and served as the treasurer of its board), but he also presided over the board of trustees of the new men's school (see the next section), which was holding its classes in the female building. With Brenton in a primary position of leadership in both institutions, it was natural that during this period the two schools became increasingly receptive to the idea of merger. When Brenton resigned the presidency to reenter politics, the official merger was virtually complete.[32]

Brenton was one of the most outstanding board members and presidents during the Fort Wayne years. Despite his somewhat precarious health he gave endlessly of his time and energy for the school during its first decade. His devotion and his ability commanded great respect. An early historian of Indiana Methodism described him as possessing "superior mental power" and as being "a true Christian"—both prime characteristics for a good Methodist college president.[33]

The faculty of the school in the early years usually consisted of three men teachers and two or three women teachers.

The faculty of the school in the early years usually consisted of three men teachers and two or three women teachers. The men taught most of the college-level courses: the president was ex officio the professor of moral and intellectual philosophy (roughly equivalent to what today we would call ethics and the social sciences), the second man instructed the students in ancient languages, and the third taught mathematics and the natural sciences. The ladies taught such "female subjects" as French, drawing, and music, and also supervised the primary department.[34]

The school expected the faculty to be willing to work long hours. The officials asked the teachers "at all times [to] exercise on the students...parental supervision." The female teachers who had no parents or relatives living in Fort Wayne agreed to "board in the college boarding house," to "govern the students," and to "aid [the students] in their studies."[35]

Faculty salaries varied widely in the beginning years. The first regular teacher recruited by the trustees received $150 and board for the 1847-48 year. President Huestis' salary as president for the period from October 1, 1847 to May 1, 1848, was $400. When prorated to a monthly basis, Huestis' salary approximately equaled President Nutt's $600 plus $100 housing allowance for 1849-50 and President Brenton's $700 for 1853-54. By the latter year the leading professors were earning $600. These figures compare favorably with those of other small Midwestern church colleges. For example, major professors earned salaries such as these: $400 at Hillsdale in 1847, $800 at Adrian in 1859, and $600 at Denison in 1865.

These, of course, are "paper" figures; as significant as the amount is whether the teachers received all of their contracted salaries. In general, professors in this period earned about as much as did preachers, but they worked with less job security than did ministers.[36]

5. THE MOVE TO COEDUCATION

The most significant organizational change in the early years of the school was the move from a female college to a coeducational institution. Officially the trustees did not make the change until 1855; however, they had been debating the subject and enrolling male students for several years before this date. As early as March, 1849, the board discussed admitting male students when Samuel Brenton proposed that the college establish a male department. The trustees temporarily tabled the subject until members of the faculty revived it the next spring. President Nutt, Vice-President Huestis, and Miss Kies sent a petition to the board asking that the school admit male students at the next term or as soon as possible; the board approved this request at its March 26, 1850, meeting. Thus in September, 1850, the school first enrolled men in Fort Wayne Female College; the male students studied in the branch of the school known as the "Collegiate Institute for Men."[37]

The most significant organizational change in the early years of the school was the move from a female college to a coeducational institution.

Meanwhile, plans were developing to change the men's division into a separate college. The delegates to the 1851 North Indiana Conference of the Methodist Episcopal Church favored this idea, and the denomination began to collect funds to make the plan a reality. The next year the female college trustees voted in favor of the plan to establish a Fort Wayne male college that held the same relationship to the North Indiana Conference as did the female college. The Indiana legislature passed an act on March 9, 1852, that incorporated the Fort Wayne Collegiate Institute as a men's school separate from Fort Wayne Female College. This incorporation became official on May 14, 1853.[38]

Despite their separate organization the schools operated as closely related institutions. The men's school held its classes in the female college building (the trustees of the collegiate institute obtained a fifty-year lease to use the recitation rooms; and they agreed to pay a rental fee of five hundred dollars for the first year and one hundred dollars for each year thereafter). The schools cooperated in the publication of their annual catalog for 1854-55, which they called *The Catalogue and Register of the Fort Wayne Female College and Fort Wayne Collegiate Institute.*[39]

The period of the dual institutions lasted for two years. On April 23, 1855, the trustees of the female college voted to merge the two schools, and shortly thereafter they agreed to assume the debts of the collegiate institute. The merger became official on October 10, 1855, and the new school took the name of Fort Wayne College.[40]

Thus ended the first period in the history of the college. After 1855 the school had a new name to reflect its changed admissions policy, and it had more stable and probably more dedicated leadership. Other factors changed little during the remainder of the Fort Wayne period. The school continued its early record of economic hardship, and it maintained its affiliation with the North Indiana Conference until 1890.

1   North Indiana Conference of the Methodist Episcopal Church, MS Minutes of the 1846 Conference (Archives of the North Indiana Conference of the Methodist Church, Marion, Indiana); *Fort Wayne Sentinel,* July 18, 1846, p. 2; Charles R. Poinsatte, *Fort Wayne During the Canal Era,* 1828-1855 (Indianapolis, 1969), p. 194; Staff of the Public Library of Fort Wayne and Allen County, *Samuel Bigger* (Fort Wayne, 1953), pp. 22-23.

2   North Indiana Conference of the Methodist Episcopal Church, Minutes of the 1846 Conference.

3   *Fort Wayne Sentinel,* October 10, 1846, p. 4; Fort Wayne Female College, MS Minutes of the Meetings of the Board of Trustees, September 28 and November 30, 1846 (Taylor University archives). Hereafter all references to the above trustees' minutes will appear as FWFCTM (Fort Wayne Female College Trustees' Minutes) for the period to October 10, 1855, and FWCTM (Fort Wayne College Trustees' Minutes) for the period after that date.

4   Indiana State Legislature, Act of Incorporation of Fort Wayne Female College, January 18, 1847 (copy in Taylor University archives); Herrick and Sweet, *North Indiana Conference,* pp. 170-71; *Laws of Michigan, 1841* (Detroit, 1841), p. 17.

5   FWFCTM, June 19, 1847.

6   *Fort Wayne Sentinel,* March 12, 1847, p. 1; FWFCTM, September 11, 1846, September 28, 1846, November 24, 1846, March 11, 1847, and March 1, 1849; FWCTM, April 18, 1856, March 31, 1858, and June 26, 1884.

7   FWCTM, October 23, 1884; Herrick and Sweet, *North Indiana Conference,* pp. 171-72; *Fort Wayne College Catalog,* 1870-71 (Fort Wayne, 1871), p. 16 and 1875-76 (Fort Wayne, 1876), p. 19. Hereafter all references to a Fort Wayne College catalog will appear as *FWCC.*

8   FWFCTM, May 11, 1847, and September 3, 1847; *Fort Wayne Sentinel,* January 22, 1848, p. 3.

9   Poinsatte, *Fort Wayne,* p. 194; Herrick and Sweet, *North Indiana Conference,* p. 172; FWFCTM, September 3, 1847.

[10] Poinsatte, *Fort Wayne*, pp. 1-3, 102-03.

[11] *Ibid.,* pp. 38, 63, 75, 77, 80, 255.

[12] *Ibid.,* pp. 227-29.

[13] *Ibid.,* pp. 132, 189-94.

[14] See Chapter 1, section one.

[15] Poinsatte, *Fort Wayne*, pp. 148-59.

[16] The Indiana Conference was not formed until 1832.

[17] F. C. Holliday, *Indiana Methodism* (Cincinnati, 1873), pp. 236-38; Poinsatte, *Fort Wayne*, pp. 160-62.

[18] United States Government Printing Office, *Biographical Directory of the American Congress, 1774-1961* (Washington, 1961), p. 1533; B. J. Griswold, *Pictorial History of Fort Wayne, Indiana* (Chicago, 1917), I, 256, 280, 326, 395, 424; Poinsatte, *Fort Wayne*, p. 215.

[19] Griswold, *Fort Wayne*, I, 254, 266, 287, 345; R. Carlyle Buley, *The Old Northwest: Pioneer Period, 1815-1840* (Bloomington, 1951), II, 320-22; Poinsatte, *Fort Wayne*, pp. 91, 155.

[20] Griswold, *Fort Wayne*, I. 260, 313, 326, 444; Poinsatte, *Fort Wayne*, pp. 161, 246.

[21] *Biographical Directory of the American Congress,* p. 846; Poinsatte, *Fort Wayne*, pp. 123, 234, 260.

[22] "James Whitcomb" in *Dictionary of American Biography,* ed. by Allen Johnson and Dumas Malone (New York, 1928-58), XX, 83; Indiana, *Twenty-Second Biennial Report of the State Superintendent of Public Instruction* (1905), p. 696.

[23] Griswold, *Fort Wayne*, I. 294, 320-21, 324, 326.

[24] FWFCTM, June 24, 1847.

[25] *Biographical Directory of the American Congress,* p. 594; Poinsatte, *Fort Wayne*, pp. 51, 183-84.

[26] FWFCTM, September, 1846–June, 1848.

[27] Poinsatte, *Fort Wayne*, pp. 233-34; Griswold, *Fort Wayne*, I, 39, 477, 486; FWFCTM, June 23, 1847, August 6, 1847, September 1, 1847, and April 22, 1851.

[28] FWFCTM, June 26, 1849 and July 30, 1849.

[29] Holliday, *Indiana Methodism*, pp. 281-85; Theophilus A. Wylie, *Indiana University, 1820-1890* (Indianapolis, 1890), pp. 99-100; James A. Woodburn, *History of Indiana University, 1820-1902* (Chicago, 1940), pp. 266-319.

[30] Holliday, *Indiana Methodism*, p. 283.

[31] FWFCTM, September 24, 1852.

[32] FWFCTM, April 16, 1853; *The Catalogue and Register of the Fort Wayne Female College and Fort Wayne Collegiate Institute,* 1855 (Cincinnati, 1855), p. 1, 3; North Indiana Conference of the Methodist Episcopal Church, *Minutes of the 1855 Conference* (Cincinnati, 1855), p. 31.

[33] Holliday, *Indiana Methodism*, pp. 139-40.

[34] FWFCTM, July 30, 1849; *Fort Wayne Female College and Fort Wayne Collegiate Institute Catalogue,* 1855, p. 7.

[35] *Fort Wayne Female College and Fort Wayne Collegiate Institute Catalogue,* 1855, p. 26; FWFCTM, April 19, 1851 and April 21, 1851.

[36] FWFCTM, July 5, 1847, September 1, 1847, July 30, 1849, and August 24, 1853; Letter, Horace Wellington to William C. Keys, April 19, 1847 (Michigan Historical Collection, University of Michigan); Adrian College Trustees' Minutes, June 1, 1859 (Adrian College archives); Schmidt, *Liberal Arts College,* pp. 95-96.

[37] FWFCTM, March 1, 1849 and March 26, 1850; Woodburn, *Higher Education in Indiana,* p. 186; Poinsatte, *Fort Wayne,* pp. 194-95.

[38] Herrick and Sweet, *North Indiana Conference*, pp. 173-75; FWFCTM, August 17, 1852 and October 10, 1855.

[39] FWFCTM, July 13, 1853; *Fort Wayne Female College and Fort Wayne Collegiate Institute Catalogue,* 1855, p. 1.

[40] FWFCTM, April 23, 1855, August 4, 1855, and October 10, 1855.

Chapter Three

FORT WAYNE COLLEGE

ort Wayne College, as the school was called from 1855 to 1890, was in many respects a typical nineteenth-century, Midwestern church college. It was small and poor, its curriculum emphasized the traditional classical studies, it enrolled many more preparatory than college students, its major social activity was the literary society, and its rules were numerous and rigid. One might wish that its course offerings had been less traditional. A curriculum so heavy in classical studies frequently was not inspiring. A more practical curriculum would likely have attracted more students, and the resultant increase in the number of students would have enlarged the tuition deposits in the college treasury. As it was, the institution frequently operated near the verge of bankruptcy. That it survived at all was due to the efforts of the college fundraisers. In the area of religious emphasis little evidence exists to indicate that the school in this period differed substantially from the typical Methodist College.

1. GOVERNING AND FINANCING THE COLLEGE

The denominations aligned with the nineteenth-century American church colleges usually displayed greater willingness to govern their schools than to finance them. This generalization applies to Fort Wayne College. The institution belonged to the North Indiana Conference of the Methodist Episcopal Church— and later to both the North Indiana Conference and the North-West Indiana Conference when the church officials divided the former conference. A joint board of trustees and conference representatives usually shared the responsibility for governing the school.[1] Periodically, the denominational officials collected offerings in the conference churches to aid the college,[2] but these irregular offerings did not represent the major economic advantage coming from the school's Methodist affiliation. More important were the enthusiastic commendations of the school that the conference could make to its members. The college leaders were highly pleased when the conference minutes called the institution a "great success" or expressed "undiminished confidence in the ability and skill of the...faculty and trustees";[3] such testimonials facilitated the efforts of the school fundraisers.

Many of the state's wealthy Methodists listened intently to the denomination's praises of its educational institutes; but at least partly because the church leaders usually sang louder praises for Asbury than for the Fort Wayne school, the large gifts almost always went to the college in Greencastle. A letter from the Fort Wayne trustees to the Education Commission of the National Association of Local Preachers in 1884 stated that recently the school had profited very little from the patronage of the North Indiana Conference because DePauw University also had been operating "under the same patronage and...[had] drawn largely on the resources of our people."[4] The trustees were referring to the specific situation in the middle 1880s, but it is indicative of how Asbury (DePauw) usually obtained most of the available resources.

Allen County Court House, 1862-1897.

While the Fort Wayne school worried about survival, Asbury concerned itself with maintaining its reputation as one of the leading educational institutions in Indiana[5] and the nation. The 1875 conference minutes talked about how Asbury "continued to prosper" with assets totaling over $313,000, while Fort Wayne "struggled...to support its campus and building." Although the Methodists owned many more churches in the state than did any other denomination, their large constituency did not possess the resources to finance adequately more than one school.[6]

The failure of Fort Wayne College to receive significant aid from the conference did not result from a lack of appeals for help. The trustees' records show the college officials constantly calling on the Methodist leaders for money to liquidate the college indebtedness. Except for the irregular "free-will" collections in the churches, however, probably no significant aid came directly from the conference. As a result, the college administrators and trustees possessed almost total responsibility for keeping the school financially solvent.

The college leaders had two choices for financing the school: they could charge the students the full cost of their education, or they could supplement reduced tuition charges with the contributions of "hoped for" benefactors. For several reasons they chose the second method. The number of potential students willing and able to pay the full cost of their education probably was not large enough to warrant the existence of the school. But the leaders believed that the institution must exist to train future ministers and other leaders, and they also

The [dire economic] experience of Fort Wayne College was not unusual. Many similar nineteenth-century schools could not find funds to enable them to operate longer than a few years. Perhaps the fact that the Fort Wayne school did survive at all should be seen as a success.

believed that an Indiana Methodist school in addition to Asbury was necessary to accomplish this purpose. Accordingly, the officials "paid" the students' part of the cost of their education to attract an adequate number of them to the school. To find sufficient benefactors to supplement the student payments was hard work. When gift income was inadequate—as it frequently was—the school officials kept the institution in operation by paying low faculty salaries or by resorting to deficit financing.

The several writers describing the financial condition of Fort Wayne College convey universally gloomy reports. A contemporary historian of Indiana Methodism wrote that the school "for many years...was seriously embarrassed by debt." An early historian of higher education in the state talked of the institution's "continuous struggle for existence." The trustees, in an unusually candid statement in 1884, remarked, "We have been struggling for so many years with inadequate supplies of aid that it seemed we were hardly out of one financial difficulty until we were in another!" One should note, however, that the experience of Fort Wayne College was not unusual. Many similar nineteenth-century schools could not find funds to enable them to operate longer than a few years. Perhaps the fact that the Fort Wayne school did survive at all should be seen as a success.[7]

Although the college survived through the post-Civil War period, it almost did not. On at least one occasion it ceased operation for an entire school year. There is evidence also that the college leaders offered the school for sale on at least two occasions.[8]

The trustees were responsible for raising the funds necessary to supplement the student payments and the Methodist Church offerings; to aid them in accomplishing this task, the trustees usually employed a full-time financial agent. Even before the opening of the school, they hired J. S. Bayless to organize fund drives in Indiana and to find benefactors. Sometimes the trustees paid the agent a regular salary, and sometimes they employed him on a commission basis. They signed a contract with the school's second agent, John H. Bruce, for the 1847-48 year for $550—a figure slightly less than the salary received by the college president. When the Rev. S. T. Stout became the agent in 1858, the board paid him thirty percent on all sums he collected provided that "the remaining seventy percent...was paid over to...the trustees as fast as collected."[9]

The St. Joseph Hospital (above) was located near the college. It was the place where legendary student Sammy Morris was to spend his last days.

The school received many gifts in the form of property, promissory notes, and advance tuition payments. Donors who contributed land property included members of such prominent Fort Wayne families as Brackenridge, McCulloch, and Rockhill. Perhaps the most common type of gift was the "scholarship." In exchange for a donation (a typical amount was $60-$100), the school gave the benefactor the right to name a student to receive a tuition-free scholarship for a certain number of years (usually three to five). The trustees stipulated that any donor not paying his scholarship in full should pay interest on the unpaid balance. Agent Bayless reportedly sold twenty scholarships valued at one hundred dollars apiece; and Samuel Brenton, during his presidency, enthusiastically promoted scholarship sales. Individuals holding scholarships in the form of pledges often did not pay the promised amount, however, but not because the trustees and agents did not place intense pressure upon them. When one scholarship holder in 1849 requested release from his note, the trustees flatly refused![10]

These scholarship sales did succeed in bringing immediate revenue to the college treasury, but the long-term results were not good. Gradually, the rejoicing over the scholarship sales changed to disillusionment. Though promissory notes often were difficult to collect, the major problem resulted from the school's borrowing future tuition income to pay current expenses. Eventually, the scholarship funds were gone, but many non-paying students remained. The fact that Fort Wayne College by 1870 was only one of many American colleges reaping the woes of earlier, short-sighted scholarship sales campaigns offered little comfort to the trustees who held personal responsibility for supplying the subsequent treasury deficits.[11]

The pressure upon the college officials to raise funds may explain the desperate measures they sometimes used to accomplish this purpose. They collected revenue from catalog advertisements that invited the readers to buy everything from paint to toilet articles. Besides this, they sometimes promoted the college with embarrassingly boastful literature. For example, the business division of the college in 1877 asserted, "We are now able to offer one of the most interesting and useful courses of educational training that has been offered the student of any age or country."[12]

Reuben D. Robinson
President
1855-65; 1869-70;
1872-77

William Yocum
President
1877-88

Throughout the Fort Wayne years the trustees struggled with a debt of several thousand dollars. When the college building was largely finished in 1848, the school owed over $9,200 of its nearly $13,700 evaluation. The indebtedness declined to $3,500 by 1868; however, it increased to $4,400 by 1876. Perhaps the nationwide depression of the early 1870s caused the debt increase after 1868. In the later 1870s and early 1880s the trustees continued gradually to reduce the debt. The success in lessening the indebtedness and increasing the number of students (three hundred by 1880) led the trustees to vote to build an addition to the college building.[13]

This addition greatly enhanced the physical appearance of the school and allowed the college to house many more students, but it also dangerously added to the indebtedness of the school. The 60' X 73' four-story addition cost $15,000, and even before its completion the school officials in 1884 were making serious plans for constructing a second building (a residence hall for women). Even though the trustees never constructed the second building, the financial burden of the addition to the original building created a major financial crisis in the late 1880s. During this critical period the trustees established a relationship with the National Association of Local Preachers of the Methodist Episcopal Church that eventually resulted in the latter group's assuming the control of the school.[14]

One positive note in the years of Fort Wayne College was the continuity of leadership at the presidential level. Two men—Reuben D. Robinson and William F. Yocum—presided for twenty-seven of the thirty-five years. Robinson, who served a total of sixteen of these years (1855-65, 1869-70, and 1872-77), was the most important figure in the school during this period. His first appointment to the presidency came at the same board meeting (August 4, 1855) at which President Brenton submitted his resignation in order to resume his former position in Congress. Robinson had previously served as a trustee and a professor of languages at the college. President Robinson assumed an active role in fundraising, and even after he left the top position he continued to serve as a college agent.

The memoirs of Burt W. Ayres provide a personal glimpse of Robinson. Like many of the Fort Wayne College officials, Robinson was a prominent Methodist clergyman, and the occasion of the acquaintance of the youthful Ayres with him was that of a Methodist presiding elder (now district superintendent) making his quarterly visits to the Hartford City Methodist Church, where the Ayres family worshipped. Ayres remembered Robinson as a large man—perhaps six feet in height and two hundred and twenty-five pounds in weight—with a light complexion and blond hair that "stood on end."[15]

William F. Yocum (1877-88) was an able educator. The quality of the academic program improved significantly during his tenure. His students spoke well of him, and he commanded respect as a person as well as an educator. He was unable to solve the continuing financial problems, however. When Yocum left the presidency in 1888, his successor was the minister of the First Methodist Church in Fort Wayne, Horace N. Herrick.[16]

Little is known of Herrick's record as president, but, as many of the school's presidents before and after him, he established a record of leadership among the Methodist clergy. He was in the middle of his career as a Methodist preacher when he presided over the college in the late 1880s. In the late 1890s he served as the Methodist presiding elder of the Muncie and Richmond districts, and in 1910 he became the historian of the North Indiana Conference. Ayres remembers

Herrick as being more of a "thought-provoking" preacher than a "heart-warming" one. During Herrick's administration the trustees made the decision to transfer control of the school to the National Association of Local Preachers of the Methodist Episcopal Church.[17]

2. THE ACADEMIC PROGRAM

Most of the small Midwestern church "colleges" in the nineteenth century had few students pursuing college-level work. Such was the case at Fort Wayne College, where the large majority of pupils studied in either the pre-college program or else in one of the non-college specialty divisions—music, business, or teacher training. A higher percentage of students enrolled in college-level courses during the period before 1870 than during the two decades from 1870 to 1890. In the school's second year of operation, thirty-one of the school's 107 students registered in the college division. The part of the student body doing college work in 1854 was only seventeen percent, but in 1870 the rate increased to nearly forty percent. After 1870 the college enrollment began to decline. During the 1875-76 school year, the names of less than ten percent of the students appeared on the college department roster. The decline of the college division in the 1870s and 1880s was due at least partly to the decision of the school officials in that period to restrict the college curriculum offerings to the freshman courses. School literature during these two decades advertised that the college offered courses that would prepare a student to enroll with sophomore status at Indiana Asbury (DePauw) University. Although the school limited its college offerings to freshman-level work, its charter giving the right to confer college degrees remained unchanged.[18]

The large majority of the American colleges in this period operated preparatory departments. In Indiana even the state university had such a

> *The decline of the college division in the 1870s and 1880s was due at least partly to the decision of the school officials in that period to restrict the college curriculum offerings to the freshman courses. School literature during these two decades advertised that the college offered courses that would prepare a student to enroll with sophomore status at Indiana Asbury (DePauw) University.*

secondary school until 1890. It was a necessity in the years before the public high school movement became widespread. The curriculum of the Fort Wayne College preparatory department included a mixture of advanced grammar-school subjects (e.g., arithmetic, grammar, reading, history, and geography) with elementary doses of mathematics and the classical languages. DePauw University accepted "without examination" the graduates of this course at Fort Wayne. The Fort Wayne school even conducted a primary department in the period before 1878.[19]

The college curriculum included large amounts of work in the Latin and Greek classics and mathematics, and a smattering of science and what today we call social science. Educators both at the Fort Wayne school and in America in general believed that the classical studies best represented the intellectual framework for an educated person. The students studied the Latin and Greek classics because they contained eternal truths and values, and they translated these ancient works because the translation process disciplined the mind. Mathematics also served to "train the mind"; therefore, it ranked next to the ancient languages in importance. Unfortunately, the undue emphasis upon mind discipline in the translation of the classics often prevented a class from giving serious consideration to the ideas of the writers.

Following the conventional practice of the day, the college offered the honorary M.A. degree. Almost all of the school's B.A. recipients could receive the degree if they had spent a minimum of three years following graduation in some profession, had generally kept out of trouble, and had paid the graduation fee.

Besides the classics and mathematics the only subject to receive serious attention was the moral philosophy course. Usually taught by the president to the seniors, it was frequently the most valuable and exciting subject. It was roughly equivalent to a combination of ethics, logic, political science, economics, sociology, and religion. The vague nature of this discipline allowed the president a maximum amount of freedom in choosing the exact contents of the course[20]

Surprisingly, the college placed minimal emphasis upon Biblical studies. Sometimes courses in ethics, natural theology, and "Evidences of Christianity" appeared in the curriculum, and the few students studying Greek sometimes worked in the New Testament as well as in the classical writings. Yet for a school that regarded the Bible as the chief source of inspiration for its existence, it showed a rather low regard for Biblical studies in its curriculum.[21]

Not all the college students enrolled in the courses in Greek. The girls of the female college studied French instead of Greek, and during part of the Fort Wayne College period a student could elect modern instead of ancient languages if enrolled in the scientific course (leading to the B.S. degree) instead of the more prestigious classical course (which led to a B.A. degree). Gradually the emphasis upon the classical languages decreased.[22]

In order to attract the largest possible number of students, the school not only offered regular academic work from the primary to the college level, but it also offered courses in vocational and special interest areas. The teacher training—or "normal"—program required two or three years to complete. Those enrolled in the teacher-training course spent the first year studying how to teach the elementary subjects. In their next year or two they enrolled in college courses in mathematics, science, and social science. Completion of the full music course took as long as three years. While the school encouraged the music students to take studies outside the music division, it did not usually require this. The music curriculum included piano, reed organ, pipe organ, notation harmony and counterpoint, vocal culture and singing, theory of music, and composition. The business division offered a one-year course. While most of its curriculum involved commercial courses such as penmanship, commercial and international law, bookkeeping, commercial correspondence, and banking, the course also included required work in geography, arithmetic, and grammar. The writer in the 1877 catalog expressed great pride that the business division offered a course in the comparatively new science of telegraphy. The division designed the one-year business course primarily for those with a grammar-school background; however, it did offer a more elementary "first grade" course for "younger people and those whose common school education has been neglected" to prepare them for entry into the regular course.[23]

The school offered a wide variety of degrees and diplomas. During the female college period the prominent advanced degree was the M.E.L. (the Mistress of English Literature). The curriculum for this degree differed little from the curriculum for the two degrees that soon replaced it—the B.A. and the B.S. Following the conventional practice of the day, the college offered the honorary M.A. degree. Almost all of the school's B.A. recipients could receive the degree if they had spent a minimum of three years following graduation in some profession, had generally kept out of trouble, and had paid the graduation fee. Those who successfully completed the music or commercial courses earned a

Mistress of English Literature

The Fort Wayne Female College was founded because the Methodist leaders saw great value in educating women. However, at the time, many doubted the appropriateness of awarding a "bachelor's" degree to a women.

Some objected to the male connotations of the word "bachelor." Others doubted whether the academic level of the work in women's colleges was sufficiently rigorous to warrant their use of the traditional degree.

Accordingly in the nineteenth century—and even into the early decades of the twentieth century —some women graduates received alternate degrees such as Mistress of Arts, Mistress of Liberal Arts, Mistress of Music, Mistress of Philosophy, Mistress of Polite Literature, Mistress of Teaching, Maid of Science, Sister of Arts, and the Mistress of English Literature.

Source: Walter Crosby Eells, *Degrees in Higher Education* (1963).

master of accounts or master (or mistress) of music diplomas.[24]

The broad range of curricular programs and the widely differing levels on which the students worked made severe demands upon the ability and energy of the faculty. The size of the Fort Wayne College faculty varied from six to fourteen members. Most of the instructors who taught the college courses held the B.A. degree (and sometimes the honorary M.A.) or the M.D. degree, while the faculty members teaching only on the non-college level usually held no degree. It is likely that most of the faculty members with degrees taught part-time in the preparatory department. By twentieth-century college standards

Fort Wayne College coeds in the 1880s.

these instructors possessed inadequate academic backgrounds. Yet in even the best Eastern schools in this period, the typical professor could claim no more training than the classical course of undergraduate studies and some theological work. Only a very few American instructors held the Ph.D. degree before 1875.[25]

Faculty salaries changed very little during the period. Contracts for major professors ranged between $600 and $850 per year. Administrators earned more—sometimes substantially more. The financial agent in 1871 earned $1,500, and President Herrick's initial annual contract called for $1,500 plus facilities in the college building for his family. Minor teachers earned less. Two female teachers in 1871 (presumably teaching non-college courses) each earned $350 plus "board and washing." The regular payment of salaries was not always certain. The trustee records of the late 1860s show discussion on the question of whether "faculty salaries will be pledged to be paid at a certain time" or whether the contracts between the trustees and the faculty members only promised "the assets of the college as security that the faculty will be paid." Apparently, experience taught President W. F. Hemenway (1865-68) that sufficient doubt existed on this point to warrant an inquiry of the trustees.[26]

One factor upon which the regular payment of faculty salaries depended was the enrollment of an adequate number of tuition-paying students. Enrollment figures for all of the Fort Wayne period are unavailable, but data for selected years appears in Figure II.[27] One should note that the figures for the years after

1870 include few college-level students. For example, enrollees pursuing the college curriculum numbered only thirteen in 1875, six in 1879, and nineteen in 1880.

The majority of the students came from Fort Wayne and the surrounding areas in northeastern Indiana and northwestern Ohio. The homes of almost all the younger students were in the immediate Fort Wayne area; however, some of the older students—especially the males—came to Fort Wayne from long distances. The 1855 catalog listed college students from Portsmouth, New Hampshire, and Santa Cruz, California. In 1870 students came from West Virginia, Pennsylvania, Maryland, Virginia, New York, and Ontario, Canada. Fourteen years later the school taught pupils from such frontier regions as Nebraska, Kansas, Dakota Territory, Indian Territory (Oklahoma) and Washington Territory. In the last year the school operated in Fort Wayne, there were students from Berlin, Germany; Minsk, Russia; and Cesaria, Turkey.[28]

Figure II

Total Enrollment at Fort Wayne Female College and

Fort Wayne College for Selected Years

1847	100	1881	395
1848	117	1882	307
1850	187	1883	327
1854	256[a]	1884	300
1855	305	1887	207
1870	253	1888	300
1875	144	1892	77
1879	225		

[a] *This figure includes the 97 men of the Fort Wayne Collegiate Institute.*

Students graduating from college with the bachelor's degree or its approximate equivalent (the Mistress of English Literature degree offered in the early years) numbered fifty-three during the Fort Wayne period (see Figure III). Not one of the first three graduates was from the Fort Wayne area. Eliza Cox and Angie Hubler came from Lafayette, and the home of Elizabeth M. Rayburn was New Carlisle, Ohio. No students graduated during most of the 1870s and 1880s because during this period, as mentioned earlier, the school offered no college courses beyond the freshman year.[29]

Figure III

Graduates of Fort Wayne Female College and Fort Wayne College

1850	3	1854	12
1852	6	1855	5
1853	5	1856	5

Of the students who attended the Fort Wayne school, perhaps none later achieved greater fame than Henry Ware Lawton. The six-foot four-inch career soldier rose to the rank of major-general during the Spanish-American War. In the Civil War he earned the Medal of Honor (now commonly called the Congressional Medal of Honor) for gallantry in the Atlanta Campaign.[30] He then participated in several frontier Indian Wars before General Nelson A. Miles in 1886 chose him to command the regiment that sought to capture the prominent Indian leader Geronimo; Lawton pursued Geronimo on a 1300-mile chase through the American Southwest before capturing him. In the Spanish-American War he was one of the commanders who accepted the surrender of Santiago, Cuba, and he subsequently became the military governor of Santiago city and province. He died in 1899, having been shot through the heart during the Philippine Insurrection.[31]

The regular school year usually continued for ten months, and it usually contained three or four terms. When the school year had four terms, each term lasted for ten weeks; when the number of terms was three, each period continued for about fourteen weeks. Summer vacation came in July and August; however, even during these months the college often operated a summer-school program.[32]

The heart of the formal learning process was the classroom. According to the catalog statements, the teachers conducted the classroom activities with a tight set of rules.[33] Each day students attended four or five classes of forty-five minutes length. The teachers required that the students attend and recite in each class, and they kept a record of each student's daily performance. There is evidence that the teachers demanded some analytic work from the students. When the faculty introduced an English literature course into the curriculum late in the Fort Wayne period, they announced that they expected the students to pass judgment

The 1870 catalog announced that "merit in scholarship and delinquency in duties will be recorded and read publicly at the close of each term."

44

on the diction, style, purpose, thought, and feeling of the author. Sometimes the school officials made student performance a matter of public record. For example, the 1870 catalog announced that "merit in scholarship and delinquency in duties will be recorded and read publicly at the close of each term."[34]

In addition to participating in classroom recitations, students learned in other ways. One was studying the textbooks during the dormitory "study hours." The textbooks assigned by the faculty included such common nineteenth-century volumes as McGuffey's reader, Quackenbus' United States History, Gray's Botany, Butler's Analogy of Religion, Haven's Mental Philosophy, and Wayland's Moral Science and Political Economy. The library afforded another important extra-classroom learning opportunity. In the late 1860s the library numbered 1600 volumes.[35]

Fort Wayne College was not all business and classes. Some of the best intellectual and most of the best social experiences took place apart from the formal academic climate. These more relaxed activities served as a necessary complement to the work of the classroom.

3. COLLEGE LIFE

Many of the Fort Wayne College students probably would have stated that the school's extracurricular activities influenced them more than did the academic program. Of major importance to the students were the religious services and the literary society meetings. Also a part of "college life" were the varied activities in the dormitory rooms, the recreational activities on–and occasionally off–the campus, and the highly authoritarian regulations that governed all phases of the college program.

The Christian faith was a major influence at the school. As long as an official agency of the Methodist Episcopal Church controlled the college, the institution did not issue an explicit doctrinal statement. Apparently, the school officials assumed that the public understood that they subscribed to the theological position of the Methodist Episcopal Church. Although Burt Ayres recalled hearing former Fort Wayne College students refer to the "pervasive

The Thalonian Society - 1898.

Thalonian Society

The Thalonian Literary Society assumed as its name "Thalonian" for the Greek philosopher Thales and as its motto "Know Thyself" for the vital principle of his philosophy.

The 1903 Gem described the society in reverent tones: *"The society somehow gets a stronghold upon the affections of its members. How much the society phase of college life means to the student! In practical value, we deem it equivalent to one of his regular day classes."*

*Know thyself! God-given forces,
Ne'er can mate with brute nor clod;
And the high stars in their courses,
Fight for him who fights for God."*
- *Thales*

Grace Husted
Professor

Christ-life" of the school, there is little evidence to indicate that the religious fervency of the institution was as intense in the period before 1890 as it became in the years after that date. While a president of Fort Wayne College might promote the school partly on the basis that a college education "pays from a money-making point of view," "enables the graduate to occupy an honorable position" in society, and "gives its possessor satisfaction," the presidents of the school in the early Upland period talked mostly about the school's ability to help the student find the "deeper spiritual life" and to educate one for a "life of Christian service."[36]

The Fort Wayne school held regular religious exercises. College officials required student attendance at weekday-morning prayers and Sunday-morning church; the student could meet the latter requirement at either a Roman Catholic or a Protestant church. There was a second daily prayer meeting, a Sunday-afternoon singspiration, and a Sunday-evening prayer meeting; but the students who attended these services did so voluntarily. In addition, the literary societies began their meetings with a devotional period, and the school sponsored a Young Men's Christian Association chapter.[37]

Except perhaps for the religious services, the most important extracurricular activities were the literary society meetings. Almost from its inception the school promoted one or more of these literary groups. The major societies during the Fort Wayne period were the Thalonian Society and the El Dorado Society. The Thalonian Society began in the late 1850s with the uniting of the older Philosophian and Excelsior literary organizations. The men's and the ladies' societies continued to meet separately until the 1870s, when the Thalonian men began admitting women to their meetings. Perhaps the chance to meet with the men led the ladies to abandon the El Dorado organization in 1878. At any rate, it ceased operation in the same year that the coeducational Philalethian Society became the second major campus literary organization.[38]

The society meetings followed a typical pattern. The chaplain opened the meeting with a Bible lesson and prayer. Then after the society heard excuses from those who were absent at previous meetings, the major activities of the evening began. The literary exercises included essays, discussions, orations, readings, and musical selections, but usually the highlight of the program was the debate.[39]

The students invested large amounts of time and effort in their society activities. They decorated their society hall with expensive furnishings, they collected their own research materials, and they likely prepared for their literary exercises with greater intellectual fervor than they used in studying for their classes. The societies also fulfilled a very necessary social function, especially after they became coeducational. The same type of energy later students would use to cheer for the athletic teams was used by this earlier generation of students in their competitive literary activities. It is interesting to note that later in Upland the demise of the societies coincided with the rise of intercollegiate athletics.[40]

Many students participated in the military drill company. Although membership in this group, which began late in the Fort Wayne period, was voluntary, the school encouraged the male students to participate. The state of Indiana supplied Springfield rifles, but the students had to purchase their own uniforms. Although a uniform cost as much as the tuition fee for one term ($14.00), the college "urgently requested" the participating males to buy them.[41]

The school leaders carefully planned the daily schedule for each student.

And then there were the informal activities. The students frequently met in the ice cream "saloons" of the city on Saturday nights and Sundays. On special occasions the male students sometimes escorted their girl friends to a favorite country spot for a picnic and a boat ride.[42]

The students spent more of their out-of-the-classroom hours in the dormitory rooms than anywhere else, as this was their center for study as well as for sleeping. The furnishings in the rooms were modest. A usual room included a bedstead, a mattress,[43] a stove, a table, chairs, a washbowl and pitcher, a mirror, and a lamp. As the enrollment grew larger, many students—usually the males— had to find housing in buildings near the campus. By the end of the Fort Wayne period the college building housed only women. While the housing could provide dormitory space for only about one hundred roomers, the dining hall could accommodate twice that number.[44]

Paying for the room in the dormitory, the seat in the dining hall, and the instruction in the classroom was one of the most painful—but also most necessary—parts of the college experience. The cost of room, board, and tuition for a school year of forty weeks ranged from about $100 in 1855 to nearly $175 in 1890. The student paid an additional sum for the fuel and lights for the dormitory room (the college sold wood and oil), and, if desired, could rent a carpet at the rate of one dollar per term per occupant. These figures applied to the student who took both room and board in the school building and who was doing college-level work. Students doing preparatory or primary work often paid cheaper tuition fees. Unlike the present-day Taylor students whose greatest expense is tuition, the Fort Wayne College students spent most of their dollars for room and board fees. As late as 1879 each college student paid only eight dollars per term for instructional costs.[45]

Some of the students found ways to reduce the costs. Students whose average scholarship and deportment in a given term averaged ninety-five percent received a five-dollar reduction in the tuition fee for the next term. Sons and daughters of active ministers could obtain a fifty-percent tuition scholarship. Self-boarding students living in off-campus rooms often could live more cheaply than dormitory students; sometimes these students formed cooperative boarding clubs for this purpose. On the other hand, some off-campus accommodations in private homes cost the students more than the regular college room and board fees.[46]

The faculty and administration closely regulated all areas of college life. The discipline may appear severe to the contemporary observer, but for several reasons one should not judge the Fort Wayne school by modern standards for college students. The pupils were younger; the majority were the equivalent of high-school students and thus needed closer supervision than did those of college age. Besides, in this period society in general believed in the general efficacy of discipline and regulation. For example, Fort Wayne town ordinances of the period provided fines for citizens convicted of "profane cursing or swearing," and hunting, fishing, or working on Sunday.[47] The denominations in general and the Methodist Episcopal Church in particular also regulated the lives of their members, and the rules at the Fort Wayne school did not differ from those of other nineteenth-century colleges, including the state universities.

The school leaders carefully planned the daily schedule for each student. They explicitly designated as study periods the hours between eight and twelve in the morning, one-thirty and four-thirty in the afternoon, and seven and ten in the evening. When the students were not attending class during these hours, the college expected them to be studying in their dormitory rooms, and no student could visit in another student's room during study hours. These study hours applied to the weekdays and Saturday afternoon and evening. The students could leave their rooms on those evenings when there were special school events, such as the literary society exercises. The school required attendance at these activities, however, so it was merely a case of replacing one mandatory activity with another.[48]

The college controlled Sunday activities no less than those of the other six days. In addition to requiring the students to attend morning church, the school also asked them to refrain from participating in certain activities on Sunday. These included making unnecessary noise, "collecting in each other's rooms for idle conversation or music," "roaming in the fields," "walking on the streets or commons for pleasure,"[49] and "frequenting the city."[50]

In a manner appropriate to the Victorian Age, the institution announced to the parents of the students that "vigilant attention will be given to the health, manners, and morals of all of the students." To aid in the achievement of this ideal, the school forbade the following practices: the use of intoxicating liquors, the use of tobacco in any form in or near the college building, dancing in the college building,[51] playing at games of chance, using profane or obscene language, visiting hotels, groceries (gin or whiskey shops), circuses, or theaters for the purpose of pleasure or entertainment, wearing firearms or other weapons,[52] and "playing any tricks which would disturb or annoy anyone."[53] Special rules existed to govern the social activities of female students. The ladies could "receive calls" from the gentlemen only in the parlor and then only in the presence of a faculty member. As late as the 1870s students could not meet with members of the opposite sex without the permission of the president and the preceptress. In the same period the ladies could not visit downtown Fort Wayne unless they went with a member of the faculty or someone appointed by a member of the faculty. Even recreational walks away from the campus were acceptable only with the permission of the lady principal.[54]

Currently existing historical marker located on the St. Mary's River at the west (back) edge of the original campus.

Apparently, the entire faculty served as members of what we would now call the student development staff. The school leaders expected the faculty at all times to supervise and control the behavior of the students as if they were their own children. This obligation gave the faculty the right to visit the rooms of the students at any time. At least as late as 1877 most of the instructors ate their meals with the students.[55]

The Fort Wayne officials thought that their students behaved comparatively well. "Owing to the fact that the large majority of our students are young men and women of maturity," the 1877 catalog boasted, "there is little of the trickery and knavery that is so annoying in many eastern institutions."[56] On at least one occasion, however, the trustees thought that the female boarding students' behavior was less than exemplary; in September, 1851, the board believed it necessary to pass a formal resolution directing President Huestis to see that the young ladies "conform to the rule on the subject of extinguishing the lights in their rooms at the designated hours."[57]

Such was life on the Fort Wayne College campus. Little remains in Fort Wayne to remind one of the school that operated there for nearly fifty years. The alumni no longer live, the campus building no longer stands, and the campus grounds now contain residential structures. Some of these homes near the major West Washington (Highway #24) thoroughfare are on "College" Avenue and "Rockhill"[58] Street. Other than these street signs, the only physical reminder of the college is the historical marker located at the point where West Wayne Street meets the eastern bank of the St. Mary's River; the plate on this marker contains the simple statement:

SITE OF
THE FORT WAYNE COLLEGE
BETTER KNOWN AS
THE OLD M.E. COLLEGE

ESTABLISHED IN 1846 AS
THE FORT WAYNE FEMALE COLLEGE
ON GROUNDS DONATED BY WM. ROCKHILL

IN 1855 THE COLLEGE CONSOLIDATED WITH THE
FORT WAYNE COLLEGIATE INSTITUTE FOR YOUNG MEN
AND IT WAS THEN CALLED THE M.E. COLLEGE

IN 1890 THE COLLEGE GROUNDS WERE DEEDED
TO TAYLOR UNIVERSITY

1 *FWCC,* 1875-76, p. 19 and 1877-79, p. 31.

2 An example of these collections was the $307.10 the conference gave the school in 1878. See North Indiana Conference of the Methodist Episcopal Church, *Minutes of the 1878 Conference* (Indianapolis, 1878), p. 29.

3 *Ibid., Minutes of the 1854 Conference* (Indianapolis, 1854), p. 16.

4 FWCTM, October 23, 1884.

5 Among Indiana colleges in the mid-1870s, only Butler University had a larger evaluation, only Notre Dame had more students, and no school had larger library holdings than did the Greencastle school. See Barnhart and Carmony, *Indiana,* II, 344.

6 North Indiana Conference of the Methodist Episcopal Church, *Minutes of the 1875 Conference* (Cincinnati, 1875), p. 48; Holliday, *Indiana Methodism,* pp. 142-43.

7 Holliday, *Indiana Methodism,* p. 239; Woodburn, *Higher Education in Indiana,* p. 186; FWCTM, October 23, 1884; Barnhart and Carmony, *Indiana,* II, 344.

8 FWCTM, September 24, 1872; North Indiana Conference of the Methodist Episcopal Church, *Minutes of the 1868 Conference* (Indianapolis, 1868), p. 31; Frederick Abbot Norwood, *History of the North Indiana Conference,* 1917-56 (Winona Lake, Indiana, 1957), p. 29.

9 FWFCTM, November 27, 1846, June 23, 1847, October 1, 1847, and November 22, 1858; Gladys Light MS, "Old Fort Wayne Methodist College" (Taylor University archives).

10 FWFCTM, November 27, 1846, November 30, 1846, July 5, 1847, July 28, 1849, and May 11, 1853; *Fort Wayne Sentinel,* March 12, 1847, p. 1.

11 FWCTM, June 29, 1870; North Indiana Conference of the Methodist Episcopal Church, *Minutes of the 1871 Annual Conference* (Cincinnati, 1871), p. 42.

[12] *FWCC,* 1877-79 (Fort Wayne, 1880), pp. 19, 35-40.

[13] FWCTM, July 28, 1849; North Indiana Conference of the Methodist Episcopal Church, *Minutes of the 1868 Conference,* p. 32; *Minutes of the 1876 Conference* (Cincinnati, 1876), p. 52; *Minutes of the 1878 Conference,* p. 28; and *Minutes of the 1880 Conference* (Indianapolis, 1880), p. 43.

[14] *FWCC,* 1883-84 (Fort Wayne, 1884), p. 33 and 1888-89 (Fort Wayne, n.d.), p. 32.

[15] Burt W. Ayres, MS "History of Taylor University" (Taylor University archives), pp. 6-8; *Fort Wayne Female College and Fort Wayne Collegiate Institute Catalogue,* 1855, pp. 1,3,7; FWCTM, August 4, 1855.

[16] Ayres, "Taylor University," p. 7; Norwood, *North Indiana Conference,* p. 39.

[17] Herrick and Sweet, *North Indiana Conference,* pp. i-iii, 166, 197; Ayres, "Taylor University," p. 8; Norwood, *North Indiana Conference,* p. 39.

[18] Herrick and Sweet, *North Indiana Conference,* pp. 172-73, 178; *Fort Wayne Female College and Fort Wayne Collegiate Institute Catalogue,* 1855, p. 17; *FWCC,* 1870-71, pp. 5, 12, 1875-76, p. 5, 1877-79, p. 23, 1881 (Fort Wayne, 1881), p. 22, and 1888-89, pp. 15, 22.

[19] Barnhart and Carmony, *Indiana,* II, p. 345; *Fort Wayne Female College and Fort Wayne Collegiate Institute Catalogue,* 1855, p. 19; Herrick and Sweet, *North Indiana Conference,* p. 177; *FWCC,* 1875-76, pp. 15-16 and 1877-79, p. 22.

[20] Schmidt, *Liberal Arts College,* pp. 43-45; *FWCC,* 1870-71, p. 13.

[21] *FWCC,*1870-71, p. 13 and 1875-76, pp. 11-12.

[22] *Fort Wayne Female College and Fort Wayne Collegiate Institute Catalogue,* 1855, pp. 19-22; *FWCC,* 1870-71, p. 13 and 1875-76, p. 23.

[23] *FWCC,* 1870-71, p. 14, 1875-76, pp. 16, 18, 1877-79, pp. 18, 21, 24-25, and 1881, p. 24.

[24] FWCTM, April 26, 1854, April 3, 1857, and April 2, 1859; *FWCC,* 1870-71, p. 17.

[25] See the faculty roster sections of the college catalogs; Schmidt, *Liberal Arts College,* pp. 70-71.

[26] FWCTM, January 2, 1868, April 27, 1871, June 22, 1871, June 30, 1871, June 20, 1888, and June 18, 1889.

[27] See the student enrollment sections of the respective catalogs; Herrick and Sweet, *North Indiana Conference*, pp. 172-73, 178; Poinsatte, *Fort Wayne*, p. 195; North Indiana Conference of the Methodist Episcopal Church, *Minutes of the 1879 Conference* (Indianapolis, 1879), p. 36 and *Minutes of the 1884 Conference* (Indianapolis, 1884), p. 57.

[28] *Fort Wayne Female College and Fort Wayne Collegiate Institute Catalogue,* 1855, pp. 9-17; *FWCC,* 1870-71, pp. 7-10 and 1884-85 (Fort Wayne, 1885), pp. 8-12; *Taylor University Catalog,* 1892-93 (Fort Wayne, n.d.), p. 12 and 1893-94 (Fort Wayne, n.d.), p. 22. Hereafter all references to a Taylor University catalog will appear as TUC.

[29] *Fort Wayne Female College and Fort Wayne Collegiate Institute Catalogue,* 1855, p. 8; *FWCC,* 1870, p. 21; *TUC,* 1890-91 (Fort Wayne, n.d.), p. 8.

[30] Another early student-turned-Civil-War-soldier was James R. Smith from Ligonier, Indiana, the only graduate (B.S., 1857) to die in the Civil War. His death came in the Battle of Pea Ridge, Missouri. See *FWCC,* 1870-71, pp. 21, 23.

[31] "Henry Ware Lawton," in Johnson and Malone, *Dictionary of American Biography,* XI, 62-63.

[32] *Fort Wayne Female College and Fort Wayne Collegiate Institute Catalogue,* 1855, p. 23; *FWCC,* 1870-71, p. 17, 1877-79, p. 33, and 1888-89, p. 39.

[33] One should recall that most of the students in both age and academic level were approximately equivalent to today's high-school students.

[34] *FWCC,* 1870-71, p. 20, 1877-79, p. 30, and 1881, pp. 33-34, 39.

[35] *FWCC,* 1870, p. 15 and 1881, p. 24; Herrick and Sweet, *North Indiana Conference*, p. 176.

[36] E. Sterl Phinney MS, "Doctrinal Statements and Slogans of Taylor University," (Taylor University archives); *FWCC,* 1888-89 (Fort Wayne, n.d.), p. 37; Ayres, "Taylor University," p. 9.

[37] *Fort Wayne Female College and Fort Wayne Collegiate Institute Catalogue,* 1855, pp. 28, 30; *FWCC,* 1877-79, pp. 30-31, 1881, p. 33, and 1888-89, p. 33.

[38] *FWCC,* 1877-79, p. 30, 1881, p. 33, and 1888-89, p. 33.

[39] *Fort Wayne Female College and Fort Wayne Collegiate Institute Catalogue,* 1855, pp. 27-28; *FWCC,* 1877-79, p. 30.

[40] *Fort Wayne Female College and Fort Wayne Collegiate Institute Catalogue,* 1855, pp. 27-28; *FWCC,* 1870-71, p. 16 and 1888-89, pp. 32-33.

[41] *FWCC,* 1881-82 (Fort Wayne, 1882), pp. 36, 37.

[42] *Fort Wayne News Sentinel,* August 14, 1921, p. 17.

[43] In the first year the school officials apparently stuffed the mattresses themselves. A trustee order called for one hundred pounds of feathers as well as fifteen double mattresses. See FWCTM, October 1, 1847.

[44] *FWCC,* 1870-71, p. 18, 1877-79, pp. 27, 29, and 1883-84, p. 37; *TUC,* 1890-91, p. 16.

[45] *Fort Wayne Female College and Fort Wayne Collegiate Institute Catalogue,* 1855, p. 24; *FWCC,* 1877-79, pp. 26-28, 1881, p. 27, and 1881-82, p. 40; *TUC,* 1890-91, p. 17.

[46] *FWCC,* 1870-71, p. 18, 1875-76, p. 19, 1877-79, p. 28, and 1883-84, pp. 38-39.

[47] Poinsatte, *Fort Wayne*, pp. 38-39.

[48] *FWCC*, 1870-71, p. 19 and 1881, p. 32.

[49] This specific prohibition applied only to the ladies.

[50] *Fort Wayne Female College and Fort Wayne Collegiate Institute Catalogue*, 1855, p. 25; *FWCC*, 1870-71, p. 19.

[51] The catalogs seemed to suggest that the college made no effort to regulate the use of tobacco or dancing by the students when they were practiced off college grounds.

[52] Apparently many students came from homes and communities where frontier practices were still in effect.

[53] *FWCC*, 1870-71, p. 19, 1875-76, p. 21, and 1877-79, pp. 31-32.

[54] *Fort Wayne Female College and Fort Wayne Collegiate Institute Catalogue*, 1855, p. 25; *FWCC*, 1870-71, p. 19 and 1877-79, p. 27.

[55] *Fort Wayne Female College and Fort Wayne Collegiate Institute Catalogue*, 1855, p. 26; *FWCC*, 1870-71, p. 19 and 1877-79, p. 27.

[56] *FWCC*, 1877-79, p. 31.

[57] FWFCTM, September 7, 1851.

[58] Rockhill Street was named for William Rockhill, who donated the land for the campus and presided over the board of trustees for many years.

Chapter Four

THE PERIOD OF CHANGE

*I*n the lives of institutions as in the lives of individuals certain periods bring many changes within a short span of time. Such a period began for Fort Wayne College in the late 1880s when a desperate search for funds to solve the worst financial crisis in its history initiated a chain of events that did not end until the school had the name of Taylor University and a location in Upland, Indiana. The change in name came with the change in ownership. When the National Association of Local Preachers of the Methodist Episcopal Church assumed control of the college in an attempt to save it from economic demise, one of the terms in the transfer of the school from the North Indiana Methodist Conference allowed the new owners to rename the institution. Thus they named their new school in honor of the only man ever to rise from the ranks of the local preachers to the bishopric in the denomination—the aging but still indefatigable missionary, William Taylor.

In addition to the new ownership, the new name, and the new location, the school adopted a new emphasis. Partly because of the influence of the Local Preachers organization and partly because of the dynamic leadership of a new president, Thaddeus C. Reade, the school changed from an institution representative of mainline Methodism to one which aligned itself with the more fervent Holiness branch of the church.

1. NEW OWNERSHIP AND CONTROL

The decision to construct a major addition to the college building led to the critical financial crisis of the 1880s. The school indebtedness had been as high as eight thousand dollars during the Fort Wayne period; and when the trustees reduced the liabilities to a comparatively modest six hundred dollars in 1884, they decided to proceed with the four-story addition to the building. This seemed

The Upland Monitor

The booster-like "extra" issue of *The Upland Monitor* in its feature story announcing the coming of Taylor gleefully boasted that Upland would be the only city in the natural gas belt to have a college. Other informational and editorial items in this number of the paper included the following;

1. The Methodist Church was "by far the largest and most attractive" of the three Upland churches, the other two being the Friends Church and the Universalist Church. President Reade was scheduled to preach to the Methodists on the next Sunday.

2. The most prominent town father was J. W. Pittinger, who with D. Lyon, operated the "most extensive mercantile business of any firm in Upland." Other major contributors to the town's "present state of progressiveness" included J. N. Johnson, James Johnson, James Linder, T. B. Lyon, and the very aged but still active town founder, Jacob Bugher.

3. Newspaper editor and publisher J. P. Richard, who charged $1.00 per year for a subscription to the weekly *Monitor*, expressed much greater support for Upland's investment in recruiting Taylor and in building the new public school building, then under construction "in a pretty grove at the southern limits of the town," than he did for the request of an unnamed railroad for a subsidy of $25,000 from the taxpayers of Jefferson Township to assure that a new line would pass through the area. In Richard's words, "We are in favor of railroads, we are also in favor of their being built by their owners."

to be a reasonable decision as the enrollment had been increasing under the capable President Yocum. Accordingly, the school officials on May 28, 1884, signed a contract with local builder William Moellering to construct the addition for $13,413. Apparently, Moellering began his work immediately as the addition was sufficiently complete by late June for the trustees to invite the local Masonic fraternity to lay the cornerstone in a Fourth of July ceremony.[1]

Whatever joy the officials experienced at the Fourth of July ceremony eventually changed to disillusionment and frustration. It gradually became apparent that the building addition was not a wise long-range investment, but rather an economic millstone hung around the school's neck. The $600 debt of 1884 became $15,000 in 1888 and $20,000 in 1890. The trustees pondered several possible solutions to their dismal economic plight. The remedy that appeared the most promising was for the institution to find a major benefactor; since 1884 the school had courted the National Association of Local Preachers of the Methodist Episcopal Church in the hope that they would assume that role. The Local Preachers seriously considered lending significant aid to the college; however, they ultimately kept the school alive only by purchasing it.[2]

The local preachers of the Methodist Church officially organized themselves as the National Association of Local Preachers of the Methodist Episcopal Church in 1858, but their existence dated from the beginning of American Methodism itself. In the frontier period the office of local preacher came into existence as a necessary supplement to the circuit-riding preacher. Of the two types of preachers, presumably the circuit rider possessed better training for the Methodist ministry, but the long intervals between his appearances at a circuit church made necessary the ministry of the less qualified but more available local preacher. Although the local preacher held a limited ordination, technically he was a layman. He could preach and receive members into the church, but he could not administer the communion sacraments. From the days of Francis Asbury the regular Methodist clergy thought that the itinerate preachers held a

A memorial to a circuit rider.

Following the example of Francis Asbury, who traveled over a quarter-milliom miles on horseback, the Methodist circuit riders were the most significant organized force in spreading the Gospel across the continent on the ever-expanding frontiers of the new nation.

Source: Elmer Clark, *An Album of Methodist History* (1952).

higher "calling" than did the local preachers. With the passing of the frontier in a given area, the circuit system gradually disappeared, and with the disappearance of the circuit system the need for local preachers declined. Nevertheless, as late as 1876 two-thirds of the preachers of Methodism were local preachers, and in the early 1890s the local preachers claimed a membership of 14,500 in their national organization.[3]

The man most responsible for introducing the Local Preachers organization to Fort Wayne College was Christian B. Stemen, a local preacher of the Wayne Street Methodist Church in Fort Wayne and a widely recognized surgeon. Stemen's interest in Fort Wayne College began at least as early as the late 1870s, when he was an instructor in physiology at the Methodist school at the same time that he was the registrar of the Fort Wayne College of Medicine. His interest in both Fort Wayne College and the Local Preachers organization grew during the next decade; in 1885 he became a trustee of the college, and in 1888 he acquired the presidency of the National Association of Local Preachers (NALP). In the same period that the college was seeking a benefactor to save it from its financial straits, a movement was mounting in the NALP to find (or found) a school that would specialize in training local preachers (or lay deacons as they sometimes were called). Stemen's role was to propose that the interests of each group could be complementary.[4]

As late as 1876 two-thirds of the preachers of Methodism were local preachers, and in the early 1890s the local preachers claimed a membership of 14,500 in their national organization.

The serious overtures between the two groups began in 1884. George W. Mooney of Brooklyn, New York, represented the national leadership of the NALP in the early stages of the negotiations with the Fort Wayne officials. During his initial visit to Fort Wayne the trustees made their first formal appeal for aid from the NALP. The Fort Wayne trustees sought a $50,000 gift, and they announced that they would use the money to pay the debt, build a girls' dormitory, repair the college building, and install new educational equipment. In exchange for the grant, the school would be willing to change its name to suit the NALP, and it would give the Local Preachers representation on the board of trustees.[5]

After the NALP further investigated the school, they recommended that each of their members consider the institution worthy of financial support. The chairman of the NALP education committee, Rev. D. H. Harding of Philadelphia, visited the college in March, 1885, and following his inspection trip the NALP leadership issued their commendation of the school. For publicity purposes the trustees then printed five thousand copies of the NALP recommendation.[6] Another helpful testimonial was a letter from Bishop William Taylor, which he wrote at the request of Mooney. The widely known missionary and former local preacher praised the school as follows: "I have known Fort Wayne College for more than a quarter of a century. I believe in its work and grand future, and recommend all my brethren of the National Association of Local Preachers and their friends to give this institution a lift toward raising the funds required to put it into more working order."[7]

> *I have known Fort Wayne College for more than a quarter of a century. I believe in its work and grand future, and recommend all my brethren of the National Association of Local Preachers and their friends to give this institution a lift toward raising the funds required to put it into more working order.*
> — **Bishop William Taylor**

The trustees recognized that favorable recommendations help in the promotion of any organization, but they hoped that the NALP would provide even more specific forms of aid, and to achieve this end they continued their courtship of the Local Preachers. In 1885 they enhanced the authority of their chief local negotiator with the NALP, Stemen, by giving him a position on the board of trustees. They invited the NALP to hold their 1886 annual meeting in Fort Wayne, and they offered the organization the free use of the college facilities. The Local Preachers accepted the offer, and the September, 1886, meeting provided the opportunity for further negotiations. The NALP voted at this 1886 meeting to adopt the school as "the" local preachers' college. This meant that the NALP would seek to aid the institution until such a time that it would be "placed on a firm financial basis"; in turn the college agreed to give special student rates to local preachers, children of local preachers, and students preparing for missionary work. The trustees accepted this offer, and they even expressed a willingness to make the NALP joint owners of the school and to give them equitable representation on the board if the forthcoming NALP aid proved to be a substantial amount. No evidence exists to indicate that the Local Preachers rendered significant financial assistance during the next few years; at any rate the economic status of the college continued to decline. The next significant event in the continuing relationship between the two groups came in 1889, when the school agreed to change its name to William Taylor College or William Taylor University and the NALP agreed to obtain for the college a $10,000 gift and a $20,000-$25,000 loan at a low rate of interest.

By the end of August, 1889, the Fort Wayne people were euphoric in their excitement about the future of the school.[8] One of the NALP Education Committee members, Chauncey Shaffer, had written that the New York Life Insurance Company was willing to grant the proposed loan, and Shaffer himself had sent a personal gift of $1,000. Stemen added to the excitement by proposing the merger of his medical school and a new law school with the college so as to make the institution a true university.[9]

The optimism was premature. The loan application failed and the anticipated major gift income did not appear. In fact, the gifts even failed to prevent a deficit in the annual budget. By the beginning of 1890 the disappointment of the trustees led them to consider a wide variety of possibilities for relieving themselves of financial responsibility for the college. They called for bids to relocate the school within the North Indiana Conference. The resultant sale of the Fort Wayne property would allow them to pay the indebtedness on it, and then they could use the balance to finance a limited amount of construction on the new site. To prevent undue competition with DePauw University, the trustees agreed not to relocate farther south than Peru or Marion. In an effort to keep the school in Fort Wayne and under the same government, the trustees offered to rename the institution Chauncey Shaffer College if Shaffer would donate an additional $25,000. The school also conducted serious negotiations with the DePauw trustees on the possibility of merging with the Greencastle college. Some of the members of the DePauw board favored this idea, but it failed to obtain majority approval. Meanwhile, the trustees had to borrow money to pay the instructors, the North Indiana Conference requested the trustees to sell the college, and President Herrick resigned from his office.[10]

In the midst of this tense climate the NALP reappeared with a firm offer to purchase the college. The Local Preachers had organized an Indiana corporation, which they called Taylor University, and through this corporation they proposed to buy the school. The NALP proposal included the following provisions: (1) Taylor University would be the legal successor of Fort Wayne College and would recognize the latter's alumni and honorary degrees; (2) the location of the school would remain in or near Fort Wayne; (3) the NALP would select one-third of the trustees, and the Fort Wayne District of the North Indiana Methodist

Christian B. Stemen

Stemen was the single most significant individual in bringing together the several organizations (Fort Wayne College, The Fort Wayne College of Medicine, and the National Association of Local Preachers) that gave birth to Taylor University in 1893.

Mr. & Mrs. Stemen

Conference would choose a similar number; (4) the new corporation would assume ownership of the buildings, grounds, and personal property of Fort Wayne College by paying a sum "sufficient to meet all the outstanding indebtedness" of the school. The indebtedness the Local Preachers agreed to assume included all of the school's liabilities, except mortgages, and it amounted to $7,592.76. This was the only offer the trustees had received by the late spring of 1890, and they accepted it unanimously.[11]

While the NALP owned the school, they temporarily shared the control of it with the local Methodists and the leaders of the institution with which the old Fort Wayne College was now merged, the Fort Wayne College of Medicine. Five men from each of the three groups served on the board of trustees of the newly reorganized school. This situation soon changed, however, and beginning in 1893 the NALP selected all the trustees. When the original Taylor University board met to select the first presiding officer of the new school, it was natural that they chose the only man who personally represented each of the three interest groups on the board, Christian B. Stemen. He served as acting president for the 1890-91 school year.[12]

The Taylor Medical School Building.

At the time the Fort Wayne College of Medicine became a part of Taylor University, it was one of the best of the Indiana medical schools and the only one in northern Indiana. In the decade after the Taylor relocation to Upland, the medical school merged into what in 1908 became the Indiana School of Medicine.

The change in the school's descriptive name from college to university reflected a major academic reorganization. The new institution advertised that it offered courses of study in seven areas. The music, business, art, and normal courses led to diplomas; the scientific and classical curriculum led to the traditional B.S. and B.A. degrees; and the medical school curriculum led to the M.D. degree. The school introduced new courses in Hebrew and Arabic languages, Biblical studies, and History of Education, and it added new departments of psychology and sacred music. The college dropped its course offerings in business, but apparently it maintained an affiliate relationship with the McDermont and Whiteleather Business College in downtown Fort Wayne, as it advised its prospective students to take their business courses in that school.[13]

The most important curriculum change was the addition of the medical school. At the time the Fort Wayne College of Medicine became a part of Taylor University, it was one of the best of the Indiana medical schools and the only one in northern Indiana. The medical students took their classroom courses at the college, but they did their clinical work[14] in the St. Joseph's Hospital, the City Hospital,[15] and the "free dispensary" connected with the college. The medical school—as did the rest of the college—admitted both men and women students. It accepted students without an examination if they had graduated from a secondary-school program or by an examination in which they demonstrated a competency approximately equivalent to that of a secondary-school graduate. Forty medical students enrolled and nineteen graduated during 1892-93, the last year that Taylor operated in Fort Wayne. All sixteen faculty members except the lecturer on pharmacy held at least the M.D. degree, and several also had the M.A. degree. Stemen served as dean of the medical school for many of its twenty-six years of independent existence. Highlights of the period of its affiliation with Taylor included the expansion of the curriculum from two years to three years, and the purchase and remodeling of the McCulloch House on Superior Street to accommodate the growing needs of the medical school. The dwelling had been one of the largest residences in the city and the home of prominent Fort Wayne banker, Hugh McCulloch, who later served as the Secretary of the Treasury under Presidents Lincoln, Johnson, and Arthur (1865-69, 1884-85). In the decade after the Taylor relocation to Upland, the medical school merged into what in 1908 became the Indiana University School of Medicine.[16]

Of the students who studied at the medical school during the years of its affiliation with Taylor, Alice Hamilton stands out for her contributions as a public health and safety crusader. After studying primarily anatomy for a year (beginning in 1890) at the Fort Wayne College of Medicine where her father, Montgomery Hamilton, had been a trustee, she earned an M.D. degree at the University of Michigan in 1893 and took further training at the University of Leipzig, the University of Munich (where she and sister Edith became the first women ever admitted), and the Johns Hopkins Medical School. From 1897 to 1919 she lived and worked at Hull House, the famous Chicago settlement house founded by her friend, Jane Addams. During this period she conducted her famous studies of workers' health and safety in factories, mines, munitions plants, and paint factories. She worked as an investigator for the United States Bureau of Labor for a decade after 1911. Her efforts persuaded both the business

Calvin English

Benefactor

An 1884 graduate of the Fort Wayne College of Medicine, Calvin English was a respected physician in Fort Wayne. For many years, the English family has served as benefactors to Taylor. In recognition of this, English Hall carries the name of Calvin's wife, Mary Tower English, and the Mitchell Theatre in the Rupp Communication Arts Center honors English's daughter and son-in-law, Betty and William Mitchell.

community and state and federal government officials of the need to provide greater protection for the nation's industrial workers. Her 1919 appointment as the first woman faculty member at Harvard University and the publication of her *Industrial Poisons* (1925) helped to confirm her reputation as the nation's leading authority in the new field of industrial hygiene. Hamilton's position at Harvard was partly in the medical school but primarily in what is now the Department of Environmental Health of the School of Public Health—the department whose present chair is Taylor graduate (1961) and current Taylor trustee, Joseph Brain. In 1995 the United States Postal Service released a 55-cent stamp in her honor as a part of its "Great Americans" series.[17]

2. A New Name

It is not difficult to understand the desire of the NALP to name their new school after William Taylor. He was a fellow local preacher of Methodism, and thus they could identify with him and his amazing missionary accomplishments; but equally important to them was the fact that Taylor accomplished his feats while ignoring—and even flouting—the somewhat autocratic official agencies of the Church. The local preachers resented the fact that the regular Methodist clergy had always treated them in a condescending manner, and they

Bishop William Taylor has been called the greatest modern world herald of the Cross, the greatest Methodist since Wesley, and the greatest missionary since Paul.
- Gem, 1924

obtained a considerable amount of satisfaction from honoring a man who could successfully "buck the establishment."

Taylor was born in Rockbridge County, Virginia, in 1821, and he gained admission to the Baltimore Conference of the Methodist Church in 1843. For over fifty years he "traveled and toiled as no other man of his denomination, becoming a missionary evangelist to all lands."[18] The first land that he sought to evangelize was western America. At the request of Bishop Beverly Waugh he sailed to San Francisco via Cape Horn in 1849 as one of the first Methodist missionaries to California, and he spent seven years in that state preaching to Gold Rush miners and other frontiersmen. Typical among his meetings were those held outdoors in front of the saloons, brothels, and lavishly decorated gambling halls in the central plaza of San Francisco. "California Taylor" would precede his preaching by standing upon a port or whisky barrel and "singing up" a crowd of hundreds by trumpeting out in his unusually powerful and resonant voice the stanzas of a gospel hymn, most typically "The Royal Proclamation":

Hear the Royal Proclamation,
The Glad Tidings of Salvation,
Publishing to every creature,
To the ruined sons of nature;
Jesus reigns, He reigns victorious
Over heaven and earth most glorious,
Jesus reigns!

With a crowd collected, he commanded their attention through an unusual combination of courage, integrity, sense of humor, even temper, earnestness, and especially an uncanny ability at repartee and turning the seeming distractions of a very public environment into an effective illustration. He always adapted his sermons to the interests and circumstances of his hearers. Taylor deeply loved the common men to whom he ministered: 1) the miners who faced intense temptations, dangers, and often deprivations while far from home, 2) the California Indians with whom he particularly identified, and 3) the sailors whose abuses at the hands of the "shanghaiing landsharks" he denounced angrily. He individually attended to many sick and broken men, helped to found a hospital to meet their needs—the first institution of its kind in California, and preached the funeral for perhaps 1,000 of them. In 1851 Taylor with two other Methodist missionaries, Isaac Owen and Edward Bannister, founded the first college in California, what is now the University of the Pacific in Stockton. David Starr Jordan, the original president of Stanford University, called Taylor the "Methodist Boanerges" and described him as "the most prominent evangelical reformer of his day, a great force for good in San Francisco". To this day, Taylor is recognized in the famous mural paintings in the San Francisco Public Library, where he appears with other prominent early Californians including mission founder Junipero Serra, author Bret Harte, Supreme Court Justice Stephen J. Field, and pioneer James "Grizzly" Adams.[19]

Bishop Taylor

He did not begin his around-the-world missionary junkets until his middle age. But Taylor was not an average middle-aged man; his six-foot, 207-pound frame possessed unusual strength and vitality. Even when nearly sixty years of age, he was able to lift over 750 pounds. He needed great stamina for his constant travels. His record of preaching and touring in such widespread areas as England, Australia,[20] Asia Minor, Syria, Palestine, Egypt, Ceylon, New Zealand, South Africa, India, Peru, and Chile is especially remarkable when one considers the slow and difficult methods of ocean travel available in the last third of the nineteenth century.[21]

Taylor believed that missionary activities should be self-supporting. He was an early advocate of the faith mission movement (which he called the "Pauline System") whereby the missionary received his support from his converts in the areas where he worked; if this method proved inadequate, then the foreign evangelist, like Paul the tentmaker, should earn the remainder of his needed income himself. Taylor supported himself and his family by the funds accruing from the sale of his many books. Among his 18 books are *Seven Years' Street Preaching in San Francisco* (1856), *Christian Adventures in South Africa* (1867), *Our South American Cousins* (1878), *Pauline Methods of Missionary Work* (1879), *Ten Years of Self-Supporting Missions in India* (1882), *Story of My Life* (1895), and *Flaming Torch in Darkest Africa* (1898), with the latter introduced by the famous British explorer Henry Morton Stanley.[22]

Taylor's missionary methods led to a major confrontation with the Methodist authorities, who called him an "incorrigible individualist." He ignored the Methodist Board of Foreign Missions when he solicited funds and helpers for his mission projects. He toured the United States gaining support for his endeavors at Holiness camp meetings from Maine to Oregon. The Methodist leaders expressed dismay that he recruited and sent abroad many missionaries who did not have "home support"; obviously the church officials did not sympathize with his "Pauline System" philosophy.[23] Friction also existed because Taylor was not an officially recognized Methodist missionary. In 1882 the Church's General Mission Committee went on record as denying Taylor (or anyone not a regular appointee) to organize Northern[24] Methodist churches outside the United States. They also specifically declared his South American congregation to be "out of order," and they demanded that the American pastors of these churches return to the United States. The Methodist leaders suffered further embarrassment when the church conference "accidentally" elected Taylor to the rank of bishop. At the 1884 General Conference held in Philadelphia an obscure delegate nominated Taylor for the new position of missionary bishop for Liberia. To the surprise of the church leaders, who had expected the election of a black man, Taylor won the election on the first ballot. To add insult to the injury, Taylor refused the $3,000 stipend that went with the position.[25]

In the years after 1890 the school began to reflect much of William Taylor's religious philosophy. It developed a keen interest in the Holiness movement, and it increasingly identified with the Holiness groups inside and outside of Methodism. It took pride in helping poor youth, and at times it claimed that its poverty was a sign of virtue. It increased its promotion of foreign missions. The college also assumed an independent Methodist denominational status. It freed itself of the control of the regular church hierarchy; yet it trained many Methodist missionaries, preachers, and lay workers. To the extent to which the aged bishop knew of these developments, he must have been very proud of his educational namesake.

Considerable controversy has existed over the years with regard to the number of times—if any—Taylor visited the school. I have found record of only one visit, but this visit was not, as tradition has suggested, on the occasion of the cornerstone ceremony of the first building on the Upland campus. The material found in the cornerstone after the building burned in 1960 showed that Taylor did not participate in the ceremony. The world missionary was midway through his eighth decade of life when he visited the college at the beginning of the 1895-96 school year. In addition, he may have visited the Fort Wayne campus five years earlier, just after the school assumed his name. The *Fort Wayne Sentinel* of October 8, 1890, reported that he "was to come" to the college during the following week, but subsequent editions of the paper did not mention that he actually came to Fort Wayne. Taylor died in Palo Alto, California, in 1902 and is buried in Mountain View Cemetery, Oakland, overlooking the San Francisco Bay.[26]

> *In the years after 1890 the school began to reflect much of William Taylor's religious philosophy. It developed a keen interest in the Holiness movement, and it increasingly identified with the Holiness groups inside and outside of Methodism....It increased its promotion of foreign missions. The college also assumed an independent Methodist denominational status....To the extent to which the aged bishop knew of these developments, he must have been very proud of his educational namesake.*

3. A New Emphasis

The earnest pietism that characterized the school in the period after 1890 was less of a "new" emphasis than an intensification of the religious fervor that already had existed at Fort Wayne College.[27] There is evidence that Fort Wayne College in the 1880s was a deeply religious institution; reports from this period speak of "daily prayer meetings largely attended" and "sweeping revivals which left few unconverted." The North Indiana Methodist Conference Committee on Education remarked in 1887 that the "revival spirit more or less prevails constantly," and President Herrick's annual report for the 1888-89 school year reported that "religious meetings have been held on nearly every evening of the week for the whole year."[28]

> *Any room is good enough for me. Is there a room nobody else wants–give it to me.*
> — *Sammy Morris*

Thus Taylor University merely expanded what Fort Wayne College had already begun, and the man who more than any other served as the catalyst of the more intense spiritual atmosphere was Thaddeus C. Reade (President, 1891-1902). One area in which the increased religious emphasis found application was the curriculum. Reade added a Bible Training School to the liberal arts and other divisions of the school. Included in the Bible School was a three-year program for ministers, a two-year program for missionaries, and a two-year program for lay preachers (this course was of special interest to the NALP). The addition of a new Bible School meant the addition of many new courses such as exegetical theology, historical theology, systematic theology, and practical theology.[29]

Despite Reade's considerable work with curriculum change, he emphasized the improvement of the students' minds less than the edification of their spirits. He displayed great pride when he could announce to the trustees that "nearly all of our students have been brought to Jesus." One of Reade's trustees expressed the President's sentiments as well as his own when he said, "Since every university seeks to become distinguished for some specific excellence, let Taylor University be distinguished for the piety and religious fervor of her students and faculty."[30]

Reade's most successful contribution to the cause of creating a school "distinguished for its piety" was the publicity he gave to the life of an African student, "Sammy" Morris. Sammy's unquestioning faith and his quest for the "Spirit-filled" life epitomized what Reade was seeking to accomplish in the lives of all his students. Even before many people knew the Morris story, Reade had been partially successful in changing the character of the school. In a sense, then, Sammy became the symbol of the already new emphasis of the college. But the young African became more than this. When Reade published his biography of Sammy Morris, it was read by many of the people who were (or could be) attracted to the type of Christianity both Reade and Morris represented. Young persons of this type began to apply for admission to "Sammy Morris' school" in increasing numbers.[31] Thus the story of Sammy Morris (more than Sammy's personal influence) was the most significant factor in effecting the type of pietistical-holiness school that Reade sought.

Just who was this Sammy Morris whose life story had been so impressive to so many people? Sammy (or Kaboo as was his native name) was born in 1873, perhaps in Guinea, as the son of a chieftain of the Kru nation which was probably based in the village of Po River in southern Liberia. An enemy army, probably of the Grebo clans, took him captive in a tribal war when he was a small child, but his people redeemed him. A second kidnapping took place when he was eleven; however, this time his tribe did not purchase him from the enemy. After a period of captivity the young lad escaped into the woods and traveled a great distance by foot until he came to a plantation on the Liberian coast. During the period of his employment on this plantation he experienced Christian conversion under the influence of a Miss Knolls, a former student at Fort Wayne College. Miss Knolls gave him the name of the Fort Wayne banker who was her major financial supporter. While this missionary lady was tutoring Sammy in his new faith, he expressed a desire to become a preacher to his own people. Another missionary, Rev. C. E. Smirl, advised him to go to America to obtain an education if he wished to preach the gospel properly.[32]

Sammy Morris

Meanwhile, Sammy met another missionary lady, Miss Lizzie MacNeil, who had recently come to Liberia from New York, and she gave him further religious training and specific advice about his proposed trip to the United States. She had come to Africa under the sponsorship of Bishop Taylor's African Mission,[33] and she had gained much of her religious philosophy from the secretary of Taylor's mission, Rev. Stephen Merritt of New York City. Merritt had placed great emphasis upon the importance of the Holy Spirit in the life of the Christian; she had absorbed his teaching and in turn passed it on to her young African pupil. When Sammy sailed for America he expressed as much interest in learning more about the Holy Spirit from Stephen Merritt as he did in finding a school that would better prepare him to preach to his people.[34]

After Sammy arrived in New York and stayed with Stephen Merritt for a while, Merritt began to look for a school he could attend. Merritt conferred with Ross Taylor, one of the Bishop's four sons and the treasurer of the Taylor mission, and they decided to write to the school in Fort Wayne to see whether the officials there would admit Sammy as a student. Reade and Stemen agreed to accept Sammy, and he enrolled in the middle of the 1891-92 school year. The student roster for that year listed him as an "irregular student," and the one for the following year classified him as a "Biblical student." Necessarily he studied primary lessons, and often he worked with a special tutor.[35]

Sammy's illness and death came during the last semester of classes held in Fort Wayne. He acquired a severe cold in January, 1893, and although he never completely recovered from the illness, he continued his studies as long as he was able to do so. Death, apparently from pneumonia,[36] came in May, 1893, and his funeral was in the First Methodist Church, the place where he had regularly worshipped. Reade described the funeral as "one of the largest...I have ever witnessed in the city of Fort Wayne." Mourners completely filled the church, and hundreds more congregated just outside the doors. His burial was in the "Negro quarters" of the Lindenwood Cemetery; however, thirty-five years later the senior class of 1928 convinced the Lindenwood officials to reinter his body in a more prominent part of the cemetery.[37]

> *Bread is one thing, stone is another thing. I once saw a stone with gold in it and they told me it was worth more than a barrel of flour; but when I am hungry I cannot eat that stone, I must have bread; so my soul cannot be satisfied with anything but Jesus, the bread of life.*
> — *Sammy Morris*

Sammy's influence became even greater in death than it had been in life. Reade's biography[38] of his life had sold over 200,000 copies by 1924. Reade probably wrote the Morris story primarily to inspire Christians and convert sinners; however, the book also brought many students and some money to the school. The profits from the sale of the book largely paid for the original Sammy Morris dormitory on the Upland campus.[39] Part of the proceeds from the book also went into a student aid fund to assist— by loans or by gifts—children of ministers, ministerial candidates, and foreign students. Some students obtained sizeable amounts of aid from this fund. For example, in 1896 the faculty voted $120.37[40] to Samuel Culpepper (who was born in British Guiana and later served as a career missionary in Puerto Rico) and $72 to Sarkis Jamkotchian of Caesarea, Turkey. Even more significant financially than the sales profits were the outright gifts from those who found the book especially impressive. Burt Ayres believed that the Morris publicity kept the school alive in this period. In terms of the funds and especially the students attracted to the school by it in the early Upland years, his view may be correct.[41]

4. A New Location

When the NALP assumed control of the college in 1890, most interested persons assumed that they would soon—and with no great difficulty— establish the school on a solid financial foundation. This, however, did not happen, although the expectation had been a reasonable one. The NALP represented a large constituency throughout the nation, and some of their members possessed considerable wealth. Yet, for some reason, the NALP leadership could not cultivate these resources for their new school, and the financial situation of the university failed to improve.[42]

The school year 1892-93 was a desperate one. Because of an order[43] to sell the property, the school officials did not hold classes in the college building; rather, they rented a structure for this purpose at the corner of Jefferson and Broadway in Fort Wayne. The limited space allowed by the small rented quarters meant a severe reduction in the number of students the college could accept. Thus the enrollment, which had numbered three hundred in 1888, dropped to seventy-seven in 1892 (see Figure II in chapter three). Meanwhile, President Reade, in an effort to keep the school alive, began looking for a city that would welcome and support it.[44] A guest-preaching engagement in the Upland Methodist Church afforded Reade the chance to meet the minister of the church, the Rev. John C. White. When White heard about the problems of the school in Fort Wayne, he became interested in persuading the college to move to Upland. He and another Upland citizen, J. W. Pittinger, were the major local residents who worked to bring the school to the community. In the spring of 1893 White negotiated an agreement between the Taylor trustees and the Upland Land Company whereby the university agreed to move to Upland and the company agreed to provide Taylor with $10,000 in cash and ten acres of land. In the summer of 1893 the school relocated in the Grant County town.[45]

It is doubtful that White would have found the local resources necessary to bring the university to Upland if the community at that time had not been experiencing the prosperity afforded by the recent discovery in the area of large

Thaddeus Reade

The President as a Poet

During his Taylor presidency (1891-1902), Thaddeus Reade brought a selfless commitment to his spiritual vision for the school. He sought to enhance the degree to which the institution was a Spirit-filled training ground for young and often impoverished ministerial candidates.

Reade was an avid writer of both prose and poetry. He wrote two books of poetry and published several of his works in hymnals. One of his hymns was included as a permanent part of the Methodist roster of hymns in 1901.

The following is from a hymn written by Reade during a time of illness:

A Song in the Night
When the storms of temptation arise,
and waves of adversity roll,
When Hope has abandoned the skies
and Joy has deserted my soul,
He gives me a song in the night,
and my darkness is turned to day:
"Lo I am thy Lord and thy Light,
Thy portion forever and aye."
- *Thaddeus Reade*

Source: Randal Dillinger, "Thaddeus Reade" (unpublished manuscript).

deposits of natural gas. The "gas boom" of central Indiana began in 1886 and continued through the 1890s before the supply began to decline about 1900. The richest deposits lay in an area bounded on four corners by Kokomo, Hartford City, Muncie, and Noblesville. The first gas discoveries in Upland were in 1888, and three years later the Upland Land Company came into existence to take advantage of the newly found resources by promoting the development of the town. In this climate of economic prosperity and community growth the Upland citizens offered to help the Taylor officials relocate the school in their town.[46]

Upland had existed for one generation, and Jefferson Township and Grant County had recorded over sixty years of history when Taylor moved from Fort Wayne to become a part of each of them. The first White resident of the Upland area was John Oswalt, who came to Jefferson Township in the early 1830s and purchased 2,240 acres including almost all the land which is now a part of Upland. He bought this large amount of land because, as a speculator, he thought that an Indianapolis to Fort Wayne canal might pass through or near his property.

The first Sammy Morris Hall.

Jacob Bugher, who moved to the township in 1851, purchased land from Oswalt. Sixteen years later, when the first railroad (the Indiana Central Railroad) passed through the township, Bugher planned the beginnings of Upland as a depot point for the railroad. The name of the town came from its reputed location as the highest point on the rail line between Columbus and Chicago. Gradually, the town grew in population and organization. By the late 1870s it had thirty families, 150 total population, one grade school, two churches, one post office, one grocery, one drugstore, three dry-goods stores, one sawmill, and one blacksmith shop. When the school moved to the community in 1893, the incorporated town of one thousand inhabitants could boast of some improved streets and carbon street lights, water and gas lines, a major glass bottle manufacturing plant, and a zinc factory. Within fifteen miles of the new Upland campus was the city of Marion, which numbered over 17,000 residents by 1900.[47]

During the first year in Upland—as had been the case in the last year in Fort Wayne—the school rented facilities in which to operate. A small wooden building on the east side of the major downtown business block contained the president's office and the dining hall, and the local churches offered their facilities for classroom purposes. The non-resident students roomed (and some also boarded) in the homes of local citizens.[48]

Two new buildings on the campus site at the south end of town greeted the students at the beginning of the second Upland year in the fall of 1894. H. Maria Wright Hall immediately became—and continued to be until it burned in 1960—the nerve center of the campus. The three-floor, 80' X 68' brick structure took its name from the wife of the current president of the National Association of Local Preachers because of her $1,000 gift for its construction. Wright Hall (later better known as the Administration Building) housed the classrooms, the science laboratories, and the chapel. Sammy Morris Hall, a white frame structure located one block north of Wright Hall, also admitted students in

Scene in the men's dormitory in the late 1890s.

September, 1894. Its first floor served as the dining hall and kitchen, and the second floor was a dormitory. The initial boarding accommodations in Morris Hall were very primitive. Each 8' X 10' room contained cheap furniture: wooden chairs, a crude study table, a small wall mirror, a dresser, a few hooks on which to hang clothes, a washstand, a bowl, a pitcher, and a slop jar. The floors were rough lumber.[49]

In the early years almost all the students lived in private homes. When Morris Hall was housing male students, it had room for only a limited number of them. Most of the students roomed in the houses in the first few blocks north of the campus. The second campus structure to serve as a dormitory was a white frame building just southeast of Morris Hall.[50] Upon its completion in the late 1890s, its second floor served as a women's dormitory; the bottom story became the new dining hall.[51]

Considering the limited amount of dormitory space in the early Upland years, one marvels that the school enrolled 158 students in the first year and 160 in 1894-95. Many of the students, however, commuted from their nearby homes; of the 160 students in 1894-95, fifty were from Upland. In this early period

The H. Maria Wright Hall opened in 1894 as the first building on the Upland property. To this day it remains the most significant building in the history of the Upland campus.

H. Maria Wright Hall.

probably no other school in the immediate Upland area offered high-school-level work.[52]

When Taylor moved from Fort Wayne to Upland, most of the major faculty members moved with it. Those who came with President Reade included Christian Stemen, C. L. Clippinger, and Grace Husted. The fact that Stemen severed his lengthy relationship with the medical school in Fort Wayne to come to Upland indicated the degree of his devotion to the NALP school. His Upland position was vice-president and professor of physiology and hygiene. C. L. Clippinger, who had been associated with the school as either financial agent or professor since 1884, became the first Upland professor of physics, chemistry, and Latin.[53]

The financial state of the university was much better in the early Upland years than it had been in the last decade in Fort Wayne. By 1895 Board President John R. Wright could report that the school owned property worth over $40,000 and held an indebtedness of only $3,000. Meanwhile, during the previous year a Mr. R. T. McDonald purchased the Fort Wayne property for $30,000. After the trustees paid the indebtedness on the Fort Wayne campus, they probably possessed a net sum to invest in the Upland campus. The school became completely free of debt on January 1, 1898. Wright, a Washington, D.C., undertaker, frequently made large gifts to the college, and a gift from him in 1898 liquidated the last one thousand dollars of liability.[54]

Thus by the mid-1890s Taylor University had its beginning in Upland. The several changes it had experienced in the previous decade largely determined the subsequent history of the school. Later events modified and modernized the Taylor pattern as it existed in 1895, but they did not greatly alter it.

[1] Herrick and Sweet, *North Indiana Conference,* p. 179; letter, Fort Wayne College Trustees to the National Association of Local Preachers Education Committee, October 23, 1884 (Taylor University archives); FWCTM, June 12, 1884, June 28, 1884, and June 30, 1884.

[2] North Indiana Conference of the Methodist Episcopal Church, *Minutes of the 1888 Conference* (Indianapolis, 1888), p. 65 and *Minutes of the 1890 Annual Conference* (Indianapolis, 1890), p. 66; FWCTM, May 29, 1890 and June 26, 1890.

[3] The National Association of Local Preachers of the Methodist Episcopal Church, *Proceedings of the Thirty-Eighth Annual Meeting,* 1895 (Pittsburgh, 1986), p. 3; Emory S. Bucke, ed., *The History of American Methodism,* 3 vols. (Nashville, 1964), I, 471-73, 504 and II, 651, 658-59; *TUC,* 1892-93 (Fort Wayne, n.d.), p. 5.

[4] E. Sterl Phinney, "Christian B. Stemen," *Taylor Bulletin,* September, 1962, pp. 6-8; *FWCC,* 1877-79, p. 40; *TUC,* 1893-94, p. 6.

[5] FWCTM, October 23, 1884.

[6] *Ibid.,* March 21, 1885 and June 9, 1885.

[7] *Ibid.,* November 18, 1884.

[8] President Herrick told a local newspaper reporter that he expected an endowment of $200,000 within a two-year period! See *Fort Wayne Sentinel,* August 28, 1889, p. 1.

[9] FWCTM, December 22, 1884, July 16, 1885, June 20, 1889, and August 13, 1889; *Fort Wayne Sentinel,* August 28, 1889, p. 1; Woodburn, *Higher Education in Indiana,* pp. 187-89.

[10] FWCTM, June 18, 1889, January 14, 1890, February 6, 1890, March 4, 1890, April 15, 1890, and May 6, 1890.

[11] *Ibid.,* May 29, 1890 and June 26, 1890.

[12] *TUC*, 1890-91, p. 2 and 1892-93, p. 5; *Fort Wayne Sentinel*, April 23, 1890, p. 1; Douglas J. Marlow, "Life, Liberty, and the Pursuit of Health Care," *Taylor Magazine*, Winter, 1994, p. 13.

[13] *TUC*, 1890-91, pp. ii, 3-4, 8-12.

[14] The school advertised that the laboratory training of the medical students included the dissection of "cold, stark, human stiff." See *Fort Wayne Sentinel*, March 25, 1891, p. 3.

[15] The location of the City Hospital was the corner of East Washington and Barr Streets.

[16] Phinney, "Stemen," pp. 6-8; *TUC*, 1890-91, pp. 17, 22-23, 25-26; Marlow, "Life, Liberty, and the Pursuit of Health Care," pp. 13-15.

[17] Barbara Sicherman, *Alice Hamilton: A Life in Letters* (Cambridge, 1984), pp. 18, 33-35; Wilma Ruth Slaight, "Alice Hamilton: First Lady of Industrial Medicine," Diss. Case Western Reserve University, 1974, pp. 11, 70; Exploring the Dangerous Trades: The Autobiography of Alice Hamilton (Boston, 1993), p. 38; "Edith Hamilton," *Dictionary of American Biography*, Supp. 7 (1981), p. 313; "Alice Hamilton," *Dictionary of American Biography*, Supp. 8 (1988), pp. 241-42; Obituary, *New York Times*, September 23, 1970, p. 50; letter, Joseph D. Brain, to author, December 6, 1995.

[18] "William Taylor" in Johnson and Malone, *Dictionary of American Biography*, XVIII, 345.

[19] *Ibid.*, XVIII, 345-46; William Taylor, *Story of My Life* (New York, 1896), p. 144; Idwal Jones, *Ark of Empire* (Garden City, New York, 1951), p. 117; George W. James, *Heroes of California* (n.p., 1910), pp. 142-43, 146-47; Rockwell Hunt, *California's Stately Hall of Fame* (Stockton, 1950), pp. 255-58; Rockwell Hunt, ed., *California and Californians* (Chicago, 1926), pp. 396-98; interview with Alan H. Winquist, Winter, 1996.

[20] Taylor sent from Australia the original seeds which established in California the wide expanse of fast-growing eucalyptus or blue gum trees. Consequently the eucalyptus became one of the most common trees in the state. See Jones,

Ark of Empire, p. 118; and James, *Heroes of California*, pp. 149-50.

²¹ "William Taylor," *Dictionary of American Biography*, XVIII, 345-46; also see John H. Paul, *The Soul Digger* (Upland, Indiana, 1928), for a detailed description of Taylor's missionary journeys.

²² "William Taylor," *Dictionary of American Biography*, XVIII, 345-46; interview with Alan H. Winquist, Winter, 1996.

²³ For a more recent critical view of Taylor's methods, see the assessment by prominent historian Geoffrey Moorhouse in his *The Missionaries* (Philadelphia, 1973), pp. 203-07.

²⁴ The Methodist Episcopal Church had split into Northern and Southern branches over the issue of slavery in 1844, and they remained apart in this period and until 1939.

²⁵ Bucke, ed., *American Methodism*, II, 192, 621.

²⁶ Letter, E. Sterl Phinney to author, June 17, 1970; *Upland Monitor*, September 12, 1895, p. 1 and October 3, 1895, p. 1; *Fort Wayne Sentinel*, October 8, 1890, p. 1; interview with Alan H. Winquist, Winter, 1996.

²⁷ The religious upswing at Taylor stood in contrast to the general decline in religious enthusiasm that characterized American colleges in general in this turn-of-the-century period.

²⁸ FWCTM, October 23, 1884 and June 20, 1889; The North Indiana Conference of the Methodist Episcopal Church, *Minutes of the 1887 Conference* (Indianapolis, 1887), p. 61.

²⁹ *TUC*, 1892-93, pp. 4-7.

³⁰ National Association of Local Preachers of the Methodist Episcopal Church MS, "Report of the President of Taylor University," Mountain Lake, Maryland, 1895 (Taylor University archives).

[31] In the early years after the school moved to Upland, almost every nonlocal student mentioned the Sammy Morris book as the primary factor in attracting him to Taylor University. See Ayres, "Taylor University," p. 11.

[32] Thaddeus C. Reade, *Samuel Morris* (Upland, Indiana, 1924 edition), pp. 310; Jorge O. Masa, *The Angel in Ebony* (Upland, Indiana, 1928), p. 19; Lindley J. Baldwin, *The March of Faith* (Chicago, 1941), pp. 19, 23; Charles B. (Tim) Kirkpatrick, MS Liberia Videotaping Safari (Taylor University archives), p. 3.

[33] Bishop Taylor had visited the Cape Palmas area on his missionary endeavors, and he was especially interested in the Kru tribes. By 1895 over fifty missionaries had gone to the area under his mission. During their 1988 Liberian trip, Professor of Communications Charles B. (Tim) Kirkpatrick and alumnus David Ryan participated in the Methodist districtwide celebration of the centennial of the establishment of the Taylor mission in the likely area of Morris' childhood. See Barclay, *History of Methodist Missions*, II, 896-97 and III, 902; Kirkpatrick, Liberia Safari, p. 1.

[34] Reade, *Morris*, pp. 11-13; Masa, *Angel in Ebony*, p. 41.

[35] Letter, Ross Taylor to C. B. Stemen, October 20, 1891 (Taylor University archives); *TUC*, 1892-93, p. 12 and 1893-94, p. 22; Reade, *Morris*, pp. 18-25.

[36] A report in the *Fort Wayne Sentinel* described Sammy's ailment as "stomach trouble, which has caused a dropsical affection" with "symptoms of dyspepsia." Taylor physician David H. Brewer stated that nineteenth century medical reports were often limited to symptomatic descriptions rather than precise diagnoses. These reports, however, led Brewer to assume that Sammy's fatal illness was pneumonia. See "Like A Romance," *Fort Wayne Sentinel*, April 14, 1893, p. 1; letter, David H. Brewer to author, May 26, 1989.

[37] Reade, *Morris*, pp. 26-27; Ayres, "Taylor University," pp. 11-12.

[38] Two later Morris biographies are Jorge O. Masa, *Angel in Ebony*, written by a Filipino member of the class of 1928; and Lindley J. Baldwin, *March of Faith*, written by a member of the 1886 class of Fort Wayne College. The Masa book appeared in 1928 and was more thorough than the earlier Reade book.

The Baldwin volume is currently the most useful of the Morris biographies.

[39] One should not confuse this dormitory with the current Morris Hall, which was constructed in 1958.

[40] This was approximately the cost of room, board, and tuition for a year in this period.

[41] Reade, *Morris*, p. i; *TUC*, 1895-96 (Fort Wayne, 1895), p. i; MS Taylor University Faculty Minutes, May 4, 1896 (Taylor University archives); Ayres, "Taylor University," p. 11; *TUC*, 1899-1900 (Upland, n.d.), pp. 30, 31; interview with Alan H. Winquist, Winter, 1996.

[42] Ayres, "Taylor University," p. 8, 10.

[43] It is unclear whether this order came from the NALP or whether it was a court order.

[44] One town whose leaders showed some interest in acquiring the school was Van Wert, Ohio. See *Fort Wayne Sentinel*, March 29, 1893, p. 1.

[45] *TUC*, 1892-93, p. 4 and 1893-94, p. 5; Ayres, "Taylor University," pp. 10, 15, 73; *Upland Monitor*, April 13, 1893, p. 1; *Taylor Bulletin*, May, 1922, p. 15.

[46] Barnhart and Carmony, *Indiana*, II, 282-84; Hugh Freese, ed., *The Upland Story*, 1867-1967 (n.p., 1967), p. 6.

[47] Rolland L. Whitson, ed., *Centennial History of Grant County* (Chicago, 1914), I, 7, 159, 165-66; Freese, *Upland*, pp. 4-6, 53-54; Barnhart and Carmony, Indiana, II, 294; *Upland Monitor*, April 13, 1893, p. 3; *TUC*, 1893-94, p. 5.

[48] Ayres, "Taylor University," pp. 16, 27.

[49] *Ibid.*, pp. 16-17; *TUC*, 1893-94, pp. 5, 19-20; National Association of Local Preachers, *Proceedings of the Thirty-Eighth Annual Meeting*, 1895, p. 15.

[50] This structure housed the campus grill and bookstore in the 1950s and 1960s.

[51] Ayres, "Taylor University," pp. 17-18.

[52] *TUC*, 1894-95, pp. 27-28 and 1895-96, pp. 26-30.

[53] *TUC*, 1892-93, p. 3 and 1893-94, p. 4; FWCTM, June 12, 1884 and September 30, 1884.

[54] National Association of Local Preachers of the Methodist Episcopal Church, *Proceedings of the Thirty-Eighth Annual Meeting*, 1895, p. 7; letter, Charles Bash to T. C. Reade, December 14, 1894 (Taylor University archives); Ayres, "Taylor University," p. 26.

Chapter Five

THE FIRST FIFTY YEARS IN UPLAND
(PART I): ADMINISTRATION AND FINANCE

The Upland school in the period before World War II primarily sought to be a religious training school for children from the common-class families; the effort to be a first-rate academic institution with a solid economic foundation was always a secondary goal. The trustees usually selected presidents who could provide religious leadership; they were less concerned about whether their appointees also possessed intellectual influence and business acumen. The result was that the school trained and inspired many future ministers, future missionaries, and other Christian youth, but it did not establish solid credentials in areas other than religious training. The failure to seek and obtain regional accreditation not only prevented the strengthening of the academic program, but it also contributed to the economic distress. Many potential benefactors and students hesitated to invest their resources in an unaccredited institution. Its announced goal of helping to subsidize the education of poor Christian boys and girls also contributed to the economic problem. In a sense this aim was highly admirable; however, it sufficiently impoverished the college so that there always was doubt about whether it would survive to educate another generation of poor (or any other type of) students. The decline in interest by the National Association of Local Preachers caused further difficulty. After the first Upland decade, the largely Eastern-based Local Preachers organization began to assume the status of absentee landlords. Their representatives on the board of trustees missed many of the biannual meetings. This neglect by the NALP eventually led to a change in ownership of the school in the 1920s.

The administrative and financial history of the college in this fifty-year period

Dr. Reade will. . . bear the expense of all repairs necessary...and ...the first party [the trustees] shall not be or become liable for any debt or expense incurred as above whatever.

Burt W. Ayres

While many other people arrived and departed from Taylor during the first half-century in Upland, one person's longevity, as well as power of character and integrity of mind, left an indelible mark on the university. More than any other single individual, Burt Ayres represented the best qualities of the institution during his time with the university (1897-1906, 1910-46).

Severe and stern when duty demands, because of justice and right, never was one able to deal with more general satisfaction to all....

- 1903 *Gem* on Burt Ayres

is full of crises. Three changes in ownership, two receiverships, and talks of relocation worked against stability and almost led to the demise of the school. Part of the difficulty developed from the general economic crisis in America during the 1930s, but some of the problems resulted directly from unenlightened institutional planning. The school continuously operated with an indebtedness in varying amounts. When the debt became sufficiently small, the officials often planned the construction of a new building. Benefactors usually helped to pay for part but never all of the new building; then the indebtedness again would increase. The situation of permanent indebtedness was not necessarily a bad one; the university always had a large balance of total assets over liabilities. The problem was that most of the assets were not liquid, and the college sometimes had considerable difficulty in paying its current liabilities. When the creditors pressed for payment in an unusually vigorous manner, the school found itself in an embarrassing and sometimes legally dangerous position.

1. THE READE ADMINISTRATION AND AFTER

Four men presided over the university during most of its first half-century in Upland. They were Thaddeus C. Reade (1893-1902),[1] Monroe Vayhinger (1908-21), John H. Paul (1922-31), and Robert L. Stuart (1931-45). Several other men also led the school, but they served either only for brief periods or else in the role of acting president.

Thaddeus Reade came to Taylor after a career of preaching and educational administration in Ohio. He spent his boyhood days near Marion, Ohio, and he was graduated with honors from Ohio Wesleyan University. He held pastorates at Sidney, Fostoria, and Zanesville, Ohio, and he served as president of Fairfield Union Academy. Reportedly, he declined an offer to become the president of Willamette College, a Methodist school in Oregon. The first Mrs. Reade must have been an interesting woman. She published many poems in the *Western Christian Advocate* (a leading Methodist periodical), and she attended the 1874 national convention of temperance women in Cleveland that organized the Women's Christian Temperance Union. Unfortunately, she died before her husband became the president of Taylor.[2]

Reade's primary contributions to Taylor were the directing of the move to Upland and the development of the enhanced religious fervor of the school; however, his role as an administrator was far from insignificant. In the decade of the 1890s, the trustees had a curious agreement with him whereby he did not merely administer the college but also held personal responsibility for collecting funds and paying debts. For example, his contract for the period 1898-1903 stated that he would "bear the expense of all repairs necessary...and...the first party [the trustees] shall not be or become liable for any debt or expense incurred as above whatever." When, about 1900, the trustees feared that the profits and gifts resulting from the sale of Reade's biography of Sammy Morris might allow the president to exploit the financial arrangement to his personal advantage, they altered the agreement to place the responsibility for all the business affairs in the hands of the board treasurer, Upland

businessman T. W. Williams. The implications of the trustees' action hurt Reade deeply. Not only did he possess great personal integrity, but he had actually contributed several thousand dollars of his own money to sustain the college. One might argue that Reade, as the author of the Morris book, justifiably could have claimed the right to the proceeds accruing from it. Instead, however, he directed the monies from it into a fund for school construction and

A view from the southeast c. 1905.

scholarship projects. The Eastern trustees, who knew very little of the internal administration of the university, had acted on the basis of an inaccurate suspicion. A short time later Reade's health began to decline, and during the last two years of his life he was able to perform the duties of his office only on a limited basis.[3]

The list of the first Upland trustees contained many names that are familiar to later generations of Taylor students and Upland residents. The Maria Wright Administration Building and Wright Avenue took their names from the original Upland board president, John R. Wright, and his wife. The Wrights were among the most generous benefactors of the school during its first decade in Upland. The college officials named the museum for Nathan Walker, who was at various times treasurer and chairman of the board. Walker, who operated a clay-pottery plant in Wellsville, Ohio, contributed many geological specimens to the museum. Two board members, Louis Klopsch and George W. Mooney, were associated with the *Christian Herald* magazine. Mooney convinced the Christian Herald Publishing Company to contribute to the university many of its own publications and books it had collected for review purposes. This contribution comprised much of the school's original Upland library, which became known as the Mooney Library. Silas C. Swallow and the wife of Christopher Sickler later provided gifts that paid for a large part of the construction costs of the first two brick dormitories, Sickler Hall and Swallow Robin Dormitory. The only faculty member other than Reade and Christian Stemen to serve on the first board was C. L. Clippinger. It was largely through his efforts that the college acquired a 10 1/4-inch reflector telescope. The building that housed the instrument took the name of Clippinger Observatory. Wright, Walker, Stemen, and Sickler had all been presidents of the NALP; and Wright, Walker, and Stemen had served as editors of the association's periodical, the *Local Preachers Magazine*.[4]

Figure IV

Presidents of Taylor University

	Christian B. Stemen[a]	1890-1891
15.	Thaddeus C. Reade	1891-1902
	John H. Shilling[a]	1902-1903
	Burt W. Ayres[a]	1903-1904
16.	Charles W. Winchester	1904-1907
	Albert R. Archibald[a]	1907-1908
17.	Monroe Vayhinger	1908-1921
18.	James M. Taylor	1921-1922
	Burt W. Ayres[a]	1922
19.	John H. Paul	1922-1931
20.	Robert L. Stuart	1931-1945
21.	Clyde W. Meredith	1945-1951
	Harold J. Wiebe[a]	1951
22.	Evan H. Bergwall	1951-1959
	Milo A. Rediger[a]	1959-1960
23.	B. Joseph Martin	1960-1965
24.	Milo A. Rediger	1965-1975, 1979-1981
25.	Robert C. Baptista	1975-1979
26.	Gregg O. Lehman	1981-1985
27.	Daryl R. Yost[a]	1985
28.	Jay L. Kesler	1985-

[a] *Acting President*

86

Also among the first trustees were Chauncey Shaffer, a major benefactor when the school was in Fort Wayne, and three prominent Upland residents: John C. White, Anson C. Bugher, and T. W. Williams. White, the minister of the Methodist Church, was the local resident most responsible for bringing the school to Upland. Bugher was the son of the Jacob Bugher who had plotted the town of Upland, and the father of John C. Bugher, who later as a medical researcher and an Atomic Energy Commission executive became one of the school's most distinguished alumni. Williams, perhaps the leading businessman of the community, was the most generous local contributor to the school in the early years. His Upland holdings included a farm, a sawmill, a brickyard, and a large hardware and implement store. Probably much of the lumber for the construction of Wright Hall and Morris Hall came as a gift from Williams' sawmill; and when Williams held the office of board treasurer, he often paid school bills from his own funds.[5]

The most important addition to the physical plant in the first decade of the twentieth century was Sickler Hall, built in 1902-03. The school officials used a five-thousand-dollar gift from the will of the widow of one of the early Taylor trustees, Christopher Sickler of Camden, New Jersey, to pay for much of the cost of the new hall. It was the desire of the Sicklers that their gift help young ministerial candidates obtain their educational preparation, and the trustees thought that the best way to implement this wish would be to provide free or very inexpensive dormitory rooms for such students in a new residential hall. Not only ministerial candidates but also children of ministers and missionaries obtained free rooms in Sickler Hall. The building remained a dormitory, however, only in the early period. Subsequently, it served as a science hall, education department center, and speech department headquarters.[6]

Several other small dormitory buildings appeared in the period before 1910. President Reade directed the construction of a number of small, low-cost, family cottages in the years before 1900 so that the school could offer cheap housing to young married ministerial candidates. These units were not well-built; they had no foundation, and the rugged Upland wind blew through the cracks in the walls. However, Reade's purpose for the cottages had been to rent them for almost nothing, and the minimum cost of their construction allowed him to do that. Gleaners Hall and Speicher Hall were house-like ladies' dormitories. The Gleaners building was built about 1903 as a project of a group of women who wished to provide rent-free rooms for female missionary candidates; however, when the women gave the building to the school it still had a thousand-

dollar mortgage. Speicher Hall originally was a private home owned by Joseph B. Speicher on the present site of Swallow Robin Dormitory. It became the property of the college by purchase in 1906.[7]

Meanwhile, changes appeared in Wright Hall. After Dr. Wright provided the funds to finish the fourth floor of the building in 1900, this top story became the chapel auditorium. The chapel room of the 1890s had been the southwest room on the second floor; this old chapel site became the new Mooney Library.[8]

Other campus improvements gradually appeared. The administrative offices obtained a telephone in 1902, and the trustees voted to install a water system in 1906. When the local supply of natural gas began to decline after the turn of the century, the officials installed a campus-wide system of steam heat. Drinking fountains, lavatories, and a sewage disposal plant also were in existence at the school by the eve of World War I. Improvements in the campus streets came more slowly; a 1907 report described them as being in "dreadfully muddy condition" during most of the year.[9]

Economically the school operated as a quasi-charity institution. The students paid only a small percentage of the costs of their education. Much of the support for the new Upland school came from the large, but irregular, gifts of people like Wright and Sickler and the large and frequent contributions of Reade and Williams. There were other benefactors, however. College officials greatly rejoiced when they obtained a $3,000 Kokomo real estate gift in 1896 and the deed to a $2,600 California farm in 1904. Sometimes donors contributed unusual gifts. A trustee from Baltimore sent (with a $500 check) a keg of oysters for the boarding students. Despite the gifts, the institution was rarely out of debt. By 1906 the debt-free status of 1898 had changed to an $11,200 indebtedness. When the ordinary means of keeping the university solvent (i.e., tuition and gifts) failed—and they invariably did[10]—the school relied upon the willingness of the faculty to accept low and irregular salary payments.[11] The listed salaries for the 1905-06 year specified $2,000 for President Winchester, and amounts ranging from $380 to $650 for the rest of the faculty. It was not unusual for the school to be tardy with its payroll; for

Mooney Library.

example, the 1906-07 year ended with more than $3,000 in unpaid salaries.[12]

The death of President Reade in 1902 initiated a leadership crisis that continued until 1908. Almost simultaneous with the death of Reade came the illness and permanent retirement from the faculty of a longtime professor and dean, C. L. Clippinger. The able and youthful John H. Shilling, who had been vice-president prior to Reade's death, served as the acting president in 1902-03; but he left after that year to pursue further graduate study in religion that would better prepare him to direct Taylor's theological program upon his return. Combining scholarly ability and diligent working habits with a pleasant disposition, he would have become an excellent president. Unfortunately, he met an untimely death in 1904.[13]

Burt Ayres succeeded Shilling as the acting president in 1903-04, but he accepted that position only when the board could not find a satisfactory permanent president by the time of Shilling's departure. This was the first of two occasions during Ayres' nearly half-century with the school that he served as interim president, but it was only one of many times when his guidance helped the college through a difficult period. Ayres more than any other single individual represented the best qualities of the institution during its first half-century in Upland. He was an inspiring teacher of philosophy and a

Combining scholarly ability and diligent working habits with a pleasant disposition, he would have become an excellent president. Unfortunately, he met an untimely death in 1904.

John Shilling

man of considerable personal integrity and wisdom. Future President Evan H. Bergwall, who was a Taylor student in the 1930s, remarked of Ayres, "He is one of four or five men who have made the greatest impact on my life...." During much of his tenure with the school (1897-1906, 1910-46), he was the unquestioned intellectual leader of the faculty. His abilities as an administrator were less outstanding. Often when he served as dean, vice-president, or acting president, he did so from a sense of duty. He was at his best when he was teaching philosophy, giving advice on academic matters, and counseling students on questions of personal values.

While Ayres temporarily guided the institution, the trustees continued their search for a permanent president. In the summer of 1903, a minister by the name of A. L. Whitcombe accepted the offer of the board to become the new president beginning in September. A few days before the opening of the term he sent a message that he was not coming. Apparently his wife prompted his negative response; she objected to the smallness of the president's house and the abundance of ragweed in Upland.[14]

When the board obtained Charles W. Winchester of Buffalo, New York, to head the institution beginning in January, 1904, the school glowed with high expectancy; this man would provide inspiring leadership! Winchester came with impressive credentials: he had graduated from Syracuse University as the valedictorian of his class, and the school later awarded him an honorary doctorate degree; he had served as the editor of the *Christian Uplook* and the *Buffalo Christian Advocate*; and he had written several books, including *The*

President Winchester with Wright Hall office staff.

Gospel Kodak Abroad and *The Victories of Wesley Castle*. When Winchester first visited Upland as the president-elect, the school welcomed him in a manner that now appears humorous but which at the time indicated the enthusiasm with which the college looked forward to his presidency. The school paper reported his arrival in this manner: "Dr. Winchester...was given a memorable greeting on his first visit to the school. Almost the entire student body marched in military array through the streets of Upland to the depot. Dr. Winchester was greeted at the train by Prof. Ayres and Mr. Duncan. The latter escorted the Doctor through the double file of cheering students to the carriage waiting." To express further the school's greetings at the depot, the girls sang the university song and the boys gave the college yell.[15]

The optimism was premature, however, as Winchester's administration brought severe disharmony on campus. The new president clashed with Dean Ayers on the issue of student discipline. Ayres saw Winchester as being "too arbitrary and authoritative in handling discipline." He believed that Winchester wanted him to be a "kind of sheriff or hangman, rather than a counselor or disciplinarian."[16] The most important issue dividing the school during the Winchester years, however, was the president's plan to move the school to Muncie. Believing that Taylor could not long survive under its impoverished condition, Winchester thought that his proposal to move the college to Muncie would alleviate the problem. During the 1906-07 school year he arranged with Muncie officials for the school to occupy the original building and grounds of what has since developed into Ball State University. The plan called for Winchester to become the president of the Muncie school and for the institution to retain the name of Taylor University. Apparently, the Muncie citizens favored the move as much as did Winchester; but the Taylor board voted against the plan, and Winchester moved back to Buffalo, New York.[17]

The 1907-08 Taylor catalog, which Winchester wrote and printed during the period when the school was considering the proposed move to Muncie, showed the independent and tactless spirit of Winchester. He wrote the catalog on the assumption that the Muncie move was already a *fait accompli*. Apparently he deemed as unimportant the fact that the trustees had not yet approved his plan. The catalog, which bore the title of "Taylor University, Muncie, Indiana," showed a picture of the Muncie campus. The section describing the Muncie location was an insert pasted over what apparently had been the printed Upland description. Because of situations such as this, several (at least seven) faculty members (including Ayres) resigned their positions during Winchester's last two years at Taylor.[18] After Winchester's three-year tenure, still another year elapsed before the school again could find a president who could provide stable, long-term leadership.

2. The Vayhinger Administration

Monroe Vayhinger began his lengthy association with Taylor in 1908, when he became the seventeenth president; he served in this position until 1921. Even after he left the presidency, he continued on the governing board at least until 1933. The son of German immigrants, he held earned degrees from Moore's Hill College (now the University of Evansville) and Garrett Biblical Institute, and honorary degrees from Moore's Hill College and Taylor University. Before coming to the Taylor presidency at the age of fifty-two, he had been a teacher and an administrator at Moore's Hill College and a minister in the Indiana Conference of the Methodist Episcopal

Culla Vayhinger   *Monroe Vayhinger*

Church. While president, he regularly used the pulpit as a public relations medium for the school; as a preacher he attracted his greatest popularity in the churches and campgrounds of the groups that especially enjoyed his "holiness" (or "second blessing") theology.[19]

The most dynamic member of the Vayhinger family was not the president but rather his wife, Culla J. Vayhinger. Five years before the Vayhingers came to Upland, she won election as the president of the Indiana branch of the Women's Christian Temperance Union; and largely due to her influence, Taylor served as the state headquarters of the W.C.T.U. during the period when her husband presided over the school. One will note that the years of the Vayhinger administration approximately coincide with the peak period of the nationwide Prohibition movement.[20]

During the Vayhinger years the college added two major buildings, Helena Memorial Music Hall and Swallow Robin Dormitory. A $7,000 bequest from Mrs. Helena Gehman of Urbana, Ohio, and a $2,400 gift from Mr. and Mrs. Israel B. Shreiner of Lancaster, Pennsylvania, paid for much of the cost of the new music hall; therefore, the university officials decided to call the building by the first name of Mrs. Gehman and the second-floor chapel-auditorium by the last name of the Shreiners. This was not the first gift by the Shreiners to Taylor. In 1910 they had paid the $800 mortgage on one of the dormitory houses near campus, and at that time its name changed from the New York House to Shreiner's Dormitory. When the music building was completed in 1912, it contained more than music classrooms, music practice rooms, and an

Swallow Robin Residence Hall.

auditorium. Its basement floor housed a new gymnasium (with dressing rooms and shower rooms).[21]

Nearly one-half of the $10,000 cost of constructing Swallow Robin Dormitory came as a gift from the Rev. and Mrs. Silas C. Swallow of Harrisburg, Pennsylvania. The benefactors asked that the university name the building for their mothers (Mrs. Swallow's maiden name was Robin). The Swallows had contributed to the school before; when the college was in Fort Wayne, they had established a loan fund (the Mrs. S. C. Swallow Loan Fund) from which students could borrow up to $50 per year. Swallow had also given the money for the construction of one of the cheap school cottages that appeared during the Reade administration.[22]

Undoubtedly, Swallow developed an increased interest in Taylor as he observed the intense Prohibition emphasis during the Vayhinger period, for the Pennsylvania minister was one of the leading Prohibition crusaders in the country. He collected 130,000 votes while running as the Prohibition Party candidate for governor of Pennsylvania in 1898, and six years later the party's national organization selected him as their candidate for the Presidency. Swallow did not limit his reform crusading to the fight against alcohol; he also militantly attacked tobacco, dancing, roller-skating, and the Republican Party machine in Pennsylvania. When he died in 1930, the *New York Times* said that the "fighting parson" was "probably one of the most ardent enemies of liquor, tobacco, and secular amusements this country has ever seen."[23]

Merritt O. Abbey, for years the head of the school's maintenance department, carefully supervised the construction of Swallow Robin Dormitory; and when it was ready for occupancy by the female students in 1917, it was the largest and the best built residence hall on campus. The four-story (including basement) mortar-and-brick structure contained twenty-five residential rooms, and its basement originally served as the headquarters for the home economics department. Although the dormitory originally housed women, over the years it has alternated between being a women's hall and a men's hall.[24]

Meanwhile, the university obtained additional land property. The original ten-acre campus was the northeastern corner of an eighty-acre tract, and in 1915 the college paid seven thousand dollars to purchase the remaining seventy acres from Charles H. and Bertha Snyder. Oliver W. Outland, a local resident who worked part time as a fund raiser for the school, persuaded Margaret McGrew of Warren, Indiana, to contribute five thousand dollars toward the needed seven-thousand-dollar purchase price. She later gave another one thousand dollars to construct a barn on the seventy-acre site. The university added another eighty

acres to its campus property in the early 1920s, when Mr. and Mrs. John Campbell of Huntington, Indiana, and Mr. and Mrs. David Speicher of Urbana, Indiana, contributed the necessary funds for the purchase of the Lewis Jones farm, which lay adjacent to the campus on the south.[25]

The poverty of the school in this period stood in stark contrast to the growing wealth of the major rival Methodist college in the state, DePauw University. An evaluation of the Taylor property in 1919 showed it to be worth over $200,000; however, the school indebtedness equaled one-fourth of this evaluation. At this same time the institution each year received about $10,000 less in tuition and rental income than it spent. Therefore, Vayhinger had to depend upon the balance to come from such donors as sympathetic ladies at

Venerable Miss Abbey

Iris Abbey '15, at 103 in 1996, is believed to be Taylor's oldest living alumna. Her father, Merritt O. Abbey, longtime head of the Taylor maintenance department, supervised the building of Swallow Robin Dormitory in 1917.

Miss Abbey is seen in 1912 at the conclusion of her piano recital in the new Shreiner Auditorium and also in December, 1995, at the lighting of the Upland community Christmas lighting display.

his Holiness camp meetings or wealthy friends from the Eastern states. Meanwhile, the large gifts from wealthy Indiana Methodists almost always went to DePauw. Periodically the Greencastle school in the early twentieth-century years received individual contributions ranging from $25,000 to $60,000, and by 1920 that college's endowment reached the $2,000,000 mark.[26]

The difficult financial situation was likely a major reason why the trustees replaced President Vayhinger in 1921; they chose as his successor James M. Taylor, a Methodist missions administrator and a former missionary. The trustees believed that Taylor's broad experience in Methodist circles would allow him to enlist an increasing number of major donors for the school. The trustees never were able to learn whether the new president's influence would have brought increased revenues to the school, because in January, 1922—after only six months in office—they voted to dismiss him.[27]

> *The new constitution permitted no more than seven of the twenty-one trustees to be from any one denomination.*

During a period in the early 1920s that included parts of the Vayhinger, Taylor, and Paul administrations, the ownership of the college changed on two occasions. For years the official governing body of the institution, the National Association of Local Preachers, had neglected their administrative responsibilities. The NALP trustees from the Eastern states showed little interest in the institution; and when they did attend meetings, they often did not possess enough knowledge of school affairs to participate intelligently. The local (mostly Indiana) trustees and the college administrators resented this neglect by the NALP, and in the early 1920s they sought to remove the school from the control of the negligent local preachers. The leader of the movement to place the college under new—and "interdenominational"[28]—control was Board Chairman Daniel L. Speicher, a real estate agent from Urbana, Indiana. Speicher convinced the trustees to agree to his plan to transfer the ownership and control of Taylor to the Alumni Association. When the NALP met in a special meeting in Philadelphia on May 6, 1922, they decided by the margin of one vote to agree to the transfer. The change in ownership did not take place with complete harmony. The local preachers expressed dismay that the new constitution permitted no more than seven of the twenty-one trustees to be from any one denomination. The NALP had hoped that the institution would somehow remain a Methodist school. New trustees on the new nondenominational board included Howard Cadle (United Brethren), the minister of the Cadle Tabernacle in Indianapolis, Indiana; Paul Rader (Christian and Missionary Alliance), an evangelist from Nyack, New York; and Elwood Haynes (Presbyterian), a resident of Kokomo, Indiana, and one of the first Americans to construct an automobile. The college remained under the control of the Alumni Association for less than two years. President Paul led the reorganization in 1924, at which time the ownership of the college passed to another nondenominational body, the Legal Hundred of Taylor University.[29]

3. THE PAUL ADMINISTRATION

John H. Paul was a congenial Southern Methodist preacher and educator. Before accepting the Taylor presidency in 1922, he had served as a minister of several churches, an evangelist, a college professor, and the vice-president of Asbury College in Kentucky. His calm, optimistic personality and his beaming countenance allowed him to make friends easily. He had a wide following among Holiness groups; and many small evangelical

The Legal Hundred of Taylor University owned and governed the university from 1924 until 1933.

denominations that possessed no college of their own also found him appealing. He greatly enjoyed writing and editing, and he once proposed that the school establish a national religious magazine—the *Globe-Review*—of which he would be the editor. He also displayed considerable interest in the public issues of the day. His public pronouncements appeared sympathetic to Presidents Coolidge and Hoover, but ardently opposed to socialism, "ethereal pacifism," and "dreamy internationalism."[30]

When Paul assumed the presidency he realized that he faced a difficult financial situation. The building and expansion projects of the preceding decade had increased the college indebtedness beyond a safe point; by the early 1920s the debt totaled $150,000 against a $400,000 evaluation. The crisis came in 1923 when payment was due on thirty thousand dollars worth of mortgage bonds for which there were no liquid resources to pay. The claimants, who would not accept new bonds, filed suit; and the list of plaintiffs included faculty members who had earlier accepted mortgage bonds as salary payments. Subsequently, the Grant County Circuit Court placed the government of the university under a three-party receivership comprised of President Paul, Trustee and School Business Manager Edward O. Rice, and the Farmers Trust and Savings Company of Marion.[31]

Paul's role in this receivership was to try both to save the college and to be as fair as possible to its creditors.[32] Indiana law permitted a new corporation to purchase an existing corporation if the new one negotiated a plan of settlement with each of the creditors of the old one. Accordingly, Paul organized the Legal Hundred of Taylor University in September of 1923; he named the new organization after the group formed by John Wesley to hold the property of English Methodism. The Legal Hundred met informally during the winter of 1923-24, and in March, 1924, it became an official corporation. The Grant County Court and the school set April 8, 1924, as the date to sell the college. The Legal Hundred submitted the only bid to buy it from the receivers; and Mrs. Ella G. Magee, a widow from Bloomsburg, Pennsylvania, paid the $50,000 purchase price for the corporation. Meanwhile, Paul had been negotiating payment plans with each of the creditors. Some of the claimants donated part of the money owed to them, some accepted notes for part of their claim, others insisted upon immediate cash payment.[33]

John Paul

Paul's role in the receivership of the university was to try both to save the college and to be as fair as possible to its creditors.

The Legal Hundred owned and governed the university from 1924 until the period of the second receivership in 1933. Despite the organization's name, it is not clear that it ever had a membership list as large as one hundred.[34] Certainly the number regularly present at its annual or semi-annual business meetings never approached that figure; the usual attendance at such meetings ranged from twenty to fifty. Most of the work of the Legal Hundred took place in the monthly meetings of its executive committee. This executive group of nine directors (or trustees) included mostly faculty members and other individuals who resided in or near Upland. Perhaps the decision of the Legal Hundred to select "local" trustees to do most of the governing of the school developed from a reaction against the absentee governorship during the period when the NALP was in control.[35]

The 1922 change in ownership had removed the university from any official connection with the Methodist Church. The 1924 change did not basically alter that new situation, but it did strengthen the unofficial connection between the college and the church over what it had been since 1922. Paul stated in his explanation of the organization of the Legal Hundred that a majority of its membership must hold membership in the Methodist Church. The president himself was a very loyal Methodist; and although he acknowledged that the school operated free from the control of any denomination, he also clearly announced that the school identified itself with Methodist doctrine and tradition. If Paul had had his way, the college would have completely returned to "the Methodist fold." At the very first meeting of the Legal Hundred he delivered an impassioned plea calling for Methodist affiliation. He argued for affiliation because almost all the students came from Methodist churches and because the families in the "old-fashioned," Holiness wing of the church wanted to have a school such as Taylor in which to educate their children. Paul also favored Methodist affiliation for financial reasons. He argued that "an interdenominational Christian college was a most unusual thing and that it would last no more than a generation or two. After that it would go in one of three directions: to the church, or to the world, or to oblivion." Even though Paul proposed Methodist affiliation, he harbored some misgivings about the outcome if the liberal branch of the church gained control: "...if it were left to the majority of authorized education leaders of the M. E. Church to mold the policies of Taylor University she would soon cease to supply the demand for a school emphasizing holiness and revivals and advocating the 'traditional' Methodist view of the Bible." This statement by Paul generally expressed the primary reason why Taylor trustees in the 1920s and in later periods chose not to reaffiliate the college with the denomination.[36]

> *An interdenominational Christian college is a most unusual thing; it will last no more than a generation or two. After that it will go in one of three directions: to the church, or to the world, or to oblivion.*
>
> *- John Paul*

A major innovation in the government of the internal affairs of the school appeared in the 1920s with the introduction of faculty committees. The committees debated and voted on issues that heretofore only the faculty as a whole had discussed; however, all committee decisions were subject to the review of the full faculty. The president, with the approval of the faculty, selected the membership of the committees. He also possessed the right to veto faculty action; if the faculty passed a vetoed measure, then the governing board made the ultimate decision.[37]

One major new housing unit appeared in the 1920s. Magee-Campbell-Wisconsin Dormitory (MCW), a four-story, "H" shaped structure with 170 rooms (and a new dining room in the basement), became the largest building on campus. Mrs. Ella Magee, who had already become the single largest contributor in the school's history, provided $50,000 toward the construction of the new hall. She presented her gift in the form of an advanced payment on an estate note she had previously willed to the university. She asked that part of the dormitory be named for her deceased son, Stanley, who if he had lived

Magee-Campbell-Wisconsin Dormitory (MCW).

would have been the sole heir to her carpet manufacturing fortune. The reason for Mrs. Magee's original interest in Taylor and the sum of the gifts she gave to the college are both unknown. A 1937 issue of the *Echo* suggests that her contributions totaled approximately $144,000; this figure probably is reasonably accurate. Upon the suggestion of Burt Ayres, the board voted to name the middle section of the new building after John Campbell of Huntington, a past benefactor of the school (see Chapter 5, section two). The third section of the new dormitory took the name of Wisconsin because a group of men from that state had helped in raising funds to finance the construction of the building. Paul also liked the idea of using the name of that state because of the "metropolitan appearance" it gave to the building and school.[38]

The completion of MCW led to several campus changes. With the school dining hall now in the basement of the new building, the old eating center at the northeast edge of the campus became the post office, mailing room, bookstore, and restaurant. In addition, the existence of 170 rooms for women in the new dormitory allowed the conversion of Swallow Robin Dormitory into a residence hall for men.[39]

A second major building project of the 1920s was the gymnasium. Construction of it began in 1926 under the supervision of the same man who had directed the building of MCW Dormitory, H. C. Miller. Because of delays in obtaining the necessary finances, the builders could not complete the new athletic structure until 1930. Maytag Gymnasium took its name from the man who contributed the single largest gift for its construction, T. H. Maytag of

Newton, Iowa. The dedication of the 2,500-seat gymnasium-auditorium took place on May 23, 1930, when the well-known evangelist William A. (Billy) Sunday delivered the dedicatory address. Sunday was the first speaker to use the new three-thousand-dollar public-address system which H. F. Capehart, a Fort Wayne businessman, had contributed to the university. At the time of the completion of the gymnasium, the other athletic facilities of the school—all located immediately west of the Maytag building—included tennis courts, a baseball diamond, and a track.[40]

The minutes of the meetings of the trustees in the 1920s and 1930s show discussion of almost nothing but financial affairs. This probably was a necessary emphasis as the college in this period almost constantly struggled for economic survival. One could compare the institution to a family that barely survived from one payday to another with little money in reserve. Consequently, routine business transactions often became major crises.

From a bookkeeping standpoint the university was always in a solvent condition. But in the year following the completion of MCW Dormitory, the liabilities totaled $270,000 while assets amounted to about $850,000; the problem was that nearly all of the assets existed in a non-liquid form. A favorable balance of total assets over liabilities meant very little to a creditor who wanted immediate cash payment; and at any given time a significant number of creditors were holding currently payable notes or accounts. Consequently, the financial officials spent much time finding ways to satisfy the least patient of the creditors. Sometimes board members personally signed notes; sometimes the school borrowed money from banks by using for collateral the endowment funds it was about to receive from wills that were in the process of settlement; and sometimes the school transferred endowment funds (those not explicitly marked as "permanent" endowment funds) into the current operating budget.[41]

The college worked hard to obtain large deferred gifts from elderly people. School "agents" such as Edward O. Rice constantly sought—especially from farmers—annuity contracts, estate notes, and will contracts. An example of the type of contract the university solicited was an agreement in 1925 with a Fort Wayne couple whereby the latter deeded $22,000 in real estate to the school, and the school agreed to pay them $110 per month for as long as they lived. The deferred giving contracts improved the future prospects for Taylor but they did not help greatly in the years when the agents wrote them; for example, in the mid-1920s the expense of having field representatives was greater than the "immediate" funds they raised.[42]

Thus the financial situation in the years before the outbreak of the Depression was not good. Even before the stock market crash, the Taylor trustees made plans for the possibility that the school might have to cease operation. With the coming of the nationwide depression, the Taylor crisis deepened. The problem was not that the debt increased, but rather that the generosity of the creditors decreased. In the summer of 1930, Taylor's claimants in Marion gathered for a "friendly" meeting to discuss the problem of the college's obligations to them. Paul became desperate enough by the fall of 1930 to ask the Legal Hundred organization to find someone to relieve him of some of the financial strain. The governing body found a man who was willing to accept the challenge of helping the school out of its financial difficulties; his name was Robert L. Stuart.[43]

With the coming of the nationwide depression, the Taylor crisis deepened. The problem was not that the debt increased, but rather that the generosity of the creditors decreased.

Stuart was an enthusiastic alumnus of Taylor, the minister of a Methodist church in Newton, Iowa, and—since 1928—an influential member of the Legal Hundred. He had successfully recruited students and finances for the school. Two of the students whom he had directed to the university were his son, Marvin Stuart, and Hazen Sparks. These two boys possessed a keen interest in athletics, and when they enrolled at Taylor in 1927 they developed a scheme to help finance the new gymnasium then under construction. They expressed their desire to see the completion of the new gymnasium to T. H. Maytag, a wealthy parishioner in the elder Stuart's church in Newton, Iowa. The boys believed that if they could convince Maytag to visit the school, then he would contribute a major gift for the construction of the building. Maytag, who belonged to the famous washing-machine family, visited the school, and subsequently contributed $25,000 toward the gymnasium construction costs. Partly because of his relationship with Maytag, partly because of his enthusiasm for fundraising, and partly because of his businesslike mind, the trustees gradually began to view Stuart as the eventual successor to Paul.[44]

The transition from the Paul to the Stuart administration came with some difficulty. Paul announced late in October, 1930, that he wished to resign at the end of the first term of that school year (1930-31); he cited "failing health" as the reason for this resignation, though the financial burdens of the college certainly contributed to his decision. When the board asked him to remain through the entire school year, he agreed to continue beyond the first semester. At the board meeting on February 2, 1931, the trustees voted to invite Stuart to become president on September 1, 1931, or earlier if he wished. Paul then expressed reservations about his original resignation, and real doubt existed as to whether Stuart or Paul would be the president at the beginning of the 1931-32 year. The trustees met in an "emotion-packed" session on April 7 to resolve the issue. They unanimously decided not to change their earlier offer of the presidency to Stuart. The board came to this decision after listening to the advice of an attorney who predicted that if they did not select a new president at that meeting, the university would be closed within ten days. Apparently, creditors had delayed taking their claims to court on the hope that a new president would improve the college's ability to meet its financial obligations. Stuart became president shortly after his election.[45]

4. THE STUART ADMINISTRATION

Robert L. Stuart led the school for fourteen years (1931-45)—a continuous[46] tenure longer than that held by any other Taylor president. In the 1930s the trustees began the practice of electing the president for five-year terms; perhaps this innovation contributed to Stuart's longevity in the office. By the early 1940s when Stuart had completed two full terms, the board nearly chose not to re-elect him. He won re-election only by a vote of eight to five; the five opposing trustees all cast their ballots for the Rev. Lloyd Nixon, a Michigan evangelist.[47]

Stuart was a large, energetic, and somewhat direct individual. His slender, 6'4", well-dressed frame appeared almost constantly to be in motion. While his straightforward nature offended some people, his incessant labor to lead the university through its worst financial crisis won him the support of many others.

The primary contribution of Stuart to Taylor was saving the college from the death-by-bankruptcy fate that came to so many institutions during the 1930s. His knowledge of business law allowed him to guide the college successfully through its second receivership in as many

President Stuart with faculty members in Shreiner Auditorium.

decades, and his knowledge of sound business principles allowed him to institute improved business practices. His administration did not turn Taylor into an affluent institution, but it did enable the college to continue its existence into the more prosperous post-World War II period.

The immediate goal of the new president following his inauguration in 1931 was to save the university from a second receivership. He succeeded in achieving this goal for two years, but by 1933 even his improved business practices could not prevent the creditors from seeking court action. One critical economic blow came in the first year of Stuart's term. His close friend and major school benefactor, T. H. Maytag, died in an automobile accident. Maytag had planned to pay Stuart's salary ($5,000 per year) indefinitely, and presumably Stuart would have been able to convince him to underwrite other Taylor projects.[48]

The receivership of 1933 actually improved the financial standing of the college. It came when L. J. McAtee and Company filed a petition in the Grant County Superior Court on June 17, 1933, for a receiver for the school. The Court appointed Marshall Williams, a Marion attorney, as the receiver. Meanwhile, the alumni and other friends of the school were organizing a new corporation, the William Taylor Foundation, which hopefully could buy the institution from the receiver with the funds Stuart was working very hard to raise. The President solicited the aid of the same lady who had provided the money for the purchase of the college at the time of the first receivership, Mrs. Ella Magee. The benefactress of the school had moved from her former home in Pennsylvania to California, and Stuart made two trips to the West Coast to see her during the crisis.[49] He convinced her to contribute the balance (approximately $32,600) of the estate note she had earlier given to the university, and the officials used most of this money to purchase the institution for the new William Taylor Foundation. At the time of the sale of the college in September, 1937, no bidders competed with the William Taylor Foundation; the new owners purchased the college for the price of $27,600. The major effect of the receivership and sale was not that the school changed owners (practically speaking, this was no change at all), but rather that the courts allowed the school to be free of much of its cumbersome debt. In the words of President Stuart, "The William Taylor Foundation...bought the property free from the mortgage and all other liens and did not obligate itself in any way to pay any claims of the holders of the First Mortgage or Annuity bonds or any other creditors of either Taylor University or the Legal Hundred of Taylor University."[50]

The change in ownership and control that came as a result of this second receivership did not change the nature or method of governance of the university. The reorganization took place because of economic necessity, not because of a desire for a change in government, religious nature, or educational goals. The

William Taylor Foundation and the Legal Hundred were similar in structure in that both were large organizations that usually approved in a routine manner the actions of the smaller board of directors. The larger group in both cases existed primarily to provide a tangible link between the school and important financial supporters (or would-be supporters). The board of directors of the William Taylor Foundation hoped that the larger group eventually would enlist a membership of 2,500. The formula for the selection of the board allowed the foundation to choose only three of the fifteen directors. The Alumni Association and the North Indiana Conference of the Methodist Church each chose a like number, and the president of the university served as a member ex officio. These ten members then selected the other five members. The foundation required each director to hold membership in "some protestant, evangelical church" and to express "sympathy with the traditional policies of Taylor University."[51]

The William Taylor Foundation board introduced several measures to require the school to operate with a greater degree of economic cautiousness than had been the case in the decades preceding the Great Depression. The foundation decreed that the debt of the college could not exceed ten percent of the total evaluation unless

To save money on the dining hall expenses, the school raised and slaughtered its own cattle and hogs.

twelve of the fifteen trustees approved such an action. The foundation also required—in obvious reaction to the practice in the 1920s—that the college hold in trust all annuity funds.[52]

Stuart achieved balanced budgets during much of the Depression, and he did this by carefully controlling expenditures and by finding new methods to attract students. The university began no new building programs during the Stuart presidency; thus it had no mortgage payments to meet. To save money on the dining hall expenses, the school raised and slaughtered its own cattle and hogs. The college did not guarantee faculty salaries. If enough students did not enroll in a class to warrant offering it, the school canceled the course, and the instructor received no payment for it; if a shortage of funds to pay faculty salaries developed, the teachers shared proportionately the available funds. Not all the instructors were willing to work under such uncertain financial arrangements. One professor—a department chairman—stated in his letter of resignation: "I wish to assure you that my...years [here] have been very pleasant, but I cannot stand any further loss or reduction in income." Reduction in faculty income, however, occurred at many American colleges during the Depression years. For example, at the generally affluent DePauw University in the second semester of 1932-33, the instructors received only one-half of the expected salaries.[53]

Recruitment of students during the Depression period, when only a limited number of young people could afford to go to college, was a highly competitive business among American institutions of higher education. Taylor offered its current students fifteen dollars for each new enrollee they could attract to the school. The college held its first "Youth Conference" in the 1930s, and a major result of this annual weekend youth revival was that it interested high-school students in applying for admission to the Upland school. One promotional medium the college used during the Depression—but which had begun before this period—was the Varsity Quartet. This singing group visited churches, religious conferences and campgrounds, and other sites where they could find potential students and the parents of potential students who would listen to their music and their explanation of the merits of Taylor. Sometimes President Stuart found that it was easier to obtain students than to obtain the students' money. For example, at the end of the 1934-35 school year the students still owed $6,200 on their accounts.[54]

Such was the financial and administrative history of the college during the first half-century in Upland. The efforts to build buildings, raise funds, placate creditors, and obtain good administrators were never easy; and often they were discouraging. Yet the school officials persevered in their endeavors because they believed that the cause of educating future Christian leaders was worth the accompanying difficulties. The process of educating these Christian young people during Taylor's first fifty years in Upland is the subject of the next chapter.

> *Yet the school officials persevered in their endeavors because they believed that the cause of educating future Christian leaders was worth the accompanying difficulties.*

[1] As noted earlier, the Reade presidency began in Fort Wayne in 1891.

[2] Ella Reade Fike MS, "Thaddeus C. Reade" (Taylor University archives).

[3] Contract between T. C. Reade, President, and the Taylor University Board of Trustees, June 3, 1897 (Taylor University archives); Ayres, "Taylor University," pp. 12-14, 26.

[4] MS Articles of Association of Taylor University of Upland, 1893 (Taylor University archives); *TUC*, 1895-96, p. 5; Ayres, "Taylor University," pp. 27, 74; National Association of Local Preachers of the Methodist Episcopal Church, *Proceedings of the Thirty-eight Annual Meeting*, 1895, pp. 3, 20. On Klopsch, also see "Louis Klopsch," in Johnson and Malone, *Dictionary of American Biography*, X, 447.

[5] *Biographical Memories of Grant County, Indiana* (Chicago, 1901), pp. 672-74; Ayres, "Taylor University," pp. 15, 26, 74.

[6] *TUC*, 1901-02 (Warsaw, n.d.), p. 38; Ayres, "Taylor University," pp. 18-20, 38.

[7] Ayres, "Taylor University," pp. 18-20; Taylor University Souvenir Booklet, 1905-06 (n.p., n.d.), pp. 7-8; MS Report of the President of Taylor University to the National Association of Local Preachers, October 12, 1906 (Taylor University archives).

[8] Ayres, "Taylor University," pp. 38-39; *Upland Monitor*, September 20, 1900, p. 4.

[9] *Upland Monitor*, March 13, 1902, p. 4; MS Taylor University Trustees Minutes, June 4, 1906 (Taylor University archives); *Taylor Echo*, March 22, 1929, p. 4; MS Report of the President of Taylor University to the Board of Trustees, June 3, 1907 (Taylor University archives); *TUC*, 1912 (Upland, 1912), p. 21 and 1914 (Upland, 1914), p. 15.

[10] The reader should note that inadequate financing has frequently plagued many institutions of higher education; Taylor's problems, while embarrassing, were not unique.

[11] The salaries were lower in this period than they had been during the era of Fort Wayne College. See Chapter 3, section two.

[12] *Upland Monitor*, October 15, 1896, p. 1, November 24, 1904, p. 4, and January 17, 1907, p. 1; Report of the President to the National Association of Local Preachers, 1906; Taylor University Trustees Minutes, June 7, 1905; Report of the President of Taylor University to the Board of Trustees, June 3, 1907; Ayres, "Taylor University," p. 26.

[13] Ayres, "Taylor University," p. 39; Burt W. Ayres, *Honor to Whom Honor Is Due* (Upland, 1951), pp. 67-68.

[14] Ayres, "Taylor University," pp. 33, 42.

[15] *Christian Herald*, June 1, 1904, p. 487; (Taylor) *University Register*, November, 1903, p. 1 and June, 1904, p. 5; Ayres, "Taylor University," pp. 49-50.

[16] Ayres, "Taylor University," pp. 49-50.

[17] Report of the President of Taylor University to the Board of Trustees, June 3, 1907; Ayres, "Taylor University," pp. 48-49, 76; Glenn White, *The Ball State Story* (Muncie, 1967), p. 36.

[18] *TUC*, 1905-06 (Upland, n.d.), p. 31, 1906-07 (Upland, n.d.), pp. 6-8, and 1907-08 (n.p., n.d.), pp. 1, 8, 12.

[19] *Taylor Gem*, 1909 (Upland, 1909), p. 13 and 1921 (Upland, 1921), p. 25; Taylor University Legal Hundred, Minutes of the June 9, 1933, Meeting (Taylor University archives). Hereafter all references to the minutes of the Taylor University Legal Hundred organization will appear as TULHM.

[20] Ernst H. Cherrington, ed., *Standard Encyclopedia of the Alcohol Problem* (Westerville, Ohio, 1930), VI, 2744.

[21] *TUC*, 1912, pp. 20-21; Whitson, *History of Grant County*, I, 308; *Upland Monitor*, February 10, 1910, p. 1.

[22] *Upland Monitor*, December 2, 1915, p. 4; FWCTM, December 4, 1887; Ayres, "Taylor University," p. 65.

[23] Ayres, "Taylor University," p. 65; "Silas Comfort Swallow," in *Dictionary of American Biography*, XVIII, 233-34; obituary, *New York Times*, August 14, 1930, p. 19.

[24] Ayres, "Taylor University," pp. 65-66; *Upland Monitor*, June 7, 1917, p. 4; *TUC*, 1920 (Upland, 1920), p. 17.

[25] Ayres, "Taylor University," pp. 66, 69, 98.

[26] *Taylor Bulletin*, November, 1919, p. 14; *Upland Monitor*, November 10, 1910, p. 4; Ayres, "Taylor University," p. 64. Also see the minutes of the annual meetings of the North Indiana Methodist Episcopal Conference during the 1900-1920 period.

[27] (Upland) *Community Courier*, June 16, 1921, p. 1; Ayres, "Taylor University," p. 87.

[28] When the college leaders used the term "interdenominational" to describe the school, they did not mean that the school was under the sponsorship of several denominations, but rather that the school freely accepted individuals from many different denominations in its student body, faculty, administration, and board of trustees.

[29] Ayres, "Taylor University," pp. 75,79, 82-83, 86, 94-95; *Taylor Bulletin*, May, 1922, p. 17; *TUC*, 1931 (n.p., 1931), pp. 14-15.

[30] *Community Courier*, August 10, 1922, p. 1; Ayres, "Taylor University," p. 129; *Taylor Echo*, October 10, 1922, p. 3; TULHM, August 30, 1929 and January 31, 1930; *Community Courier*, June 16, 1927, p. 1; *Taylor Echo*, February 8, 1927, p. 1 and March 4, 1931, p. 1.

[31] Ayres, "Taylor University," pp. 87-89; *Community Courier*, July 19, 1923, p. 1.

[32] Paul compared the receivership to "the Old Testament law providing a city of refuge to which some person apparently guilty may escape from an impulsive avenger." See *Community Courier*, July 26, 1923, p. 1.

[33] Ayres, "Taylor University," pp. 96, 104-09, 113; *Community Courier*, July 19, 1923, p. 1; *Laws of the State of Indiana* (Fort Wayne, 1921), pp. 730-31.

[34] One member was Sergeant Alvin York of Jamestown, Tennessee, the deeply religious, quasi-pacifist, World War I hero and Congressional Medal of Honor winner. For an able biography of York, see David D. Lee, *Sergeant York: An American Hero* (Lexington, Kentucky, 1985).

[35] *TUC*, 1926-27 (Upland, 1926), p. 8 and 1928 (n.p., 1928), p. 8; also see the attendance records in the minutes of the meetings of the Legal Hundred.

[36] John Paul, ed., *Taylor University Government* (Upland, 1926), pp. 6-16; *TUC*, 1928, p. 8; TULHM, September 13, 1923.

[37] *TUC*, 1926-27, p. 85.

[38] *TUC*, 1926-27, p. 91; Ayres, "Taylor University," pp. 105, 140; TULHM, June 17, 1924; *Taylor Echo*, October 30, 1937, p. 1; Taylor University Legal Hundred Board of Directors, Minutes of the December 26, 1924, meeting. Hereafter the minutes of the meetings of the Board of Directors (the Trustees) of the Legal Hundred will appear as TULHDM.

[39] *TUC*, 1926-27, p. 85.

[40] TULHDM, June 29, 1926 and October 27, 1926; *Community Courier*, May 15, 1930, p. 1; *Taylor Echo*, February 12, 1930, p. 1; *TUC*, 1931, p. 17.

[41] TULHDM, October 28, 1925, October 30, 1925, December 8, 1925, April 29, 1927, September 30, 1927, and November 28, 1930.

[42] TULHDM, October 15, 1925, June 17, 1926, August 17, 1926, and September 30, 1927.

[43] TULHDM, February 22, 1929 and September 26, 1930; Ayres, "Taylor University," p. 109; *Taylor Echo*, November 20, 1929, p. 1.

[44] Ayres, "Taylor University," pp. 117-18, 124; TULHM, October 31, 1928 and June 11, 1929; *Taylor Echo*, November 20, 1929, p. 1.

[45] TULHDM, October 29, 1930, February 27, 1931, and April 7, 1931; Ayres, "Taylor University," pp. 125-26, 130.

[46] Reuben D. Robinson was president of Fort Wayne College for a total of sixteen years.

[47] TULHDM, October 28, 1933; Ayres, "Taylor University," pp. 147-48, 150.

[48] *Community Courier*, October 8, 1931, p. 1; TULHDM, June 22, 1931; Ayres, "Taylor University," p. 138.

[49] On both trips Stuart convinced railroad officials that they should give him a free pass and thus "help a small struggling college that needed very much to have him get to California." See Ayres, "Taylor University," pp. 140-41.

[50] TULHDM, October 21, 1933 and May 22, 1934; Ayres, "Taylor University," pp. 138-43.

[51] *TUC*, 1936 (Upland, 1936), p. 12; William Taylor Foundation Board of Directors Minutes (Taylor University archives), June 4, 1934. Hereafter the minutes of the meetings of the board of directors of the William Taylor Foundation will appear as WTFDM.

[52] WTFDM, June 1, 1934.

[53] Ayres, "Taylor University," p. 150; WTFDM, November 13, 1933 and August 15, 1935; Manhart, *DePauw*, II, 350.

[54] WTFDM, March 14, 1934, May 31, 1935, June 3, 1935, and June 24, 1935.

Chapter Six

THE FIRST FIFTY YEARS IN UPLAND
(PART II): RELIGION, RECITATIONS, AND RECREATION

One will recall the classic suggestion of a Reade-era trustee, "Since every university seeks to become distinguished for some one specific excellence, let Taylor University be distinguished for the piety and religious fervor of her students and faculty." The trustee's wish became a reality. Even before Reade left the presidency, he acknowledged that what attracted people to Taylor (in addition to its low rates) was its "universal religious influence." When the students attending the school during the 1930-31 year expressed in a poll the reasons they chose to attend Taylor, the number who reported that they came because of the "Christian spirit" was three times as large as the number who stated that they enrolled because they were primarily attracted to the academic program. By comparison with its religious emphasis, the college gave only secondary attention to its curricular and extracurricular activities (that is, those not related to religious endeavors). It is true that by the 1930s the university was seeking regional accreditation and it had begun participation in intercollegiate athletics; however, the most significant gains in the academic and recreational programs came after World War II.[1]

1. THE TAYLOR PROFILE

The Upland school in the period before World War II was a devoutly religious college that placed special emphasis upon "Holiness" theology, the Prohibition movement, and the training of young men and women from the "common man" class to be teachers, preachers, and missionaries. From the early Upland years the promotional literature presented Taylor as an intensely religious institution. For example, the 1893-94 catalog announced the determination of the college to "bring the spirit of every student to the Great Master, who alone can transform and develop for a useful life and happy eternity."[2]

Contemporary Events 1895-1945

1890s-WW I	The peak period of the college-based Christian associations: the YMCA, the YWCA, and the Student Volunteer Movement.
1896	The first intercollegiate basketball game.
1906	The Azusa Street (Los Angeles) Revival launches the modern Pentecostal movement.
1918	The general education movement in higher education curriculum begins at Columbia.
1920-1933	National Prohibition
1925	The Scopes Evolution Trial
1939	The reuniting of the Methodist Episcopal Church North, the Methodist Episcopal Church South, and the Methodist Protestant Church.
1943	The founding of the National Association of Evangelicals
1944	The passage by Congress of the GI Bill

The periodic revival continued to be one of the most important methods of bringing "the spirit of every student to the Master." Once, twice, or maybe three times a year the college sponsored protracted revival meetings, some of which became very emotional. Sometimes the school leaders dismissed classes to allow the students to give complete attention to the state of their souls; often the revivalist could announce that "nearly all of our students were brought to Christ."[3]

It was during the period discussed in this chapter that the Modernist-Fundamentalist conflict raged. In a sense, Taylor was a Fundamentalist college. Its leaders sympathized with Fundamentalist doctrine, and when questioned they could clearly issue statements such as: "We...have no use for higher criticism." Yet the university did not place major emphasis upon defending the traditional faith from its liberal Protestant critics; rather, it promoted orthodoxy on the assumption that it was valid, and it gave minimum attention to the theological conflict. Perhaps the school sensed no need to enter the fray because its constituency was not a highly educated group, and thus probably little attracted to the ideas of liberal Protestantism. Whatever the reason for it, Taylor spent much less time in these years rationally defending its faith than it did emotionally experiencing it.[4] The following mystical poem by President Reade (written just before his death) better than any polemic treatise symbolizes the type of religious emphasis that characterized the school in this period.

> *Since every university seeks to become distinguished for some one specific excellence, let Taylor University be distinguished for the piety and religious fervor of her students and faculty.*

AT REST

In Faith's kingly builded palace
Standing, I shall soon be blest;
If I fall not on the threshold
of my long sought promised rest.

God, Thou knowest what befits me;
Portion Thou my weight of care;
'Tis the burden to my shoulders;
For my heart the grief prepare;

Then in Thy Dear Name I'll bear it
For Thou sendest what is best;
And when burden-worn I languish
Thou wilt send the weary rest.

—Quoted from Ayres, "Taylor University," pp. 28-29

The pre-1945 Upland school served the Holiness branch of the Methodist and other churches. In the early Upland years almost all of the students came from Methodist churches, and even after the college dropped its Methodist affiliation in 1922, it continued to enroll a majority of Methodist students. Presumably, most of the Methodist students came from the theologically conservative churches that sympathized with the Holiness movement. In addition, smaller Holiness denominations—such as the Evangelical Church,[5] the Christian and Missionary Alliance, and the Mennonite Brethren in Christ—began to send an increasing number of students to the school in the years after 1922.[6]

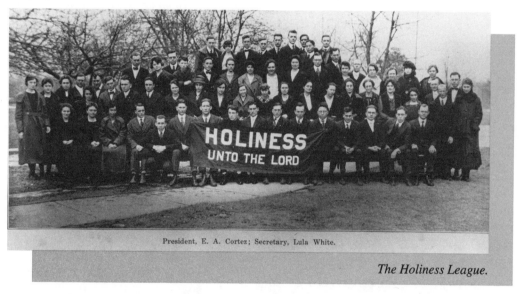

President, E. A. Cortez; Secretary, Lula White.

The Holiness League.

The Holiness theology Taylor preached placed prime emphasis upon the necessity for the Christian to experience a "second work of grace." Sometimes this religious event took the name of "sanctification" or "the baptism of the Holy Spirit"; it sought to render the individual free from sin. The university's statement of faith expressed this theological position, and as late as 1935 the members of the board of directors endorsed the Holiness view that one may be "cleansed from all sin and filled with the pure love of God" as the result of an "instantaneous work of Grace...subsequent to regeneration." The college received the official approval of several Holiness associations, and it served as host to national Holiness conventions. Visiting revivalists usually sought to persuade the Christian students to seek the "baptism of the Holy Spirit."[7] One of the major student organizations was the "Holiness League," and student orators annually vied with each other for cash prizes offered to those who delivered the best messages on "Entire Sanctification." The Holiness emphasis at the school gradually decreased in the period after 1945; this trend coincided with the decrease in the percentage of students coming from Methodist churches.[8]

Another major emphasis of the college in this period was the training of ministers and missionaries. A larger percentage of the Taylor students entered these "full-time Christian service" professions during this first half-century in Upland than in either the preceding or the succeeding eras. The 160 students in 1895 included thirty ministerial candidates and nine missionary trainees. Twenty years later 123 out of 316 students were preparing to be preachers or missionaries. During the period from 1908 to 1919 forty-one youths left the school to become missionaries, and over four hundred students became ministers. Most of the alumni who went abroad in the period before 1927 served in China, India, or Africa. Approximately ten percent of all Taylor graduates in the period before 1949 worked on a mission field. During many of these years the university maintained a close contact with John C. Wengatz, one of its early missionary graduates. Wengatz was a pioneer missionary to Africa; and his humility, wit, and dedication to God and his alma mater won the respect and affection of the students. The school leaders saw him as a prime example to present to the students to encourage them to consider a missionary career. One student who likely gained inspiration from Wengatz was Ralph E. Dodge, a 1931 graduate who went to Africa in 1936 and later became Bishop of the Methodist Church for Central and Southern Africa. Dodge produced three influential books that reflected his experiences, *Unpopular Missionary* (Westwood, New Jersey, 1964), *Pagan Church: The Protestant Failure in America* (Philadelphia, 1968), and *The Revolutionary Bishop* (Pasadena, California, 1986).[9]

> *Wengatz was a pioneer missionary to Africa; and his humility, wit, and dedication to God and his alma mater won the respect and affection of the students.*

Sometimes the Taylor emphasis upon the training of Christian workers led the general public to conclude that the college educated only ministers and missionaries. This conclusion is understandable, but inaccurate. Nearly as many students entered the teaching and other service professions as became ministers and missionaries. A study of 589 graduates in the period before 1953[10] showed the following vocational distribution:

Ministry		37.2%
Ministers	193	
Minister's wives	26	
Education	149	25.3%
Missions	50	8.5%
Business, Industry		
and Research	42	7.1%
Medicine	28	4.8%
Homemaking	28	4.8%
Armed Services	22	3.7%
Religious Education	15	2.5%
Social Service	14	2.4%
Miscellaneous	22	3.7%

Not only did Taylor train many Christian young people in the traditions of Holiness Methodism, but it also instilled in them an intense enthusiasm for the Prohibition movement. Probably no other Indiana college matched the Taylor zeal in the antiliquor cause. In the period before the beginning of national Prohibition, the Taylor faculty and staff almost always participated in temperance activities. Burt Ayres nearly gained election as Prohibition mayor of Dunkirk, Indiana, in 1890; he defeated future President Vayhinger as the party nominee for state superintendent of public instruction in 1900; and he later ran for the United States Congress on the Prohibitionist ticket. The Indiana Prohibition Party selected Reade as the honorary chairman of its state convention in 1900, and it chose President Vayhinger as the party nominee for state senator in 1914. It was Mrs. Vayhinger, however, who more than anyone else made Taylor a hotbed of Prohibitionist activity. Culla Vayhinger served as state president of the Women's Christian Temperance Union during the entire period when her husband led the school, and in 1915 the W.C.T.U. moved its state headquarters to the Taylor Music Hall. The state convention chose her as its nominee for the United States Senate on September 9, 1920—only two weeks after the ratification of the women's suffrage amendment to the Constitution! Mrs. Vayhinger withdrew from the race three weeks before the election because national Prohibition was then in effect and neither of the major party senatorial candidates proposed any change in the antiliquor amendment. Her withdrawal did not end her political ambitions, however, for in 1922 she declared herself a candidate for the Republican nomination for the state senate. She won the primary election in May, but lost to the Democratic nominee, Ora C. King, in the fall.[11]

The students also participated in the Prohibition cause. In the 1900-20 period most of them enrolled as members of the Intercollegiate Prohibition Association. The members met regularly in classes to study the alcohol problem. A writer in the school paper in 1906 believed that "a year's work in the class will equal in value a term's regular classwork in Political Economy" and that, "the knowledge gained would serve as the 'Battering-ram' to crash thru 'King Alcohol's walls.'" The highlight of the association's activities each year was the oratorical contest. When the Taylor chapter determined a local winner, that student advanced to the state contest to seek to denounce alcoholic beverages more effectively than the representatives from the other Indiana colleges. Sometimes this state contest took place in Shreiner Auditorium. Almost invariably the Taylor representative would win over rivals from such schools as Wabash, Earlham, Franklin, DePauw, Butler, and Valparaiso. Sometimes the Taylor orators who won first prize in the state contest also performed very well at the Inter-State contest. Probably the best Taylor orator was Barton Rees Pogue, who was the national collegiate champion in 1918—the year of the Prohibition Amendment—and the third place finisher in the 1920 national contest. The Taylor students also worked to gain community support for the Prohibition candidates. For example, in 1916 when Republican presidential nominee, Charles Evans Hughes, came to Marion, his visit aroused little enthusiasm among the students; but when the Prohibitionist aspirant for the Presidency, J. Frank Hanly, visited the county, the Taylor students obtained transportation for elderly residents and others wishing to see the candidate.[12]

After the adoption of the Eighteenth Amendment in 1918, enthusiasm for the temperance cause declined. It is true that ardent Prohibitionists—including Indiana W.C.T.U. president Elizabeth Stanley—continued to serve on the Taylor board of trustees and that the Prohibition speech contests continued for several decades; however, never again did the crusade so completely dominate the thoughts and energies of the faculty and students as it did before and during World War I.[13] While most of the zeal for reforming society found application in the Prohibition movement, at least two other causes—woman suffrage and

> *A writer in the school paper in 1906 believed that "a year's work in the [Prohibition Association] class will equal in value a term's regular classwork in Political Economy" and that, "the knowledge gained would serve as the 'Battering-ram' to crash thru 'King Alcohol's walls.'"*

peace—found some support. The local newspaper in 1913 recorded that Mrs. Vayhinger defended the cause of the franchise for women in a debate with a woman from Alexandria. In 1915 Taylor students held a Peace Oratorical Contest in Shreiner Auditorium where they argued the cause of nonviolence in declamations such as "Militarism," "The Passion of War and the Spirit of Peace," and "Peace Viewed from Calvary."[14]

Prohibition League.

Taylor intentionally sought to train boys and girls from the lower economic classes.[15] Promotional literature included such statements as "Taylor University is the school for the poor boy and girl" and "Taylor is the school of the plain people." While the institution also welcomed the enrollment of children of the "well to do," it urged them to "provide for themselves a simple wardrobe...in the interest of...school democracy."[16] The styles of the wealthy students did not cause difficulty, however, because they comprised only a small segment of the student body. Professor John H. Furbay in 1931 conducted a study of the occupations of the students' fathers; while his survey included only a part of the student body in that year, it is likely that the homes of his sample group were representative of the backgrounds of all of the students in the early Upland decades. The results[17] are as follows:

Farmers	78	53%
Preachers	34	23%
Merchants	10	7%
Laborers	10	7%
Mechanics	8	5%
Teachers	7	5%

While the institution also welcomed the enrollment of children of the "well to do," it urged them to "provide for themselves a simple wardrobe...in the interest of...school democracy."

Often a student could gain admission to the school simply by expressing a desire to attend. President Reade in particular accepted students who had no money and very limited intellectual background; he then gave them a job to earn money, found them a private tutor—perhaps another student—and began their Taylor education at whatever level of ability they possessed. The institution especially sought to aid ministerial candidates. Sometimes these candidates were adult men who possessed little formal training. One such man enrolled with his son in the Taylor elementary department. Many people realize that the school gave special tutorial and financial help to Sammy Morris, but the Morris case was not unique; rather, it was typical of what Taylor did for many.[18]

The costs to attend the institution were minimal. While similar church colleges in Michigan as early as 1865 charged students $130-$150 per year, the Taylor expenses did not exceed such a figure until the end of World War I. For many years the Upland students obtained their education more cheaply than had the Fort Wayne College students. Ministers' children often paid even less than the regular rates. For example, such students received an $18 reduction in the $100 total costs for the 1893-94 year. In addition, during the midst of the Depression when the school desperately needed money, it gave the graduate theological students free rooms in Morris Hall.[19]

While similar church colleges in Michigan as early as 1865 charged students $130-$150 per year, the Taylor expenses did not exceed such a figure until the end of World War I.

Even though the cost to attend Taylor was very low, many students needed to work to help pay their expenses. For example, future President Evan H. Bergwall worked forty-five hours per week during his four years of study in the 1930s. Students did much of the maintenance, housekeeping, and clerical work on the campus, and some of them worked in the community stores and factories and on nearby farms. Students with skills sufficient to enable them to work as a secretary to the President earned twenty cents per hour in 1902. The college paid typists twenty cents and stenographers thirty cents for each hour of work in 1933. In the early years of the century, a number of male students formed a "Co-operative League" for the purpose of organizing their money-making efforts. The men in the League did such tasks as carpenter work; the printing of the school newspaper; and the production, promotion, and selling of ironing boards. The students produced as many as fifty to one hundred ironing boards a day, and their product, reportedly "a model of efficiency," was an invention of a Taylor professor, C. E. Smith.[20]

One method of measuring the character of the school is to note whom the college officials invited to the campus as guest lecturers. The speakers who came to Taylor in this period were primarily preachers and religious leaders, of whom the better known included Paul Rader, Paul S. Rees, Harry Rimmer, E.

Stanley Jones, and William Jennings Bryan. Rader advised the students in 1922 that "God is raising up Bible schools and colleges such as Taylor, to 'stop the tide' of German rationalism and materialism." Rimmer, during the height of the modernist-fundamentalist conflict, told the Taylor audience that "there is not a thing in the scriptures that cannot be proved scientifically."[21]

The visit of Bryan was a major event. The exact date of the trip to Upland by the three-time Presidential candidate and former Secretary of State is uncertain, but

The college farm in the 1920s.

The mooing of cows greeted the students on their way to classes. The farm buildings were located near where the Nussbaum Science Center now stands.

This picture was taken by Dr. G. Harlowe Evans ('27) sometime during his undergraduate years. However, the film was not developed until 1974, so the exact date of the picture is unknown.

probably it was in the early 1920s. He planned to speak in a regular Sunday evening service in Shreiner Auditorium, but his train did not arrive on time. The crowd waited and waited, but still he did not come. When he finally reached the lecture hall about midnight, the overflow audience was still there. After he spoke to the group in the auditorium, he dismissed them and invited the crowd waiting outside to come in and listen to him repeat his address.

Partly because he sympathized with the goals of Taylor and partly because he had practiced the political art all of his life, he began his address by giving the school high praise: "Parents all over this nation are asking me where they can send their sons and daughters to school knowing that their faith in God and in morality will not be destroyed. I find that this is a college where they teach the Bible instead of apologizing for it, and I shall, for this reason, recommend Taylor University to inquiring Christian parents."[22]

His address was a critique of Darwinian evolution. He traced the "descent of Darwin" from a believer in orthodox Christianity to a theist to an agnostic. The moral of the lecture was that what Darwinism did to Darwin, it can do to anyone.[23]

2. Degrees, Courses, and Professors

During the first three decades in Upland the university offered instruction from grade school to graduate school. In these years most of the pupils studied in the academy, or secondary school. With the growth of the public high school system in Indiana and the nation, the need for the Taylor Academy decreased;

accordingly, it ceased operation during the 1923-24 school year. In this early period the academy prepared students for common (grade) school teaching as well as for entrance into college. Few students enrolled for either elementary or post-graduate work; for example, the 1914 catalog showed fourteen pupils pursuing the "pre-academic" program, and there were only three graduate students in 1926. The graduate programs led to M.A., M.S., Ph.D., and B.D. degrees. The college offered the master's degree program in many areas; the requirements of this program included one year of study (generally in residence) beyond the B.A. level and a thesis of a minimum of five thousand words. The Ph.D. program in theology appeared in the curriculum for a brief period around the turn of the century. Graduate work in theology was available during most of the pre-World War II years. Until the 1920s, ministerial students wishing advanced work could take the three-year B.D. program; after the 1920s the school offered neither the B.D. course nor any M.A. program except the one in theology. The college offered the M.A. degree in theology only until World War II.[24]

The Taylor graduate program in theology was always less popular than the nondegree English Bible course. A student did not need a high-school diploma to enroll in this Bible program, and it especially appealed to older students. While the school encouraged ministerial students to enroll in a curriculum leading to the B.A. degree in religion, it acknowledged that a less thoroughly educated preacher could be very effective: "When one has providential grounds for choosing this (non-degree) course instead of regular college work it may often follow that a providential supplement through nature and the actual aid of the Holy Spirit will compensate for disadvantage and bring him into a large degree of usefulness."[25]

The school offered correspondence work to a large number of students for a brief period at the turn of the century. President Reade administered this program largely by himself. He greatly desired to help people—especially aspiring preachers—obtain an education in one way or another. Burt Ayres suspected that the correspondence students sometimes earned their degrees with shoddy work by taking advantage of the generous nature of Reade and the carelessness of the non-resident examiner. One correspondence paper that came to Ayres for evaluation was an essay copied verbatim from William James. Also during this early twentieth-century period two organizations sought and obtained affiliate status with Taylor. For a few years the Primitive Methodist Church and the Chinzei Gakwan Seminary of Japan gave Taylor degrees and diplomas to their students; in neither case were the Taylor faculty members involved in the instruction of the students.[26]

While the school scheduled a wide variety of programs other than the regular college work, the college curriculum itself included several degree programs. In the early Upland years the institution offered the two-year philosophical course (Ph.B.), as well as the B.A., B.S., and M.E.L. degrees it had offered in Fort Wayne. Between the World Wars the music division had its own bachelor's degree (B.Mus.) program. After 1945 the college offered only general B.A. and B.S. curriculums. Beginning in the 1930s the B.S. degree ceased to be a second classical degree and became the degree for students majoring in teacher education.[27]

The transition from the old, prescribed, heavily classical curriculum to the modern curriculum organized by departments and courses began in the second Upland decade. This change coincided with the introduction of the elective system, and the first mention of it appeared in the 1898 catalog. By 1909 the B.A. students elected one-fourth of their courses, but by the mid-1920s one-half of a student's subjects were electives and an additional one-fourth were chosen from specified academic areas.[28]

The election system meant more course offerings. The 1909-10 catalog listed a surprisingly large number of courses for the small number of students who were doing college-level work: fifteen courses in Bible; twenty-three in science; thirty-seven in languages; and abundant offerings in the departments of art, commerce, English, history and political science, mathematics, philosophy, and systematic theology.[29]

Gradually, courses in new curricular areas and new departments appeared. These included physical education courses in 1909, and economics and Hebrew language courses in 1914. Also in 1914 physical education and social science (with courses in sociology and the church and social problems[30]) became departments, and the school reorganized the old science and language departments to form new departments in astronomy, biology, chemistry, geology, physics, French, German, Greek, Hebrew, and Latin.

Domestic Science Department

The Domestic Science (also known as Domestic Economy or Home Economics) department sought to prepare young women to be able teachers, homemakers, wives, and mothers.

In 1922 the department included classes on cooking, food and dietetics, household administration, home nursing, sewing, textiles, millinery, and methods of teaching home economics.

The 1922 *Gem* reported that, "The girls of this department are one of the happiest groups of girls found in Taylor University. Some of the young men have become so interested in the work that they have also enrolled and have found it very practical and interesting."

The Domestic Science Department in 1923.

The 10 1/4-inch reflector telescope was a very good instrument for its day.

In addition, the School of Education assumed the status of a department. Six years later the college added a department in domestic economy (home economics).[31]

One of the most significant changes in the curricular requirements during the period was the gradual reduction of language, mathematics, and science requirements. At the beginning of the Upland era the college students took more work in the classical languages and mathematics than in the other curricular areas; by World War II they could graduate without one course in either of these areas. The end of the language (classical or modern) requirements for students not on the B.A. program came with the introduction of the B.S. in Education program in 1931. As late as 1920 the B.A. students took forty percent of their work in mathematics and science. By 1931 they needed only twelve hours of science, and by 1936 they could graduate with a minimum of eight hours in it.[32]

The science division provided the students with a number of practical laboratory and field experiences. In the late 1890s Professor C. L. Clippinger and his astronomy students obtained a 10 1/4-inch reflector telescope for the school. It was a very good instrument for that day; originally it may have been one of the best telescopes in Indiana. Clippinger Observatory, a small sixteen-sided structure that housed the telescope, remained just east of the Ayres Building until the 1960s. It was also in the early years that the Rev. Nathan Walker gave Taylor a collection of minerals and fossils valued at $2,000; the school placed these specimens in a room in the Administration Building, which became known as the Walker Museum. Other exhibits that later appeared in the museum included elephant, llama, lion, and mastodon skeletons, which the students helped to assemble. The mastodon skeleton attracted much attention partly because of its size and partly because of the manner in which the school obtained it. A young lad visiting a farm three miles from the Taylor campus on March 18, 1928, discovered the first of seventy remaining mastodon bones in a freshly washed-out gully. Biology Professor John H. Furbay quickly paid seventy dollars for the right to unearth and retain all of the bones of the animal, which in life had weighed approximately ten tons. Three national film companies, Twentieth-Century Fox, Paramount, and Pathe News Service filmed thirty-five Taylor students participating in a re-enactment of the original digging. The skeleton appeared at the Kiwanis Circus in the Marion Coliseum before Furbay brought it to the Walker Museum. Less exciting than a telescope or a mastodon, but nevertheless very useful, was the instruction in scientific farming which students obtained on the college farm. With the location of the school in a rural area and with many of the students coming from farm homes, it seemed appropriate when, in 1931, the college began a department of agriculture with courses in agricultural chemistry, soils, and farm crops. In addition, by 1940 the biology department had constructed a greenhouse.[33]

The academic quality of the Taylor faculty members improved as the period progressed. By 1920 many of the regular faculty members had graduated from large Methodist schools such as Boston, Syracuse, Northwestern, Illinois Wesleyan, and Dickinson; and most of them held M.A. degrees. Professors with earned doctorates began appearing on the faculty rosters in the 1920s. They numbered four of twenty-five instructors in 1926, five of twenty-one in 1936, and eleven of twenty-three in 1940; and they came from such graduate schools as Yale, North Carolina, Ohio State, Chicago, Cornell, Johns Hopkins, and the University of California.[34]

The teaching loads of the faculty were heavy in the early part of the century when the institution was giving instruction primarily to non-college students. Burt Ayres recalled that the teachers taught almost every period of a long day except during the chapel hour. Another early instructor listed his teaching load as thirty hours each week. Sometimes the school helped the regular faculty by hiring senior college students to do part of the teaching of the preparatory and non-degree students.[35]

One of the best-known professors was Barton Rees Pogue, instructor of speech and theatre from 1921 to 1932. During his teaching tenure the Speech Department offered a broad variety of courses. He was in the early part of his literary career when he taught at Taylor, but already he was showing considerable creative ability in written and oral expression. Pogue specialized in the folksy type of humorous poetry that appealed to a wide range of people. Eventually,

The mastodon skeleton attracted much attention partly because of its size and partly because of the manner in which the school obtained it.

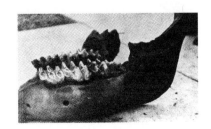

125

Barton Rees Pogue

Student and Professor

As a student and as a professor, Barton Rees Pogue ('18) brought much recognition to Taylor and Upland. As a student, he won state and national debate awards. As a professor, he made significant improvments in the Speech Department. During his Taylor teaching career (1921-32) and later, the "Hoosier Poet" became known widely for his folksy type of poetry.

(above) Pogue in 1919, shortly after graduation.

(right) Pogue as a professor in 1929.

he read his poems before three thousand audiences in twenty states, published six books of poetry, had his own radio programs on stations WIBC in Indianapolis and WLW in Cincinnati, and distributed his poems through a syndicate to many newspapers in the 1930s. Despite these many successful activities, the "Hoosier Poet" (as he was popularly called) late in life stated, "...coming to Taylor to teach was the only 'must' of my life."[36]

Faculty members with lengthy periods of service in this period included Olive M. Draper, George E. Fenstermacher, Theodora Bothwell, and James Charbonnier. Draper's forty-one-year tenure at Taylor surpassed that of anyone else except Burt Ayres. Both Fenstermacher and Bothwell taught for a quarter of a century, and Fenstermacher's twenty-five years included nine years as Dean of Men.

The school acquired regional accreditation in 1947; however, efforts to achieve this recognition began many years earlier. In 1930 the Indiana Board of Education recognized Taylor as a first-class standard college of liberal arts, but this certification was for teacher-education purposes only. The first known study of the quality of the total academic program came during World War I when the University Senate of the Methodist Church examined the college and reported that its educational standards were low. In the mid-1930s the school began working seriously to achieve accreditation with the North Central Accrediting Association of Colleges and Universities, and by the late 1930s a representative from the North Central Association was visiting the college. George Fenstermacher believes that the accrediting officials delayed recognition until after the Stuart presidency primarily because of a personality conflict between themselves and Stuart rather than because the school was not qualified earlier.[37]

3. THE EXTRACURRICULUM

As had been the case in Fort Wayne, the religious meetings and the literary society events were the major extracurricular activities. Many students attended the daily chapel service, the Sunday-afternoon campus meeting, the worship services in local churches on Sunday morning and evening, and the once or twice weekly Prayer Band. In addition, students could enroll in the religious organizations such as the Young Men's Holiness League, the Young Women's Holiness League,[38] the Student Volunteer Band, and the Women Evangels. These last two groups especially appealed to missionary candidates. Other religious activities included the annual Youth Conference (beginning in 1934) and the meetings conducted by small student groups that preached and sang in neighboring churches and campgrounds. Professors frequently (although not by rule) began their classes with prayer or singing or both.[39]

In many ways the literary societies functioned as they had during the Fort Wayne years. The Philalethean and the Thalonian Societies continued to be the major literary groups, and the format of the meetings did not change. The societies continued to debate on a combination of "joke" topics (e.g., "Taylor girls should be compelled to keep a wave in their hair," or "Taylor students should build and operate an electric railway between Matthews and Upland") and serious subjects dealing with the vital issues of the day (e.g., "The policy of our government toward our recent possessions from Spain [The Philippine Islands] is not in accord to American principles of government as formerly practiced," or "United States senators should be elected by direct vote of the people"). One major change came when the college replaced the intersociety debates of the Fort Wayne era with intercollegiate debates in Upland. As early as 1910 a Taylor team engaged in a debate with another school—Moore's Hill College (now Evansville University)—and the local paper reported that the event "drew a large crowd from the community." By the 1920s a victory by the debate team was important enough to serve as headline material for the school paper. In the nineteenth century a debate comprised only one part of the exercises of a literary society meeting; during the early part of the twentieth century it attracted sufficient interest in itself that the students formed clubs

The Intercollegiate Debate Team

From the colonial period, student debate teams had been one of the most prominent extracurricular activities in American higher education.

At Taylor, during the early Upland decades, the traditional debates of the literary societies led to separate debating societies, and then, by the 1910s, to the development of an intercollegiate debate team. Intercollegiate debating at Taylor reached its peak in the 1920s prior to the advent of intercollegiate athletics.

Intercollegiate Debaters - The Affirmative (1922).

Intercollegiate Debaters - The Negative (1922).

1906

1947

1963

1995

devoted exclusively to the forensic arts, such as the men's Eulogonion and Eureka Debating Societies, and the ladies' Soangetaha and Mananka Debating Societies. These clubs competed with the older literary societies for the attention of the students. Further detracting from the literary societies was the very popular Prohibition League, which also emphasized the persuasive skills.[40]

Gradually other organizations began to appear. The music division had an orchestra by the time of the First World War, and shortly thereafter it also sponsored a choral society, a band, and a glee club. Later in the period almost every curricular division sponsored a club for students majoring in—or just interested in—their discipline. These academic interest clubs included an Education Club (later called Future Teachers of America), an English Club, a Foreign Language Club, a Music Club, a Science Club, and an International Relations Club.[41]

With the increase in the number of new school activities, the interest in the literary societies declined. Especially detrimental to the societies was the competition from the intercollegiate activities of the debate groups and the athletic teams. The decline had begun by the 1930s. Professor Pogue in a 1932 *Echo* editorial lamented the fact that whereas the societies of his student days had provided an intellectual experience, those of the 1930s "were more for amusement than intellectual pursuit." But the societies continued to exist— probably beyond their time—until the Student Organization Committee voted to disband them in 1955.[42]

Student publications began during the first Upland decade. The first yearbook, the *Gem*, appeared in 1898; the second *Gem* appeared three years later. "Annuals" were then published during alternate years from 1901 until 1919; after World War I the *Gem* became a yearly publication.

The original school newspaper—the *University Journal*—first appeared in 1902; later the paper became the *University Register* before it assumed its present label, the *Echo*, about 1915. The newspaper, which appeared monthly in its early years, contained a combination of sermons, news about Taylor evangelists, faculty news, campus news, literary and historical articles, "locals," jokes, and advertisements. The early *Echo* editions were thirty-two-page monthly magazines that published much literary material (poems and short stories), as well as reports of society meetings, alumni news, news from other colleges, letters from missionaries, and editorials promoting "moral uplift." Sometimes student writers contributed articles of excellent quality.[43] By the 1930s the *Echo* had adopted a small newspaper format of four pages and appeared bimonthly. The first page of these later *Echo* editions featured the major school events, the second page presented the editorials and alumni news, the third page discussed world news and Taylor activities of secondary importance, and the last page contained the sports news.[44]

Most of the news items and editorials reflected a naive but pleasant spirit of generosity and optimism. For example, an article in a 1922 edition described the President's addresses in this manner: "Dr. Paul's sermons were of the majestic type and we felt that we were sitting at the feet of a Prince of Preachers." Sometimes, however, the papers contained criticism. An editorial in the January, 1917, issue criticized the school's "double standard" of "Letting girls watch boys in athletics in their gym suits but not vice-versa." On one occasion, because a student editor expressed criticism of the administration, the faculty voted to forbid the succeeding editor to publish articles that criticized administrative policy or faculty members.[45]

Most of the news items and editorials reflected a naive but pleasant spirit of generosity and optimism.

Student government originated in 1920, when the faculty chose and the students approved members of a student council whose function was to represent the students' viewpoints to the faculty, president, and trustees. The members of this first student council included future faculty member George Fenstermacher and future trustee A. Wesley Pugh. By the mid-1920s the students expressed discontent that the council possessed only an advisory role; they wanted more power to initiate action. The administration refused their request, however, stating, "It is no special virtue of democracy for an ever-changing group to revise the policies of its predecessors and type the order for its successors. Taylor is not a commonwealth...but a family made up of sons and daughters." The limited degree of student influence in the governance of the school was only one of several student complaints during the 1920s. Part of the student body also asked for fraternities and intercollegiate athletics. The students never did convince the administration of the desirability of having the Greek letter organizations, but intercollegiate athletics became a reality even before the student council was able to increase its power.[46]

Intramural athletics began very early in the Upland period. At least as early as 1898 the school sponsored baseball, bicycle, and tennis clubs, and an annual field day of track events. By 1909, the Taylor officials "strongly encouraged" the students to participate in basketball, baseball, and tennis; and in the wintertime, many students walked the two miles to the Mississinewa River to ice skate. In the period before the introduction of intercollegiate athletics, the late-spring track meet between representatives of the two literary societies (the Philo-Thalo Meet) served as one of the sports highlights of each year. While the college encouraged intramural athletics in the early years, it strongly discouraged the specific sport of football and all intercollegiate athletics. One should note that football in the early twentieth century was a much rougher sport than it is today. President Theodore Roosevelt, himself a former Harvard player, warned that if the colleges did not "clean up" football he would abolish it by executive order. Several large schools—such as Columbia, California, and Stanford—temporarily abandoned the sport. Reade, Ayres, and Winchester argued that many schools overemphasized even the more humane sports. The 1914 catalog stated that the objective of sports at Taylor was "primarily health," and it warned against "undue emphasis in this area." Accordingly, the college did not participate in intercollegiate athletics before the 1930s.[47]

The ladies' basketball team played against the Upland High School ladies' squad over two decades before male teams competed with athletes from other schools.

Surprisingly, the athletic program for women in the early years was at least as advanced as that for men. During the first year that Taylor held physical education classes (1905-06), probably only the women participated. Furthermore, the ladies' basketball team played against the Upland High School ladies' squad over two decades before male teams competed with athletes from other schools.[48]

The school had three gymnasiums in this period. Between 1905 and 1911 the top floor of Wright Hall served as both chapel hall and physical education room. The gymnasium during the decades of the 1910s and 1920s was the 33' X 65' X 15' basement floor of the Helena Music Hall. Maytag Gymnasium became the center of indoor athletic action just three years before the intercollegiate competition began.[49]

The influence of President Stuart and his sons was a major factor in the decision to begin athletic competition with other schools. One will recall that Stuart and his oldest son, Marvin, earlier had helped to convince T. H. Maytag to contribute funds to aid in the completion of the new gymnasium. Marvin Stuart's younger brothers also acquired a keen interest in athletics; thus when their father became the Taylor president in 1931, he had a personal reason for leading the institution into intercollegiate athletic competition. The board of trustees on October 28, 1932, unanimously endorsed a plan to allow the school to participate in intercollegiate basketball, baseball, and track. By the mid-

1930s tennis and cross country teams and a "T" club for the letter winners were organized.[50]

The first coach was A. Herschel Cornwell, who came to the college in 1931 with eight years of coaching experience. He directed the Taylor athletes in their first intercollegiate basketball game on November 4, 1933, a 29-20 verdict over Concordia College of Fort Wayne. Other victories in the inaugural ten-win, five-loss season came against Anderson College, Huntington College, Wheaton College, and the Ball State College freshmen.[51]

The leading athletes in the 1930s and 1940s included Art Howard, Philip Miller, Chuck Stuart, Paul Stuart, Don Odle, and Taylor Hayes. Howard, Miller, and Chuck Stuart played on the first basketball squad,

The 1933-34 intercollegiate basketball team.

and in 1933 Stuart became the first winner of the Gates-Howard Trophy, which the school has since awarded annually to the most distinguished male senior athlete. In the 1941-42 season, Odle broke Paul Stuart's one-season basketball record of 204 points by accumulating a total of 313 points.[52]

In the area of student behavior, the college continued to regulate the lives of the pupils. While the Upland students possessed more freedom than the Fort Wayne students had had, the alumni of Fort Wayne College generally believed that the twentieth-century school was "still true to its ideals." When many of the Fort Wayne College graduates visited the Upland school in 1926, they expressed great satisfaction: "There is no jazz and gin, no flapperism and no Charleston experts at Taylor. The boys don't carry flasks or cigarette cases. They don't hide poker chips and deal under the mattresses. The girls don't rouge their cheeks. They don't have to. They carry the ruddy glow of healthful living and clean thinking. They don't roll their stockings or wear men's socks... Taylor, like an oasis on a desert, offers spiritual drink in a University world charged with a barrenness of fundamental Christian living."[53]

In the early Upland years the rules were little different from those that existed during the Fort Wayne period. Even though the school was removed from "the city attraction...where the theatre, dancing hall, and other places of amusement

From the 1934 *Gem:* "It was thought advisable last fall to add a controlled program of intercollegiate athletics. . . . The results. . . have been very satisfactory....First, there was the elimination of a division in the student body. As there are only two societies, Philo and Thalo, which had become largely athletic, new students naturally joined one or the other with not even a third choice to relieve the intensity of the feeling. Now we have a 'common goal.' And the spirit of the campus indicated a marked difference early in the year. We have made our societies more literary and our athletics more collegiate."

Coach Cornwell

131

are calculated to allure the young away from their studies," the students were not allowed to visit the town without permission except on Saturday afternoons between one and five o'clock. Even in areas of conduct that did not involve morality, the college sought to control behavior. The list of twenty-seven dining-hall rules approved by the faculty in 1909 included these: "Do not appear in the dining hall until you have attended minutely to every detail of the toilet," "Do not bring to the table anything but pleasant looks and words, and agreeable topics of conversation," and "Do not have lips open while eating, or make a noise with the mouth."[54]

The girls don't rouge their cheeks. They don't have to. They carry the ruddy glow of healthful living and clean thinking.

Although by the second half of the period Taylor was becoming less regulatory, it still maintained a rigid set of rules. While the school continued to designate "study hours," it did not require students to study during this time; rather, it merely requested that they not visit other students' rooms or play games during those hours. A good indicator of what the pre-World War II college officials considered to be unacceptable student conduct was the record of the faculty committee on discipline. In the period between 1936-43 this committee (which included the president, the vice-president, and the deans among its membership) expelled students for stealing, drinking, being insolent, and "being out all night with a boy from Hartford City." This committee also heard cases involving smoking, lying, cheating, refusal to sit in the right chapel seat, removing the doors between the men's and women's sections of MCW Dormitory, "trying to stir up insurrection among students," "climbing the girls' fire escape with the encouragement of a girl," "being a 'go-between' between Taylor girls and off-campus men," and "having Mississinewa River parties without permission."[55] Perhaps the most famous (or infamous) prank of the period occurred in the fall of 1933, when a cow suddenly appeared on the second floor of the Administration Building; the *Echo* proudly announced that its own managing editor, business manager, and headline editor, the *Gem* editor, and three members of the Varsity Quartet were the culprits who "were guilty of this foul deed."[56]

The two World Wars affected campus activity. The Fuel Administration during World War I would not permit the university to heat classrooms or public buildings. Accordingly, during the coldest months of the winter of 1917-18 the school conducted many classes in the residence halls, the dining room and kitchen, and in faculty homes. The college organized a Student Army Training

Corps (SATC) company in the fall of 1918; however, many of the students did not entirely approve of it. One student later recalled that "many of the SATC members were not sanctified and some were pretty rough, at least according to Taylor's standards." While not all Taylor students showed enthusiasm for their local military unit, most of them approved the American war effort. The *Echo* editions during the war conveyed a sense of patriotism. For example, the masthead of a 1918 paper showed the American flag beside the Biblical inscription "Greater love hath no man than this: that a man lay down his life for his friends." The wartime issues printed "honor rolls" listing the names of former students who were fighting in the war, and they featured letters from these students. One criticism of wartime policy that appeared in the paper was an editorial attacking the practice of ending the use of the German language in the schools. This action "is not patriotism," said the editorial, "but nonsense." Probably the most dramatic incident on campus during this sensitive wartime period occurred in a chapel service during the month preceding the American declaration of war. While Professor David Shaw Duncan was addressing the students on the subject of "Ingratitude," a voice from the audience suddenly interrupted him. Israel Cechanowitz, a Russian Jew attending the school, boldly announced, "If I was to fight I would fight for Germany." Dean Ayres shouted, "Send him back"; and Professor Newton Wray added, "Shame on him!" Shortly thereafter the local sheriff and his deputies came to campus to investigate the incident.[57]

The World War II interruptions were less dramatic but just as profound as those of the First World War. The enrollment level dropped to the lowest point of the century—only 159 students in 1944-45. With the decrease in male students, Taylor reduced its involvement in intercollegiate athletics. The school did not sponsor a military unit on campus during this second war, perhaps largely because during the 1930s the college decided against including military science in its curriculum. Coach William H. Crawford in 1935 stated that the school's physical education and recreation program sought "to offer students enjoyment, not preparation for war."[58]

4. THE STUDENTS

The annual enrollment figures in the period before World War II were similar to those at Fort Wayne College; both institutions usually taught between two hundred and four hundred students annually (see Figure V). Significant decreases in enrollment came following the controversial Winchester

Harold Ockenga (1927)

Safara Witmer (1929)

Ted Engstrom (1938)

administration, during the World Wars, and during the receivership crisis in the midst of the Depression. One should note that while the total enrollment remained relatively constant throughout this fifty-year period, the number of students who were doing college-level work continually increased. When the school first moved to Upland only a small percentage of the enrollees were seeking B.A. or B.S. degrees. In the years just before World War II, there were very few students who were not pursuing a regular college program.[59]

While Fort Wayne College was primarily a local and regional school, the Upland institution has always attracted students from a wide geographical area. For example, the 230 students in 1901-02 came from thirty states, and by 1926 less than one-third of the pupils were from Indiana. Almost all the non-Hoosier students came from Midwestern or Central Atlantic states. The change in the geographical background of the student body resulted from the changes in the nature of the institution in the late nineteenth century. The new owners, The National Association of Local Preachers, encouraged its nationwide constituency to send boys and girls to the college. In addition, parents who were interested in having their children obtain an education cheaply in a Holiness school were scattered throughout the country.[60]

During the first Upland decade mostly males enrolled in the school; the boy-girl ratio ranged from three-to-one to six-to-one. Burt Ayres recalled that this condition led the young men to become "quite adhesive" in their dating patterns "lest an opening...lead to a loss of priority." A very different situation existed during World War II, when only one-third of the 1944-45 students were men; this situation lasted only briefly, however, as the GI influx after the war gave the men a three-to-two ratio advantage by 1949.[61]

Figure V

Enrollment at Taylor University, Upland, 1900-1995

Year	Total Students	College Students	Year	Total Students	College Students	Year	Total Students	College Students	Year	Total Students	College Students
1900-01	565[a]	27	1924-25	310	190	1948-49	578	578	1972-73	1429	1429
1901-02	230	26	1925-26	375	256	1949-50	613	613	1973-74	1445	1445
1902-03		36	1926-27	365	262	1950-51	597	597	1974-75	1437	1437
1903-04	253	25	1927-28	348	255	1951-52	505	505	1975-76	1467	1467
1904-05	241	37	1928-29	375	254	1952-53	469	469	1976-77	1491	1491
1905-06	212	35	1929-30	361	274	1953-54	438	438	1977-78	1525	1525
1906-07	212	25	1930-31	353	254	1954-55	542	542	1978-79	1539	1539
1907-08	206	21	1931-32	298	250	1955-56	559	559	1979-80	1587	1587
1908-09	163	12	1932-33	298	203	1956-57	594	594	1980-81	1582	1582
1909-10	264	31	1933-34	181	181	1957-58	624	624	1981-82	1591	1591
1910-11	272	33	1934-35	191	191	1958-59	681	681	1982-83	1470	1470
1911-12	272	33	1935-36	201	201	1959-60	757	757	1983-84	1559	1559
1912-13	291	59	1936-37	259	259	1960-61	848	848	1984-85	1473	1473
1913-14	293	76	1937-38	321	289	1961-62	857	857	1985-86	1424	1424
1914-15	316	78	1938-39	353	311	1962-63	835	835	1986-87	1492	1492
1915-16	342	96	1939-40	325	289	1963-64	848	848	1987-88	1532	1532
1916-17	357	122	1940-41	322	298	1964-65	843	843	1988-89	1661	1661
1917-18	293	98	1941-42	273	269	1965-66	1050	1050	1989-90	1708	1708
1918-19	245	146	1942-43			1966-67	1244	1244	1990-91	1729	1729
1919-20	296	97	1943-44	164	164	1967-68	1281	1281	1991-92	1780	1780
1920-21	270	96	1944-45	159	159	1968-69	1358	1358	1992-93	1817	1817
1921-22	406	156	1945-46	231	231	1969-70	1404	1404	1993-94	1844	1844
1922-23		172	1946-47	429	429	1970-71	1426	1426	1994-95	1831	1831
1923-24	269	178	1947-48	522	522	1971-72	1420	1420	1995-96	1892	1892

[a] *This total enrollment figure for 1900-01 includes the 265 students in the non-resident and affiliate college programs.*

Joseph Blades
Student

Robert E. Brown
Professor

Taylor educated only a small number of African-American students; however, some of the Blacks made significant contributions to the school, and generally the white students defended them from racial discrimination. Perhaps the second best-known African-American student (Sammy Morris, of course, was the best-known student-Black or White—in the school's history) was Joseph P. Blades. Blades came from Barbados, British West Indies, to attend the institution during the 1910s, and the story of his life appears in a biography by Ayres entitled *Honor to Whom Honor Is Due.* Blades, as well as most other Black Taylor students, experienced the humiliation of being denied public services because of his skin color. When Blades fell on the ice and broke his cheek bone during an Upland winter, a local doctor refused to treat him. The physician came to the room where Blades was waiting, took one look at him, and walked away without uttering a word. The bone healed with only the aid of chemistry professor Robert E. Brown. Before the beginning of the modern Civil Rights movement, Taylor students peacefully protested the discriminatory practices of Indiana bowling alleys, swimming pools, and restaurants when these businesses refused to allow entrance to the Blacks in the student groups. Unfortunately, a few students did not accept the idea of racial integration. On one occasion a number of students who had transferred from a school in the South objected to having seats at the same dining-hall table where the few Black students ate. The most influential Taylor person to speak in favor of segregation was President Paul, who had been born in Louisiana and had been a college instructor in Mississippi. He argued, "The contention for the social intermingling of the white and black races of the United States in the name of Christian ethics is a fallacy. Their temperament and antecedents are such that they do better...in separate homes, and separate schools...." Most Taylor faculty and students did not share Paul's view; rather, they concluded that integration at Taylor had been beneficial for both races. Not only Sammy Morris but other Black students set admirable spiritual and social examples for the majority Whites. Ayres stated in 1951, "In the half-century of my connection with Taylor University, I have never known a negro student to be guilty of any social offense...."[63]

Many of the Taylor students were graduated. Figure VI[64] shows the number of graduates in the period between the move from Fort Wayne and the celebration of the institution's 125th anniversary. The Upland school awarded more B.A. and B.S. degrees in the quarter century after World War II than it did in the half-century before the war. Approximately thirty percent of those who did academy or college work in Upland before 1960 earned a degree or a diploma.[65]

Several of the Taylor graduates during the pre-World War II period later achieved prominence in their vocations. John C. Bugher (B.S., 1921) and Charles W. Shilling (B.S., 1923) both spent their boyhood years in Upland, both earned M.D. degrees from the University of Michigan, and both became deputy directors of the Atomic Energy Commission. Bugher probably has been the most outstanding scientist to be graduated from Taylor. He was an authority on the pathological effects of radiation, and he conducted extensive research on yellow fever. Shilling, whose father had been the acting president of Taylor in the early 1900s, succeeded Bugher in 1955 as the director of the division of biology and medicine of the Atomic Energy Commission.[66]

Figure VI

Degrees, Diplomas, and Certificates Granted

Taylor University, Upland, 1894-1971

Degrees in Course

A.B.	2812	(1896-1971)
B.S. in Ed.	1671	(1930-1971)
Ph.B.	52	(1895-1901)
M.A.	35	(10 in Theology:1899, 1904, 1914-1940)
B.SCI.	31	(1895-1901, 1920-37)
B.MUS.	27	(1918-43)
B.TH.	16	(1937-39)
B.D.	10	(1900-1923)
B.REL.	9	(1934-41)
B.L.	8	(1898-1901)
M.S.	2	(1920-1923)
B.LITT.	2	(1899, 1905)
Ph.A.	1	(1906)
Ph.D.	1	(1907)
	4677	

Honorary Degrees

D.D.	138
LL.D.	28
D.H.L.	9
D.S.C.	5
LITT.D.	7
Ph.D.	4
M.A.	1
Th.D.	1
D.MUS.	1
H.H.B.	2
A.B.	<u>2</u>
	198

Non-Resident Earned Degrees

Ph.D.	59	(1896, 1897, 1902)
M.A.	44	(1902)
Ph.B.	29	(1896, 1897, 1902)
S.T.D.	18	(1902)
A.B.	5	(1897, 1902)
Ph.M.	2	(1896)
LL.D.	2	(1902)
M.A.	1	(1897)
B.D.	<u>1</u>	(1902)
	161	

Diplomas & Certificates, 1894-1929

Academy	297	(1894-1924)
Commercial	73	(1894-1922)
Expression	38	(1909-31)
Eng. Theol.	29	(1897-1911)
Grk. Theol.	22	(1903-13)
Music	13	(1898-1906)
Piano	13	(1904-16)

Latin, Theol.	10	(1897-1903)
Normal Dept.	8	(1898-1906)
Eng. Bible	7	(1915)
Voice	7	(1906-14)
Dom. Sci.	4	(1918)
Evan. Sing.	3	(1926, 1927)
Sub. Fresh.	3	(1925)
College Prep.	3	(1926)
Missionary	2	(1907, 1922)
Pub. Sch. Mus.	2	(1916-18)
Bible Inst.	2	(1913-32)
Eng. & Grk. Theol.	1	(1901)
Lit. Musical	1	(1910)
Sewing & Draft	1	(1916)
2 Yr. Elem. C.	1	(1924)
	540	

Total — 5576

Sam Wolgemuth (1938)

Evan Bergwall (1939)

Milo Rediger (1939)

Eight graduates who acquired wide influence as religious leaders include Albert E. Day (1904), Harold J. Ockenga (1927), Ralph Dodge (1931), R. Marvin Stuart (1931), Theodore W. (Ted) Engstrom (1938), and Samuel (Sam) F. Wolgemuth (1938), Paul Clasper (1944), and Virgil Maybray (1944). Day earned a citation from the *Christian Century* magazine as one of the six leading preachers in America, and he received honorary degrees from five schools including the University of Southern California. Ockenga was a long-term minister of the historic Park Street Congregational Church in Boston, the first president of the National Association of Evangelicals, a co-founder and president of Fuller Theological Seminary, and the president of Gordon College and Seminary. Dodge and Stuart, both discussed earlier, became Methodist bishops. Dodge in Africa and Clasper in Asia became missionary statesmen known for their promotion of intercultural sensitivity as well as evangelism.[67] Maybray became the executive secretary of the Mission Society for United Methodists and a leader of the Good News movement, an evangelical caucas within the United Methodist Church. Engstrom served as the third president of Youth for Christ International (1957-63), and a long-time major leader (beginning in 1963 and including a tenure as president) of the relief and mission organization, World

Vision. Wolgemuth, led Youth for Christ as president, during the period 1965-1973.[68]

Seven graduates became college presidents or chancellors. Three of these—Robert L. Stuart (1906), Evan H. Bergwall (1939), and Milo A. Rediger (1939)—presided over their own alma mater. David S. Duncan (1900) became the chancellor of the University of Denver in 1935 after spending many years on the Taylor faculty. Safara A. Witmer (1929) became president of Fort Wayne Bible College in 1945 and continued in that position until 1957, when he resigned to become executive director of the Accrediting Association of Bible Colleges.[69] Arthur M. Climenhaga (1938) served as president both of Upland College and Messiah College. Norman A. Baxter (1945) became the president of Fresno State College in 1970.[70]

By 1945 Taylor was ending one era in its history and beginning a new one. The years of the unaccredited college were over, the period of the Holiness Methodist college was coming to an end, and the days of the poor people's school were now numbered. In the post-war years the university gradually became an institution that appealed to a broad range of evangelical Protestants in the middle-income classes. Gradually, the educated public began to place a higher value upon the Taylor academic program; and gradually, the general public began to identify Taylor as the school that uses athletics as a means to promote Christian witness.

[1] Report of the President of Taylor University to the National Association of Local Preachers of the Methodist Episcopal Church, 1895 (Taylor University archives); Annual Report of the President of Taylor University, 1897 (Taylor University archives); *Taylor Echo*, March 4, 1931, p. 1.

[2] *TUC*, 1893-94, p. 6.

[3] *TUC*, 1895-96, p. 7; *Upland Monitor*, March 17, 1910, p. 4; *University Journal*, January, 1905, pp. 9-10.

[4] Thaddeus C. Reade, *The Elder Brother* (Hartford City, Indiana, 1900), p. 47.

[5] In 1946 this Church became a part of the new Evangelical United Brethren denomination.

[6] *University Journal*, January, 1904, p. 1; *Taylor Echo*, December 14, 1934, p. 5 and October 11, 1938, p. 5.

[7] A 1904 survey listed eighty-five percent of the students as "converted" and fifty percent as "sanctified," See *University Journal*, January, 1904, p. 1.

[8] *TUC*, 1901-02, p. 8, 1907-08 (n.p., n.d.), p. 11, and 1926-27, pp. 92-93; WTFDM, May 31, 1935; *Upland Monitor*, November 11, 1909, p. 4; *Community Courier*, April 24, 1930, p. 1; *Taylor Echo*, January 15, 1938, p. 2.

[9] The National Association of the Local Preachers of the Methodist Episcopal Church, *Proceedings of the Thirty-Eighth Annual Meeting*, 1895, p. 15; *Taylor Bulletin*, November 1949, pp. 2, 6; *Taylor Echo*, January 11, 1927, p. 3, May 27, 1929, p. 5, and May 17, 1934, p. 1; *Taylor Magazine*, November, 1956, p. 10, and Summer, 1981, pp. 2-7.

[10] *Taylor Bulletin*, March, 1954, p. 2.

[11] Ayres, "Taylor University," pp. 59-60, 77; *Marion Chronicle*, January 26, 1958, p. 1; *Upland Monitor*, May 3, 1900, p. 4, October 10, 1912, p. 4, March 12, 1914, p. 4, June 11, 1914, p. 1, and November 4, 1915, p. 4; *Community Courier*, September 9, 1920, p. 1, October 14, 1920, p. 1, May 4, 1922, p. 1, and November 9, 1922, p. 1.

[12] Ayres, "Taylor University," p. 59; *University Journal*, February 10, 1906, p. 1 and March 10, 1906, p. 1; *Upland Monitor*, May 24, 1906, p. 4; *TUC*, 1920, p. 19; *Community Courier*, January 8, 1920, p. 1; *Taylor Echo*, November, 1916, pp. 18-19.

[13] Ayres, "Taylor University," p. 106.

[14] *Taylor Gem*, 1915, p. 148; *Upland Monitor*, November 27, 1913, p. 4.

[15] This practice contrasted with the goal of DePauw University to recruit students from the families of wealthy Methodists.

[16] *TUC*, 1901-02, p. 6; *Taylor Bulletin*, January, 1928, p. 4; *TUC*, 1936, p. 25.

[17] *Taylor Echo*, March 4, 1931, p. 1.

[18] Ayres, "Taylor University," p. 21.

[19] William C. Ringenberg, "The Protestant College on the Michigan Frontier" (unpublished Ph.D. dissertation, Michigan State University, 1970), p. 102; *TUC*, 1913 (Upland, 1913), p. 36 and 1893-94, p. 6; WTFDM, March 14, 1934.

[20] *Upland Monitor*, April 3, 1902, p. 1; Minutes of the Faculty Committee on Clerical Help (Taylor University archives), June 5, 1920; *Upland Monitor*, February 26, 1903, p. 1; *University Journal*, January, 1904, p. 11; *TUC*, 1920, p. 28; WTFDM, November 13, 1933.

[21] *Taylor Echo*, October 10, 1922, p. 2; *Upland Courier*, May 3, 1923, p. 1; *Taylor Echo*, April 12, 1931, pp. 1, 3, January 18, 1933, p. 1, and September 14, 1935, p. 1.

[22] William Jennings Bryan, *Darwin's Confession* (Upland, n.d.), p. 4.

[23] *Ibid.*, pp. 1-4.

[24] *TUC*, 1898-99 (Upland, n.d.), p. 20, 1909-10 (Upland, 1909), pp. 60-61, 1914, p. 137, and 1926-27, pp. 7, 106; *Taylor Bulletin*, June, 1932, p. 15.

[25] Ayres, "Taylor University," pp. 22-23; *TUC*, 1898-99, pp. 8, 33.

[26] Ayres, "Taylor University," pp. 24-25; *TUC*, 1898-99, pp. 8, 33.

[27] *TUC*, 1892-93, pp. 5-6, 1895-96, pp. 8-14, 1936, p. 30, and 1945, p. 39; Ayres, "Taylor University," p. 21.

[28] *TUC*, 1898-99, pp. 9, 12-15, 1909-10, p. 77, and 1926-27, pp. 22-23.

[29] *TUC*, 1909-10, pp. 19-45.

[30] It is interesting to observe that a conservative Protestant college would offer a course on the church and social problems during the height of the period of the Social Gospel Movement. Perhaps the course primarily emphasized the problem of alcohol.

[31] *TUC*, 1893-94, p. 8, 1909-10, p. 81, 1914, pp. 55-128, and 1920, pp. 34-36.

[32] *TUC*, 1920, pp. 32-33, 1931, pp. 35, 94-95, and 1936, p. 33.

[33] *TUC*, 1897-98 (Fort Wayne, n.d.), pp. 5-6, 23 and 1898-99, p. 8; *Upland Monitor*, February 3, 1898, p. 1; William J. Jones, "A Brief History of the Indiana Mammouth and the Taylor University Mastodon" (unpublished manuscript, Taylor University archives); *TUC*, 1931, p. 38 and 1940 (Upland, 1940), p. 18; *Fort Wayne News Sentinel*, December 13, 1947, p. 22.

[34] *TUC*, 1907-08, pp. 6-7, 1920, pp. 8-9, 1926-27, pp. 10-17, 1936, pp. 79, and 1940, pp. 7-10.

[35] Ayres, "Taylor University," pp. 39-40, 53; *Taylor Magazine*, Spring, 1965, p. 28.

[36] *TUC*, 1931, pp. 76-77; *Taylor Echo*, November 21, 1936, p. 1; *Hartford City News-Times*, March 1, 1965, pp. 1, 6; *Taylor Magazine*, Spring, 1965, p. 28.

[37] *Taylor Echo*, February 12, 1930, p. 1; Norwood, *Indiana Conference*, pp. 146-47; *Taylor Echo*, January 1, 1939, p. 1 and November 30, 1940, p. 1. Also

see George Fenstermacher, "What Accreditation Would Mean to Taylor," *Taylor Echo*, November 21, 1935, p. 1.

[38] These two Holiness groups later merged.

[39] *TUC*, 1909-10, pp. 14-15 and 1931, p. 19; *Taylor Gem*, 1934, p. 60.

[40] *Upland Monitor*, February 21, 1901, p. 4 and February 17, 1910, p. 4; MS Minutes of the Thalonian Literary Society, December 9, 1904 (Taylor University archives); *Taylor Echo*, January 1, 1926, p. 1; *TUC*, 1914, pp. 24-26.

[41] *TUC*, 1914, pp. 24-26, 1931, p. 92, and 1940, pp. 18-19.

[42] *Taylor Echo*, April 13, 1932, p. 2; *Taylor Bulletin*, April 3, 1955, p. 1.

[43] See, for example, Barton Rees Pogue's humorous account of a trip of a few students in "an automobile of poor repair" to Marion to hear presidential nominee Charles Evans Hughes during the 1916 campaign (Barton Rees Pogue, "A Trip with a Peck of Trouble," *Taylor Echo*, October, 1916, pp. 4-6).

[44] *Upland Monitor*, January 16, 1902, p. 4 and January 23, 1902, p. 4.

[45] *Taylor Echo*, January, 1917, pp. 11-12 and November 14, 1922, p. 2; letter, J. Arthur Howard to Everett Shiliday, June 6, 1928 (Taylor University archives).

[46] *Community Courier*, June 17, 1920, p. 1; *Taylor Echo*, May 14, 1926, p. 2; *TUC*, 1926-27, pp. 86-87; *Taylor Echo*, January 15, 1938, p. 2.

[47] Ayres, "Taylor University," pp. 54-55; *University Journal*, February 10, 1906, pp. 8-9; *TUC*, 1907-08, p. 11, 1909-10, p. 81, and 1914, p. 30; Rudolph, *American College and University*, p. 376.

[48] Ayres, "Taylor University," pp. 54-55; *Upland Monitor*, April 22, 1909, p. 4.

[49] Ayres, "Taylor University," pp. 54-55.

[50] WTFDM, October 28, 1933; *Taylor Echo*, September 28, 1935, p. 6; *TUC*,

1936, pp. 18-19.

[51] *Community Courier*, September 10, 1931, p. 1; *Taylor Echo*, November 3, 1933, p. 4; *Taylor Gem*, 1934, pp. 93-94.

[52] *Taylor Echo*, June 4, 1935, p. 4 and March 12, 1942, p. 4.

[53] *Taylor Echo*, January 1, 1926, p. 3.

[54] *TUC*, 1893-94, p. 16 and 1894-95 (Marion, 1894), pp. 23-24; MS Minutes of the Taylor University Faculty Meetings (Taylor University archives), January 18, 1909.

[55] *TUC*, 1936, p. 27; MS Minutes of the Faculty Committee on Discipline, 1935-43 (Taylor University archives).

[56] *Taylor Echo*, November 3, 1933, p. 3.

[57] Ayres, *Honor to Whom Honor Is Due*, pp. 45-46; *Community Courier*, October 10, 1918, p. 1; *Upland Monitor*, October 25, 1917, p. 4; *Taylor Echo*, April 11, 1918, pp. 1-3 and June 13, 1918, pp. 1-3.

[58] *Taylor Echo*, September 28, 1935, p. 6 and April 10, 1943, p. 6; *Upland Monitor*, October 25, 1917, p. 4; *TUC*, 1941 (n.p., 1941), p. 97 and 1945 (Upland, 1945), p. 100.

[59] See the enrollment sections of the school catalogs.

[60] *TUC*, 1902-03 (Warsaw, Indiana, n.d.), p. 10 and 1926-27, p. 106.

[61] Annual Report of the President of Taylor University, 1897; The National Association of Local Preachers of the Methodist Episcopal Church, *Proceedings of the Thirty-Eighth Annual Meeting*, 1895, p. 15; Ayres, "Taylor University," pp. 43-44; *TUC*, 1945, p. 100 and 1949 (Upland, 1949), p. 107.

[62] A March 7, 1950, *Echo* editorial reported: "Last Wednesday night one of our colored students was made the object of discrimination in an Indianapolis

restaurant. We wish to commend those twenty or more students who walked out of the establishment after quietly informing the managers that they could not patronize a place that would not cater to all Taylor students on an equal basis. Only by such acts can we hope to break down the forces of segregation that are a threat to both democracy and Christianity."

[63] *Taylor Echo*, January 9, 1924, pp. 2, 9; Ayres, *Honor to Whom Honor Is Due*, pp. 23-24; *Taylor Magazine*, September, 1949, p. 3; *Community Courier*, August 10, 1922, p. 1; *Taylor Echo*, October 10, 1922, p. 3.

[64] The source for the dates in Figure VI is the office of the Taylor University registrar.

[65] Letter, E. Sterl Phinney to B. Joseph Martin, January 25, 1961 (Taylor University archives).

[66] *American Men of Science*, 6 vols. (New York, 1965), I, 661 and V, 4881; *Taylor Magazine*, Spring, 1967, p. 20.

[67] See Dodge's works listed earlier in this chapter and Clasper's award-winning *Eastern Paths and the Christian Way* (New York, 1980).

[68] *Taylor Bulletin*, May 1952, p. 3 and May, 1954, p. 1; James Hefley, *God Goes to High School* (Waco, Texas, 1970), pp. 70-84; alumni files, Taylor University Alumni Office.

[69] See S. A. Witmer, *The Bible College Story: Education with Dimension* (Manhasset, New York, 1962).

[70] *Who Was Who in America*, 1897-1942 (Chicago, 1943), p. 345. *Who's Who in America*, 1970-71 (Chicago, 1970), p. 423; *Higher Education Directory*, 1970-71 (Washington, 1971), p. 22.

Chapter Seven

THE POST WAR GENERATION

*J*ust as Burt Ayres had been the leading figure at the college during the first Upland period, so Milo A. Rediger (dean, 1945-48, 1952-65; president, 1965-75, 1979-81) became the single most influential person at Taylor during the generation after 1945. Each man was the academic and intellectual leader; each held a longer tenure than did anyone else during his respective period; each interrupted his service to the university briefly when a major conflict developed with the college president; and each during his absence served as dean of a college in Iowa. There also were differences. While both men were deans for many years, Ayres spent more time in the classroom than did Rediger. During Ayres' years the school was still small enough so that the dean could do a considerable amount of teaching. While both men played a major role in determining school policy, Rediger's role was larger. Ayres never became the actual president as did Rediger. Even before 1965, when Rediger became the twenty-fourth president, he often exerted greater influence than did the president.

Although Rediger was the major figure in the period, other men also made vital contributions to the college. President Evan H. Bergwall (1951-59) commanded deep respect for his integrity and spiritual earnestness, and he and Rediger brought a degree of intellectual leadership to the presidency that it had not seen since the days of Thaddeus Reade. President B. Joseph Martin (1960-65) worked hard to enhance the long-range financial resources, but his two major projects to achieve this goal—the move to Fort Wayne and reaffiliation with the North Indiana Conference of the Methodist Church—both failed. Also significant were the unusual athletic programs of Don Odle and Robert W. (Bob) Davenport, and it is possible that these innovative sports endeavors attracted as many students to the school as did the improvements in the quality of the academic program.

A great loss

January 16, 1960 will always be remembered as one of the most tragic days in Taylor's history. The 67-year old administration building suddenly became a flaming torch.

The fire started at 4:00 a.m. with such force that it was immediately out of control. The local volunteer fire department was on the scene within minutes after the blaze began, but its efforts were severely hampered by a lack of water pressure. In only four hours nothing remained of the the historic structure but a smoke-filled network of gutted brick walls.

The nerve center of Taylor, with its administrative offices, nine classrooms, the chemistry, mathematics, art and drama departments, printing and mailing department, several faculty offices, the telephone switchboard, a well-stocked supply room, and a museum, suddenly were no more.

Source: Wilbur Cleveland, "Holocaust Tests College" (unpublished manuscript).

Celebrating the achievement of accreditation.

The 1947 *Gem* described the acquiring of institutional accreditation as "The Event of the Year." In a sprightly manner, editor Alyce Rocke (Cleveland) detailed the events of the campus celebration: "On March 26, the ringing of the tower bell announced that Taylor had received full accreditation from the North Central Association, Professors pressed in the lectures to offer prayers of thanks; students broke into songs of praise.

"That evening the campus met in Shreiner Auditorium. Testimonies of the spirit that Taylor had in individual lives thrilled our hearts. The achievement of accreditation was a climax of the delightful labors of many over a period of years. Everyone present sensed a deeper loyalty to their school.

"Realizing the significance of this event, the students desired a celebration. A spirit of exaltation permeated the room. With a grand spirit of unity, the students and faculty made plans to meet Dr. Meredith and Dr. Rediger at the train station. Under the direction of the Student Council arrangements were made for a colorful parade."

1. Maturing of the Academic Program

The single most important development in the improvement of Taylor's academic program was the acquisition of regional accreditation by the North Central Association of Colleges and Secondary Schools in 1947. President Clyde W. Meredith (1945-51) and Dean Rediger defended the application for association membership at the March 26, 1947, meeting of the organization's board of examiners in Chicago, and within minutes after the climactic hearing, the board granted the school full accreditation. The joyous Taylor administrators immediately called the anxiously waiting faculty and students in Upland, and shortly thereafter the Administration Building tower bells rang out the celebration with unusually loud pealing.[1]

The achievement of membership in the North Central Association represented the culmination of many years of hard work to upgrade the quality of the institution. Meredith gave special praise for the accomplishment to Marion E. Witmer, who had served as business manager during the previous ten years; many individuals, however, had contributed to the effort to improve the areas of weakness that the North Central Association examiners had criticized in their 1939 study of the college. The criticisms of the 1939 examining committee had included the following: (1) the library was weak for the professional growth of the faculty, (2) the physical plant for instructional activities was unattractive and inadequate, (3) the financial history of the school was a source of considerable embarrassment to the governing board and the administration, (4) the salary schedule was very low, (5) the student personnel services, while well conceived and properly organized, lacked maturity, and (6) the student health service needed to be expanded.[2]

In many respects Meredith was a good man to lead the college in its effort to obtain accreditation. His Holiness Methodist background pleased the Taylor constituency, and his solid academic credentials and pleasing manner favorably impressed the accrediting officials. He had been graduated from Houghton College, and at the time that the trustees offered him the Taylor presidency he was a professor at Marion College and the pastor of the Jonesboro, Indiana, Methodist Church. He held a seminary degree from the Winona Lake School of Theology and graduate degrees from Butler University and the Illif School of Theology of Denver University. With his Th.D. degree from the latter school, he was the first Taylor president to have an earned doctorate degree.[3]

The gaining of accreditation was the high point of Meredith's administration; during the second half of his tenure, school morale declined sharply. In the late 1940s and early 1950s the faculty became as deeply divided as they had been at any time since the 1906-07 Winchester controversy. The major issue of division was a disagreement between Meredith and Rediger on the degree of freedom with which Rediger could administer the academic program. Rediger resigned the deanship in 1948, and two years later he left his Taylor teaching position[4] to become the Dean of Dubuque University in Iowa. Meanwhile, the board of trustees became as divided as was the faculty. In 1950, when the board voted to continue to have Meredith lead the school, they made the decision by a one-vote margin. One year later the sudden death of one of Meredith's supporters on the board led to a situation whereby the trustees voted by a 7-6 margin to ask the president to submit his resignation.[5]

The trustees found it very difficult to obtain a qualified man to accept the Taylor presidency in 1951. The recent divisions and the still not healthy financial situation made the position an unattractive one. After the board of directors considered several possible candidates, they offered the post to one of their fellow trustees whom they greatly respected, Evan Bergwall. Bergwall reluctantly accepted the presidency, and he later reported that had he known the full financial situation at the time, he probably would have declined the offer.[6]

Bergwall came to the presidency with excellent scholarly credentials. After he had graduated *summa cum laude* and first in the Taylor class of 1939, he pursued graduate studies at Yale Divinity School, New York University, Emory University, and Oxford University. Yale awarded him the Tew Prize in Literature, the Julia Archibald high scholarship award, the Day Fellowship, and *cum laude* graduation honors.[7]

One of Bergwall's first actions to strengthen the college was to invite Rediger to return as the academic dean. Bergwall and Rediger worked well together as an administrative team; thus in the early 1950s Rediger first experienced the degree of freedom he wished to have to develop the academic program in the ways he believed

Clyde W. Meredith

President

The Meredith presidency (1945-51) featured the achievement of institutional accreditation by the North Central Association in 1947 and the construction of the Ayers Alumni Memorial Library in 1950.

During his years at Taylor, Dr. Bergwall became deeply appreciated by alumni and many other friends of the university for his intellectual and spiritual leadership, deep sincerity and devotion to the strengthening of Taylor's entire program.

-Wilbur Cleveland

151

Milo Rediger

Milo Rediger served Taylor in five different decades and in many roles, namely Instructor of Philosophy and Religion, Dean of Students, Academic Dean, President, and Provost. His primary contributions include these: 1) he led the effort to include students in the institutional governance process in a period when such a practice was not common in higher education, 2) he was the most important factor in the growing academic maturity of the institution after World War Two, and 3) he was very effective in representing Taylor to both the academic community and the general Christian community in a way that caused them to increasingly appreciate the university's effort to promote intellectual rigor no less than spiritual experience.

would improve the school. Rediger sought to lead Taylor from "an academic level of indoctrination to an academic level of education"; he sought to strengthen the quality of the faculty; and he sought to introduce the concept of "community government" into the governance of the institution. As a student in the 1930s, Rediger had perceived Taylor as a school where a student did not possess complete freedom to raise certain questions and where faculty members sometimes avoided an honest examination of difficult intellectual issues (i.e., those which challenged Christian orthodoxy). As dean—and later as president—he sought to create a learning climate in which the philosophical premise was that "all truth is God's truth, and the Christian does not fear it—nor is he afraid of where it will lead him." Somewhat related to this increased openness in the search for truth was the gradual de-emphasis in the postwar years of Taylor's traditional relationship to a specific church (Methodist) and to a specific theological system (Arminian).[8]

Rediger believed that the school could increase the quality of instruction if it would increase the faculty salaries. He thought that minimum budgets in the past had often made it difficult to hire and retain excellent teachers. He also argued that it was unfair to expect the faculty (by their low salaries) to subsidize the students' education. Accordingly the salaries gradually increased. The highest professorial salaries, which had been $2,200 in 1945, became $3,500 in 1950 and $5,150 in 1958. The median salary, which had been $4,100 in 1958, grew to $6,900 in 1964, and to $9,400 by 1970. Also significant in this postwar period was the addition of insurance and retirement benefits; such supplementary remuneration had not existed as late as 1945.[9]

To pay for the higher salaries the college increased the tuition rates. Tuition costs, which had been $170 per year in 1945, became $300 in 1950, $390 in 1955, $800 in 1961, $1,240 in 1967, and $1,698 in 1971; the total annual costs that had amounted to $495 per year in 1945 rose to $774 in 1950, $992 in 1955, $1,500 in 1961, $2,100 in 1967, and $2,800 in 1971.[10]

Thus by the 1970s the college was no longer a "poor man's school." Many believed that the change in the economic nature of the school resulted in the acquisition of a better faculty, which in turn resulted in a better education for the students; however, not all expressed enthusiasm about the results of the continually increasing student costs. Former President Bergwall, who by the late 1960s was a Methodist district superintendent in Indiana, lamented the fact that many Methodist ministers who had been graduated from Taylor could not afford to send their children to their alma mater.

There is no doubt that by the early 1970s the university offered a better education to its students than it had provided in 1945, but it is difficult to judge the extent to which the improvement came as a result of the changed economic policy. The percentage of faculty holding doctorate degrees did not increase during this period despite the salary increases; however, the larger financial base allowed the school to decrease the average teaching load to 12 hours by the early 1960s. Part of the improvement in teaching came when the college grew large enough to allow the professors to teach primarily within the area of their training. For example, Grace D. Olson, who had taught all of the history and political science courses (seventeen hours) during her first semester at the school in the fall of 1945, taught mostly the modern European history courses by the late 1960s. One result of the improvement of the academic level and economic status was a decrease in the turnover rate of faculty and staff. By the school's 125th anniversary in 1971, individuals who recently had served the college for fifteen or more years included: Hazel Butz Carruth, Wilbur Cleveland, Virginia Cline, Lily Haakonsen, Alice K. Holcombe, Paul Keller, Gordon M. Krueger, Herbert G. Lee, Jennie Andrews Lee, Fred H. Luthy, Elmer N. Nussbaum, Don J. Odle, Grace D. Olson, Jack D. Patton, E. Sterl Phinney, Elisabeth Poe, Milo A. Rediger, Frank H. Roye, Hilda L. Steyer, Julius J. Valberg, Lois A. Weed, and Vida G. Wood.

It was better for Taylor to have Dr. Rediger than to have been given $10,000,000. His colleagues had an enormous respect for him....

Not only did the university increase spending for instruction, but by the late 1960s it was also increasing its expenditures for instructional facilities. The new Liberal Arts Building (1966) and Science Center (1967) offered the students more attractive classrooms and such new education units as a media center and a computing center.

When Rediger first became the university dean in 1945, that position included the function of dean of students as well as academic dean. One of his major goals for the school was a system of community government in which the students and faculty—as well as the administration—would participate in the decision-making process. Prior to the mid-1940s the faculty committees had wielded limited influence and the student council had existed primarily to promote social functions. Under Rediger's leadership the old faculty committees became administration-faculty-student committees that possessed the authority to initiate policies in such areas as academic affairs, student conduct, and religious events. In a similar manner the student organization became a legislative body, and by 1947 it possessed a written constitution to define its new authority. Beginning in 1955 the new student judiciary allowed student representatives to participate in the enforcement of the school policy that for a decade they had been helping to make. Thus by the 1940s and 1950s the Taylor administration because of conviction was giving the students "a piece of the action"; many other colleges granted

People are more important than paper and policy; caring is better than manipulation; serving is better than power. In fact those who desire power should not have it; those who have it will not enjoy it; those who enjoy it will abuse it. Delegation is essential, the delegation must be respected, and accountability must be required.

- Milo Rediger

similar authority to their students only by the late 1960s and early 1970s, and then only under duress. When Rediger was visiting numerous colleges as a coordinator for the North Central Association Liberal Arts Study in the 1957-63 period, one of the questions that representatives from other schools most frequently asked him was, "What is Taylor's 'community government' concept, and how is it working?"[11]

Just as was the case in the pre-World War II period, the type of guest lecturers the Taylor officials invited to the school was an indicator of the general intellectual nature of the college. Before 1945, most of these speakers had been popular preachers or Bible teachers. After the war, Taylor continued to welcome the popular preachers, but it also frequently invited religious leaders who could communicate rational as well as mystical Christianity (e.g., Elton Trueblood) and speakers who represented civic concerns (e.g., Governor Matthew Welsh and Senator Birch Bayh). Also in the later period the school sponsored an increasing number of programs that showed an interest in the broad public issues of the day (e.g. a forum that brought agricultural leaders and representatives from the national media to the campus for a consideration of the topic "The Farmer's Dilemma: Surpluses and Security").[12]

Most of the scholarly research in this period was done by members of the

Science Division faculty, many of whom worked with government and/or industry research grants. As early as 1950 chemist Manly J. Powell was experimenting with vitamins A and E for Research Corporation; however, the Atomic Energy Commission and other governmental agencies financed most of the science research projects. Faculty members involved in these government projects included A. J. Anglin, Stanley L. Burden, Elmer N. Nussbaum, Donald H. Porter, and Vida G. Wood. Nussbaum spent his summers during the 1960s teaching at the Oak Ridge, Tennessee, Institute of Nuclear Studies, and his reputation as a physicist aided his efforts to bring prominent scientists to the campus each year (beginning in 1957) for the highly profitable Science Lecture Series.[13]

One additional project of note in the Science Division was the development of the biology field station. In the early 1950s, Clinton J. Bushey taught field biology to Taylor students at Camp Oskejo in Watersmeet, Michigan; however, in the 1960s the school under the leadership of Harold Z. Snyder developed its own biological field station at Big Twin Lake near Mancelona, Michigan. The station operated a science camp for boys as well as a college program for the Taylor students.[14]

In general the Taylor faculty members during this period spent little time writing articles and books for publication, though there have been some noteworthy exceptions. The best of the faculty publications included an article in one of the leading history journals, the *Mississippi Valley Historical Review* (now the *Journal of American History*), by Paton Yoder;[15] the multi-volume *Wesleyan Bible Commentary* (Grand Rapids, 1964-69), which Charles W. Carter edited; and a psychology textbook, *An Introduction to Psychology* (Grand Rapids, 1952) by Hildreth M. Cross.

The teacher-education division of the college became much more prominent after World War II than it had been in the previous period. In the late 1940s an elementary-education department was added, and by 1950 one-third of the students were preparing to be primary or secondary teachers. For two decades after the mid-1950s, the division reached the peak of its prominence with approximately one-half of the Taylor graduates earning the teacher-education B.S. degree; the primary leaders of the education program in this period were Jennie Andrews Lee and George Haines. Originally the practice-teaching part of the curriculum involved only a three-hour credit course in which the senior student taught a single class per day in one of the Upland, Hartford City, or Marion Schools. By the late 1950s the elementary student teachers were working

Harold Snyder

Professor

Jennie Andrews Lee

Professor

George Haines

Professor

Grace D. Olson
Professor

Hazel Butz Carruth
Professor

In the best tradition of Burt Ayers and Milo Rediger, these two revered ladies during lengthy Taylor careers modeled the expectation of academic rigor. Grace Olson's students—particularly those at the upper division level—learned quickly that whatever their previous experience may have been, they now must face the necessity of becoming independent, critical thinkers. Hazel Butz Carruth, raised on the rugged South Dakota plains, early learned an exacting work ethic that she expected of her students no less then she expected of herself. Early in her career she taught at the Fort Wayne Bible Institute; thus when in 1992 that institution (as Summit Christian College) merged with Taylor, she personally provided an important symbolic link in the common tradition of the uniting colleges.

in their assigned schools during the entire day and living in the community in which they were teaching. The secondary student teachers moved to the full-time residential experience in the late 1960s. The rising prosperity of the Education Department did not please everyone at Taylor. Especially in the 1950s and 1960s tension existed between those who wished the school to be primarily a liberal arts college and those who preferred that the college become predominantly a teacher-training institution. This conflict was not a new one in this period, however, for as early as 1926 a very pointed *Echo* editorial entitled "Is This a College or a Normal School?" expressed the hope that Taylor would "again become a 'college' rather than allow her position to slide down [in]...status...[to that of] merely another Normal School." Since the mid-1970s only approximately one-fourth of the graduates have completed the elementary or secondary education curriculum.[16]

Several changes in the calendar occurred during the post-war period. In the mid-1930s the college had replaced the three-term school year it had brought to Upland from Fort Wayne with the two-semester school year. Although the summer session ceased operation in the mid-1950s because of lack of demand, summer classes were resumed in 1968. Also in 1968 the college changed the calendar by creating an "interterm" during the month of January. This new "4-1-4" division of the regular nine-month school year provided the opportunity for creativeness and experimentation in course offerings and learning methods during the interterm while still retaining the two-semester concept during the remainder of the year. In the late 1950s and early 1960s the college seriously considered adopting the "tri-mester" plan. In 1957 Rediger first proposed the three-semester, year-round calendar concept for Taylor; at that time he saw it as a means of educating more students, giving full-year employment to the faculty, and better utilizing the already existing physical plant. In the early 1960s when the college leaders thought that the school would return to Fort Wayne, they planned to introduce the tri-mester plan at the time of the move. After the 1965 decision to stay in Upland, the school leaders, who learned that institutions that already had tried the plan were experiencing problems with it—especially with the summer "mester"—decided against introducing it at Taylor.[17]

Many alumni who studied at Taylor during this post-war period have made noteworthy contributions to society. Among the more visible of these are several college and seminary presidents: Timothy Warner (1950), Fort Wayne Bible College; David LeShana (1953), George Fox College, Seattle Pacific University, and Western Evangelical Seminary; Jewell Reinhart Coburn (1955), University of Santa Barbara; Kenneth Gangel (1957), Miami Christian College; Jay Kesler (1958), Taylor University; Charles Ford (x 1960), University of New England; Benjamin Sprunger (x 1960), Bluffton College; John Oswalt (1961), Asbury College; Thomas Atcitty (1963), Navajo Community College; Eugene Habecker (1968), Huntington College; and Gregg Lehman (x 1969), Taylor University. Kesler also served as president of Youth for Christ (see chapter ten). Atcitty presided over the first college owned and operated by American Indians, and in 1995 he became vice president of the Navajo Nation, the largest Indian tribe in the country. Also recently Habecker has become president of the American Bible Society. Other leaders of major Christian organizations have included Billy Melvin (1951), executive director of the National Association of Evangelicals and Daniel Southern (1976), president of the American Tract Society. Scientists of note have included Robert Schenck (1951) and Raymond Isley (1957). Schenck, based at Chicago's Rush Medical College and Rush-Presbyterian-St. Luke's Medical Center, has become widely recognized for his skill in reconstructive hand microsurgery and his promotion of hand injury prevention programs. Isley, working with the Research Triangle Institute (North Carolina) was cited by international health officials for his important contributions to the improvement of water sanitation conditions in tropical Africa.[18]

Figure VII			
Library Holdings			
1902	4,000	1956	31,000
1911	6,000	1961	36,000
1921	7,000	1967	63,400
1926	9,000	1971	89,000
1930	11,000	1976	112,700
1936	13,500	1981	129,300
1941	17,200	1986	142,400
1945	21,800	1991	157,500
1951	26,000	1995	176,000

David LeShana

Alumnus

Thomas Atcitty

Alumnus

Eugene Habecker

Alumnus

Alice Holcombe

Librarian

Lois Weed

Librarian

The Ayres Building served as Taylor's library until 1986.

2. THE SEARCH FOR FINANCIAL SECURITY

During the Meredith and early Bergwall years the same old struggle for survival continued; after the early 1950s the financial status gradually improved. Worry about immediate economic survival gradually was replaced with concern about how to obtain money to construct non-income-producing buildings and how to assure the long-range survival of the institution. During Meredith's tenure many of the private colleges in Indiana agreed to unite their efforts to seek financial support from the state's business and industrial organizations. To facilitate their cooperative efforts, the schools organized themselves as the Associated Colleges of Indiana; however, they did not admit Taylor to original membership. Much of the improved financial position of the college, however, came because the 1950s were prosperous years for the American economy in general and higher education in particular. When Bergwall resigned the presidency in 1959 to return to the Methodist ministry, he did so primarily because, as he said, "I was weary of fund raising" and "it was not my calling to be a fund raiser."

When the board met to choose Bergwall's successor, it sought a man who possessed interest and ability in the financial aspect of college leadership. B. Joseph Martin seemed to be the right choice. He was a Methodist minister, held a Ph.D. degree from the University of Southern California, and his mother and father-in-law (John A. and Jennie Duryea) had formerly worked on the Taylor staff; however, it was his financial success as President of Wesleyan College in Macon, Georgia, that most interested the trustees. He had established an impressive record of fund raising and construction of new buildings while he presided over that school (1953-60).[19]

Most of the story of Martin's presidency is an account of his efforts to make the institution more affluent. One of the methods he hoped to use to accomplish this purpose was to return the school to the ownership—and financial responsibility—of the North Indiana Conference of the Methodist Church. The two groups on several occasions had shown interest in each other since their separation in 1890, but the reunion overtures of the early 1960s were unusually serious. During much of the period after 1890, Taylor, in fact, had operated as an "unofficial" institution of Indiana Methodism. Many faculty members (e.g., Burt Ayres, George Fenstermacher, Jesse W. Fox) had been leaders in Indiana Methodism. The two groups had seriously considered merger during the 1915-22 period, and beginning in the mid-1950s the North Indiana Methodist Conference annually contributed $6,000 to the college in recognition of the school's role in the training of many of the conference ministers.

It is somewhat ironic that these serious reunion talks came in the 1960s because by this period the school was "less Methodist" than it had ever been. Martin in 1962 cited as one of the reasons for reunion the fact that twenty-four percent of the students were Methodist. What he perhaps did not realize was that even as late as the early 1950s the Methodist Church could claim as many as thirty-five to forty percent of the students. In the years after 1945 the plurality of Methodist students became smaller as an increasing number of enrollees came from Baptist and Independent churches.[20]

Early in his administration Martin began working to convince the Taylor trustees, the general Taylor constituency, and the North Indiana Conference Methodist officials that reunion would be beneficial. He argued correctly that traditionally "the underlying financial structure of the university has been one

B. Joseph Martin

President

of sheer instability," but he incorrectly implied that this situation had not improved during the 1950s. If he expressed undue pessimism in his implication that the school was approaching the "financial rocks" and needed Methodist affiliation to survive, he conveyed great optimism in his vision of what reaffiliation would mean. He saw the Methodist Taylor of the future as becoming "the" great evangelical university. In January, 1961, the Taylor trustees appointed a committee to meet with representatives from the North Indiana Conference to consider the possibility of a closer relationship between the two groups. Both groups expressed a mixed reaction to the Martin proposal. Many trustees shared the fear of former President

Most of the story of Martin's presidency is an account of his efforts to make the institution more affluent. One of the methods he hoped to use to accomplish this purpose was to return the school to the ownership—and financial responsibility— of the North Indiana Conference of the Methodist Church. Martin's second plan to improve the financial status of the college was to relocate it. The impetus for this idea came from the fire—the worst in the school's history—that destroyed the Administration Building on January 16, 1960, just two weeks after Martin had assumed the presidency.

The Death of a Legend (1960)

Bergwall that reaffiliation would gradually result in the loss of the school's dynamically evangelical character, and many of the Methodist leaders hesitated to identify the conference with the institution because of the high degree of uncertainty involved in Martin's plan to move the school to Fort Wayne. When in 1965 the school decided to remain in Upland and Rediger replaced Martin as the head of the institution, the reunion negotiations ended.[21]

One result of the rejection of the reaffiliation plan was that the school continued to become even less of a Methodist institution than it had been in the early 1960s. By 1970 the Methodist students totaled only eighteen percent—a figure less than half that of the Baptist and Independent students. During the Bergwall administration one-half of the new preachers (approximately fifteen to twenty) entering the North Indiana Methodist Conference each year had been graduated from Taylor; by 1970 Taylor was sending the conference only one or two new ministers per year.[22]

Martin's second plan to improve the financial status of the college was to relocate it. The impetus for this idea came from the fire—the worst in the school's history—that destroyed the Administration Building on January 16, 1960, just two weeks after Martin had assumed the presidency. The student night watchman, Daniel Freeman, discovered flames in the basement chemistry laboratory about 4:00 on that cold Saturday morning, and when the Upland Fire Department arrived on the scene it quickly extinguished the flames. Just as the firemen were preparing to leave, an explosion shot the raging fire out of control, and the oldest and most important campus building was doomed. The school leaders immediately moved the administrative offices to the basement of the library, they moved the classes that had been meeting in the Administration Building to the basement of MCW Dormitory, and—with the campus "nerve-center" now gone—they soon began to consider the idea of moving the university from Upland. Apparently a letter from the Rev. Maurice Berry of Sarasota, Florida, first gave Martin the idea of relocating the institution.[23]

Martin had greater success in convincing the trustees that they should move the school than he had in obtaining their approval for reaffiliation with the Methodist Church. Initially, the board considered several possible relocation sites including Clearwater, Fort Myers, and Port Charlotte, Florida; however, by their June, 1960, meeting the trustees voted to relocate only within Indiana.

Seven months later they decided to move the university to Fort Wayne—hopefully within a three-year period. The Taylor officials decided to leave Upland primarily because they had not succeeded in their efforts to raise funds to replace the Administration Building. Secondary reasons for leaving included the fact that the college had been growing large without an accompanying growth of local church, school, transportation, shopping, and student employment facilities; also, to remain in Upland would necessitate an immediate large capital investment for the construction of new campus sewer and water systems. The board chose Fort Wayne as the new site primarily because the businessmen of that city offered the school $1,500,000 plus the purchase cost of the new campus site. The trustees believed that a city of Fort Wayne's size would offer more opportunities for student employment and the promise of greater community financial support than could the town of Upland. When the trustees met for their spring, 1961, meeting, they selected as the new campus site a seven-hundred-acre plot southwest of Fort Wayne near the present intersection of U.S. Highways #24 and #69.[24]

Meanwhile, the college sought a buyer for the Upland property. A professional appraisal of the school lands and buildings in August, 1961, placed the value of the facilities at $2,325,000. In early 1963 a newly formed school, Indiana Industrial University (later Indiana Northern University of Gas City, Indiana) agreed to purchase the Upland property, and the two institutions decided that they would both hold classes in the Upland buildings until Taylor constructed the new Fort Wayne campus.[25]

The flames were leaping so high that you could see them clearly. When the bell broke free and tumbled through the burning building, it clanged as it fell; it was the most awful sound....
- Betty Freese on the 1960 Administration Building fire

The original optimism toward the proposed move gradually changed to pessimism and then to a decision against relocation. When the trustees chose the Fort Wayne site in 1961, they expressed the hope that Taylor would begin classes in the new city in the fall of 1963. As this target date approached, it became obvious that more time would be needed, and as 1963 changed to 1964 many of the board members became increasingly skeptical of the possibility of financing the move. Gradually, Martin lost his ability to sell the idea of his project to the Fort Wayne citizens and the Taylor constituency; and in January, 1965, he resigned from the presidency. When Martin left the college the idea of relocation left with him, and Board President Lester C. Gerig announced the

Paton Yoder
Professor

Elisabeth Poe
Professor

William Green
Dean of Students

decision to remain in Upland on March 12, 1965. The difficulty of financing the move was not the only factor involved in the decision against relocation. Several of the disadvantages of remaining in Upland disappeared during the early and middle 1960s. The completion of Interstate Highway #69 brought a major transportation artery near the college; a new public school consolidation (Eastbrook School District) and a new modern secondary school plant offered improved facilities for the children of the faculty and staff members; a major new industry located in Upland; and the municipality constructed a new water and sewage system. In the meantime, Indiana Industrial University defaulted on its purchase payments for the campus property; thus Taylor again had no buyer for its Upland plant.[26]

One result of the plan to move was that the relations between the college and the Upland community became as strained as they had ever been. Cordial relations between the two groups during the relocation talks would have been difficult under any circumstances, but Martin further increased the tension by placing undue emphasis upon the disadvantages of remaining in Upland. Part of the mutual resentment between "town and gown" that surfaced in the early and middle 1960s had its roots in long-standing grievances. At least since an 1898 faculty resolution deploring the existence of a saloon in "our otherwise quiet and law-abiding University town,"[27] the setting existed for conflict between the forces of idealism (i.e., the Taylor community) and those who resented the implications of that idealism (i.e., primarily the non-church-oriented townspeople). The Uplanders often interpreted (sometimes justifiably, sometimes not) the Holiness theology of the Taylorites as meaning that "we Taylor people are holier than you Upland people." Creating this same impression were the rigid rules of the early Upland years that carefully regulated the times and conditions under which the students could visit the Upland stores and socialize with the Upland people. Money had also been a sensitive issue. A difference of opinion existed between the town and the college with regard to how much the former had financially aided the latter, and the community never forgot that the receiverships of the 1920s and 1930s had resulted in considerable loss for some local merchants. Differences in educational and cultural values— a major factor in many "town-gown" conflicts throughout American history— probably were not a large factor in Upland because Taylor for so long had presented itself as a "common man's school." No matter how one explains the conflict of the 1960s, the fact remains that it was intense. The situation improved significantly, however, after Rediger succeeded Martin as president in 1965.

Rediger was a diplomatic person, and he had lived in Upland for a quarter of a century; thus the townspeople viewed him as one with whom they could identify rather than as an "outsider."

Meanwhile, the search for other sources of financial aid continued. The school finally gained admission to the Associated Colleges of Indiana in 1966; by 1970 the annual revenue resulting from this membership amounted to approximately $50,000. Early in the 1970s Taylor joined nine other colleges in organizing a Christian College Consortium, the functions of which included cooperative fund-raising endeavors. The university's endowment level approached the one-million-dollar mark by 1970; income from this source helped to provide the nearly twenty percent of institutional expenses for which the students did not pay. Taylor also participated in some of the federal government's programs to aid higher education. The GI Bill and the National Defense Education Act primarily benefited the students, and the science research grants primarily aided specific faculty members; however, the college directly benefited from the federal government loans for the construction of the new Morris Hall and the food service center in 1958, the Science Center in 1967, and the new dining commons and women's residence hall in 1971. The philosophy of the school leaders with regard to accepting federal government aid was that they were willing to examine carefully the government programs to see which of them Taylor could participate in without having to compromise its educational and religious goals.[28]

As the school ended its first 125 years, it struggled with the economic problem of how to raise the funds necessary to construct a new library, a new chapel-auditorium, and a new gymnasium. To obtain large loans for non-income-producing buildings such as these was difficult. As early as 1950, President Meredith had called for a new chapel: "We cannot accommodate all our student body and faculty together in Shreiner

Early in the 1970s Taylor joined nine other colleges in organizing a Christian College Consortium....

Auditorium any longer";[29] by the late 1950s the college began holding its chapel exercises in the more spacious, but less appropriate, Maytag Gymnasium. The increasing use of the Maytag building for a variety of functions by the increasing number of students led to the decision in 1965 to construct a low-cost, dirt-floor field house west of the gymnasium. The new structure eased the pressure on the overused and by then undersized Maytag structure while the university awaited the opportunity to construct a new athletic center.

3. THE RISE OF ATHLETICS

The sports program took on a role of major importance in the period after the early 1950s. In a manner characteristic of many of the large universities, athletics at Taylor served as a principal point of contact with the general public. Especially unique was the manner in which the Venture for Victory basketball teams and the Wandering Wheels bicycle program used athletic skill and stamina as a means to promote evangelistic endeavors. By the early 1970s probably more people associated Taylor with its athletic evangelism than with any other aspect of its program. The college, however, did not neglect its regular schedule of intercollegiate athletics. The students especially enjoyed basketball, and former professor Barton Rees Pogue, who lived near the campus during his entire adult life, may have been thinking of the students who crowded into Maytag gymnasium on winter evenings to watch the varsity team compete when he wrote the following verse:

The basketball Trojans c. 1960.

HOOSIER HYSTERIA[30]

They're packed to the ceiling,
They're rocking and reeling,
They're quite running over with cheers,
They're screaming for baskets
They're blowing their gaskets,
And stripping their vocals of gears!

They're basketball crazy,
They're a little bit hazy
On Latin and English and Speech,
They're up on the rule books,
They're down on their school books
They hammer each other and screech!

They're goofy a bit, but don't mind it
They're happy, as ever you'll find it,
In the Ides of March they're the worst,
But from mid October
They're only half sober,
With basketball ardor they burst!

'Tis the Hoosier Hysteria some name it,
And not many Hoosiers disclaim it,
All units are storming the gates,
This "hoop infiltration"
Has taken the Nation,
We're fifty hysterical states!

Don Odle, who coached the Taylor contribution to "Hoosier Hysteria" during most of the post-war years, produced such Little All-American athletes (first or second team) as Forest Jackson and Carl Honaker in the mid-1950s. One of the highlights of this period came during the 115-59 win over Huntington College in the 1952-53 season when Jackson tallied 63 points to set the school single-game scoring record.[31]

Two major innovations in the late 1940s were the introduction of intercollegiate football in the fall of 1948 and the admission of the college into the Hoosier College Conference (HCC) in the spring of 1949. Controversy surrounded the decision to begin football. When Odle began his coaching career at the school in 1947, the addition of the gridiron sport was one of his major goals. Although President Meredith supported his proposal, former Dean Burt Ayres and several board members did not. When Odle fielded Taylor's first football squad in 1948, he may have wished that a majority of the board members had opposed his request for the new sport, because he faced problems that were almost insurmountable. Eight of his starting eleven had not played on a high-school squad, the players used second-hand equipment that high-school teams had discarded, and the team had to play its "home" games in Marion. After a winless first season the team surprised everyone the next year by finishing second in the HCC. Don Granitz, a member of those first two football teams, won letters in football, basketball, baseball, and track in 1948-49, thus becoming the first Taylor athlete to win such recognition in four sports in one year.[32]

The athletic teams achieved greater success than ever before in the 1960s.

Bob Davenport's football teams won five conference championships during the decade; however, the development of the minor sports was equally significant. In the ten year period ending in 1970-71, conference crowns came to George Glass's track teams in seven years, Glass's cross-country teams in six years, Jack King's baseball teams in five years, and Dale Wenger's and Robert Blume's tennis teams in five years. Two of Glass's runners won national championships in the National Association of Intercollegiate Athletics (NAIA) organization. Phil Captain won the three-thousand-meter steeplechase in the spring of 1969, and Ralph Foote defeated all other cross-country runners in the fall of the same year. Wrestling was added in the 1960s, and by the end of the 1970-71 season Coach Thomas Jarman's squad had accumulated twenty-one straight victories in dual meets.[33]

The Venture for Victory basketball program was the first Taylor effort at athletic evangelism. The idea for the program originated in the minds of two Oriental Crusades missionaries in Taiwan (Formosa), Richard Hillis and W. Ellsworth Culver. In 1952 these two men discussed their idea of basketball evangelism with Ted Engstrom, then a Taylor board member and a leader of Youth for Christ International (see chapters six and eight); and Engstrom suggested that they contact the Taylor basketball coach, Don Odle. Hillis and the Youth for Christ organization invited Odle to organize a squad of Christian basketball players, obtain their finances, and bring them to Taiwan during the summer of 1952; the plan was that on the Asian island they would use their ability to play basketball as a means to gather crowds who would listen to their half-time and post-game Christian messages. That 1952 squad included five Taylor players—Don Grantiz, Howard Habegger, Norm Holmskog, Forest Jackson, John Nelson—and one former Wheaton College athlete—Bud Shaeffer. Each player raised his own finances (approximately two thousand dollars each), and the team spent the summer playing and speaking twice daily to crowds that averaged four thousand people per contest. The squad found help in the active encouragement of Madame Chiang Kai-shek, and they were able to convince seven thousand Taiwanese to respond to their invitation to Christian commitment and to enroll in a Bible correspondence course. After the first year Odle used athletes from many schools in addition to Taylor to comprise the teams he sent to Taiwan and other countries each summer. In 1965 he transferred the leadership of the organization to the Overseas Crusades Mission.[34]

It is difficult to determine the exact effect of the Venture for Victory organization upon the college. Certainly it introduced many people to Taylor.

It probably did not directly help Taylor financially, and at times it may have hurt the school by competing with it for aid from some of the same individuals. On balance, however, the Venture for Victory teams—as well as the Wandering Wheels programs that began later—did much good for the school. The publicity they attracted was a factor in the increasing number of student applications coming to the Admissions Office in the 1950s and 1960s.

The Wandering Wheels bicycle program began in 1964[35] as an effort by Bob Davenport to offer young people a group experience that would combine adventure and physical vigor with Christian fellowship and witness. In the early years most of the riders came from Taylor; however, gradually an increasing number of students from

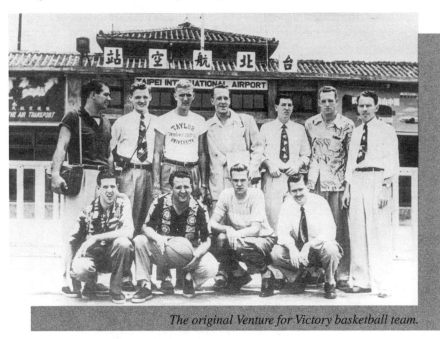

The original Venture for Victory basketball team.

other colleges and high schools began to join the growing number of tours. As Davenport's cycling program became increasingly popular, many other groups organized their own trips, and by the summer of 1971 over fifty such "off-shoot" bicycle organizations were in existence. The nature and length of the excursions varied from leisurely one-hundred-mile trips to rugged three-thousand-mile, coast-to-coast treks,[36] to overseas riding voyages in England, continental Europe, Russia, China, and Israel, to long-term (8-10 month) work-study-cycle 10,000-12,000 mile "Circle America" experiences. Beginning in the late 1960s the standard equipment for each ride included Schwinn Super Sport bicycles, Harley-Davidson motorcycle escorts, and a custom-built trailer with forty-eight lockers and a built-in kitchen. Davenport operated Wandering Wheels on a part-time basis until 1969, when he resigned his position as football coach to devote full attention to the growing bicycle program.[37] In addition to organizing the trips, he spent much of his time in public-relations work to obtain the necessary operating expenses.[38]

The purpose of the organization stemmed from Davenport's personal philosophy. He believed in the importance of physical exercise, the value of group devotional periods, and the desirability of communicating the Christian faith to non-Christians; but his philosophy included more than these things.

Like the traditional ascetic he believed that planned physical hardship and deprivation was a spiritually virtuous discipline. "To grow up," he argued, "a person needs to court danger and discouragement in order to watch God take him through it."[39]

The unusual nature and the high visibility of the Wandering Wheels trips helped to bring the program wide publicity. Sometimes the riders found articles about and pictures of themselves in such prominent newspapers as the *Washington Post* and the *Louisville Courier-Journal*, but some of the most favorable and influential publicity appeared in the papers of the many small cities and towns through which the cyclists rode. Representative of the small-town reports was the February 2, 1971, article in the Naples, Florida, paper which praised the cyclists as "not 'ordinary kids' out for a bicycle ride but a band of devoted Christians traveling in a bicycle pack speaking on Jesus Christ and the Bible to all with whom they come in contact." The article also expressed the relief of the town residents

Wandering Wheels riders sing in front of President Johnson.

that the riders were not a "group of Protesters" but rather "good clean kids." The program gained further publicity when riders sang before President Johnson and Former President Truman, when they appeared with announcer Joe Garagiola on the National Broadcasting Company's "Today Show," and when Governor and Mrs. Edgar D. Whitcomb of Indiana pedaled fifteen miles through southern Indiana with the 1970 transcontinental riders; however, it probably was the Julian Gromer film that most effectively introduced the public to Wandering Wheels. Gromer, a photographer and travelogue circuit artist, made the film to use on his professional tour. Taylor and the Schwinn Bicycle Company also showed many of the twenty-five copies of the film in the years after its release in 1968.[40]

While athletic evangelism was the major new method of Christian outreach begun at Taylor during this period, there were other innovative programs designed both to present the Christian message and to promote the school. The Sammy Morris biographical film, which adapted an old public-relations idea to a new communications medium, introduced Taylor and its most famous student to many people who knew little about either. The idea to produce the film originated with President Bergwall, and the first showing of it came during the middle of his administration. The Taylor World Outreach (TWO) program began spontaneously on a small scale at least as early as 1960, when several students began spending their summers in some type of Christian service in this country or abroad. Gradually the number of students participating in such summer endeavors increased, and during the 1967-68 year the first college pastor, Peter Pascoe, organized, expanded, and gave a name to the program. By the summer of 1968 almost one hundred students engaged in evangelistic projects in twelve states and six foreign countries.[41]

4. YEARS OF GROWTH

Most American colleges experienced their greatest period of growth in the years after 1945.[42] World War II veterans took advantage of the G.I. Bill, and education-conscious parents took advantage of the nation's unparalleled economic prosperity to send their sons and daughters to college in record numbers. The growth at Taylor reflected this national pattern; by almost every standard of measurement the school increased in size. The enrollment of 159 in 1944 grew to 429 in 1946, 613 in 1949, 624 in 1957, 848 in 1960, 1050 in 1965, 1281 in 1967, and 1426 in 1970 (see Figure V in Chapter 6, section four). The number of full-time faculty members, which had been 24 in 1945, became 38 in 1949, 47 in 1957, 57 in 1961, and 95 in 1967. The size of the administrative staff also increased sharply. At the beginning of the period the dean served as the registrar, the director of admissions, and the director of student affairs, as well as the leader of the academic program; by the 1960s there were separate offices and staffs for each of these functions. A development office, an alumni

Kollege Korner: the post office, bookstore, and grill.

secretary, and a public relations director appeared in the early post-war years; and by the 1960s the school had such staff members as a university minister, a student financial aid counselor, and a director of campus security.[43]

The physical plant also grew to accommodate the increasing size of the student body and faculty and staff. Many of the new students in 1945 and 1946 were married war veterans; accordingly the university converted Morris Hall into an apartment building and opened a trailer court north of the bookstore. In 1948 the federal government gave the college an 80' X 40' two-story wooden barracks building from the Fort Wayne Baer Field military station, and the school placed it on the north side of Reade Avenue. The structure became the science building[44] after the school divided it into two classrooms, three laboratories, and three faculty offices. The major new building in the immediate post-war years was the Ayres Alumni Memorial Library. The college originally made plans for the building in 1940; however, the war caused delay, and construction began only in 1949. The financing for it came largely from fund drives among the alumni, students, and other friends of the institution; by the time the building was complete in March, 1950, the college had received over $100,000 from donors.[45]

Aerial shot of campus in the late 1940s.

The school first developed a long-range growth and construction plan in the mid-1950s. Working with the advice of the Gonzer and Gerber Consultant Firm of Chicago, the Taylor officials established an extensive fifteen-year development plan, which they designed to culminate in 1971, when the school would celebrate its 125th anniversary. The plan gave top priority to the construction of a new men's residence hall, a food service center, and a science building; but it also included a chapel, an auditorium, a fine arts building, a classroom building, an administration building, and a student center. The men's residence hall and the dining hall and food service center were the only new units in existence when the plan to move to Fort Wayne temporarily interrupted the development of the Upland campus. After the decision to remain in Upland, the university officials developed a revised campus master plan.[46]

The new Sammy Morris Residence Hall for men, the Storer Food Center, the large Camp Dining Hall, and the small Kerwood Dining Hall were built in 1958. The architectural attraction of this combination structure was the dome-shaped dining area with its circular glass wall. The four-story residence hall accommodated 176 men in eighty-eight double rooms. The school financed the nearly $800,000 construction and furnishings costs primarily through a

$600,000 Federal Housing Administration loan.[47]

Other new buildings in the late 1950s and early 1960s were the Fairlane Village Apartments and the Chemistry Building. The Ford Foundation granted the institution $103,000 in 1957, of which $50,000 was used to purchase thirty-nine officers' cottages from Camp Atterbury (Indiana). Located several blocks north of the campus, most of these two- and three-bedroom units served as residences for married students or groups of three to six male students. A cement-block Chemistry Building (located immediately north of MCW Dormitory) replaced the chemistry laboratories and some of the classrooms that were lost in the Administration Building fire. This structure, as enlarged, later housed the Art Department, the Development Department and the Office of Buildings and Grounds.[48]

When the college decided to cancel the plans to move to Fort Wayne, it immediately launched the largest building program in its history. Seven buildings—four of them major structures—appeared in the next two years. These included Wengatz Hall for men (1965), the Art Building (1965), the Field House (1965), East Hall for women (1966), the Liberal Arts Classroom Building (1966), the President's Home (1966), and the Science Center (1967). The university financed the $1,400,000 science facility with the help of a $512,000 federal loan and a $410,000 federal grant. The combined cost of the Liberal Arts Building and the two residence halls surpassed two million dollars. The Liberal Arts Building contained twenty-six classrooms, thirty-seven offices, and a Media Center; and the two new three-story brick residence halls each could accommodate about three hundred students.[49] This rapid increase in the size of the school plant allowed the enrollment to increase quickly from the 850 level, where it had been during the early 1960s, to over 1,400 by 1969. In the late 1960s an increasing number of students began residing in the two privately owned, but school-controlled, apartment complexes north of the campus.

In 1971 two new buildings were constructed at the southern edge of the campus near the eight-acre

Sammy Morris Hall after its opening in 1958.

Taylor had been gradually changing from a school known primarily for its religious fervor toward one whose intellectual pursuit of truth was not to be distinguished from the aforementioned piety as the two became integral components of the quest to know and embrace God and His world.

campus lake. South Hall, a women's residence designed with six-student suites instead of two-student rooms, opened in the fall of 1971, and the new 1,060 capacity dining commons was completed near the end of 1971. The cost of these two new buildings totaled $1,750,000. In the same year, the college purchased an eighty-acre tract of land adjacent to the northwest quarter of the campus.[50]

When Taylor celebrated its 125th anniversary in 1971 it was a very different institution than when it entered the post-war era. The most obvious differences were in the physical plant, which in the previous six years alone had grown by nine of the ten buildings that were to be added during the Rediger presidency.[51] These physical changes were representative of the less visible but equally real evolution in the academic climate and general reputation of the school. For Taylor had been gradually changing from a school known primarily for its religious fervor toward one whose intellectual pursuit of truth was not to be distinguished from the aforementioned piety as the two became integral components of the quest to know and embrace God and His world. More than any other one person, the leader in these changes in this period was Milo Rediger, and many in the northcentral Indiana area and the external academic community increasingly appreciated Taylor because of how they saw him representing it.[52] At Rediger's retirement in 1975, another college president noted "It was better for Taylor to have Dr. Rediger than to have been given $10,000,000. His colleagues had an enormous respect for him...."[53] This developing institutional emphasis upon the nurturing of both spirit and mind and on broadening the base of those who appreciated this dual focus, was to continue into and through the most recent twenty-five years of the Taylor experience.

[1] *Taylor Echo*, April 2, 1947, p. 1.

[2] *Marion Leader-Tribune*, March 27, 1947, p. 1; letter, A. G. Brumbaugh to Robert L. Stuart, March 21, 1939 (Taylor University archives).

[3] *Taylor Bulletin*, April, 1945, p. 1; *Marion Leader-Tribune*, March 27, 1947, p. 1.

[4] Officially Rediger left the school in 1950 on a leave of absence.

[5] *Marion Chronicle-Tribune*, June 5, 1951, pp. 1-2.

[6] *Taylor University*, MS Minutes of the Meetings of the Board of Trustees, July 11, 1951 and October 31, 1951 (Taylor University archives). Hereafter all reference to the above trustees' records for the period since 1951 will appear as TUTM.

[7] *Marion Chronicle-Tribune*, August 24, 1951, pp. 1-2 and March 27, 1959, p. 1; *Taylor Bulletin*, October, 1952, p. 1.

[8] Milo A. Rediger, "What Is a Christian College?" (address given at Spring Arbor College, May 1, 1963). Also see Milo A. Rediger, "Why Christian Education is Necessary Today," *Taylor Magazine*, February, 1961, pp. 4-7.

[9] MS Annual Report of the President of Taylor University, 1950 (Taylor University archives); MS Taylor University Faculty Contracts, 1958-59 (Taylor University archives); *American Association of University Professors Bulletin*, Summer, 1965, p. 278 and Summer, 1971, pp. 254-55.

[10] *TUC*, 1945, p. 25, 1950-51 (Upland, 1950), pp. 27-30, 1955-56 (Upland, 1955), pp. 33-35, 1961-63 (Upland, 1961), pp. 33-35, 1967-68 (n.p., n.d.), pp. 41-43, and 1971-73 (n.p., 1971), p. 17.

[11] *Taylor Echo*, April 2, 1947, p. 1; *Taylor Magazine*, Spring, 1966, p. 5.

[12] *Taylor Magazine*, January, 1957, p. 3; *Taylor Bulletin*, January, 1960, p. 1, March, 1960, pp. 6-8, and October, 1961, p. 1.

[13] *Taylor Bulletin*, March 1950, p. 5, July, 1956, p. 1, and May, 1960, p. 1; *American Men of Science*, 1965, IV, 3932.

[14] *Taylor Bulletin*, April, 1951, p. 6 and May, 1963, p. 3.

[15] See "Private Hospitality in the South, 1775-1850," *Mississippi Valley Historical Review*, XLVII (December, 1960), pp. 419-33.

[16] *Taylor Echo*, October 1, 1926, p. 2; *TUC*, 1936, pp. 57-58, 61-62; Annual Report of the President of Taylor University, 1950; interview with Jennie Andrews Lee, Winter, 1996; interview with Thomas G. Jones, Winter, 1996.

[17] *Taylor Echo*, January 12, 1935, p. 1; TUTM, October 28, 1960; *Taylor Bulletin*, November, 1960, p. 6.

[18] Alumni files, Taylor University Alumni Office; letter, Betty Freese to author, Winter, 1996.

[19] *Taylor Bulletin*, January, 1960, p. 1.

[20] Norwood, *North Indiana Conference*, pp. 39, 146-48, 312-15; B. Joseph Martin MS, "A Statement Concerning the Possible Affiliation of Taylor University with the North Indiana Conference of the Methodist Church," September, 1962 (Taylor University archives); *Taylor Magazine*, November, 1955, pp. 11-12.

[21] Martin, "A Statement Concerning Affiliation"; TUTM, January 5, 1961; North Indiana Conference of the Methodist Church, *Minutes of the 1964 Annual Meeting* (n.p., n.d.), pp. 223-24 and *Minutes of the 1966 Annual Meeting* (n.p., n.d.), p. 812.

[22] MS "Religious Affiliation of Taylor Students, September, 1970" (Taylor University Registrar's Office).

[23] B. Joseph Martin MS, "The Decade of the Sixties and the Future of Taylor University" (Taylor University archives); *Marion Chronicle-Tribune*, January 17, 1960, p. 1.

[24] Martin, "Decade of the Sixties"; *Taylor Bulletin*, July, 1960, p. 1; TUTM, June 9-10, 1960, October 28, 1960, January 6, 1961, and June 8, 1961; *Marion ChronicleTribune*, January 8, 1961, pp. 1-2; *Taylor Bulletin*, July, 1961, p. 1.

[25] MS, "Physical Plant Appraisal, 1961" (Taylor University archives); *Taylor Bulletin*, May, 1963, pp. 1-2.

[26] TUTM, January 29, 1965; *Indianapolis Star*, February 1, 1965, p. 19; *Taylor Echo*, March 15, 1965, p. 1.

[27] MS Taylor University Faculty Meeting Minutes, 1897-99 (Taylor University archives), May 3, 1898.

z

[29] "Annual Report of the President of Taylor University, 1950."

[30] Barton Rees Pogue, *The Rhyme Book of a Real Boy* (Upland, 1965), p. 26.

[31] *Taylor Gem*, 1953, p. 101, 1954, p. 95, and 1955, p. 98.

[32] *Taylor Echo*, May 17, 1949, p. 1 and May 24, 1949, p. 3.

[33] See the athletic sections of the *Taylor Gem* for the respective years; also, on Foote's performance see "Faces in the Crowd," *Sports Illustrated*, January 19, 1970, p. 65.

[34] *Taylor Bulletin*, January, 1953, pp. 2, 5, 13 and July, 1957, p. 4; "Look Magazine Applauds Venture for Victory," *Look*, June 30, 1953, p. 23; Donald J. Odle, *Venture for Victory* (Berne, Indiana, 1954), pp. 12-13, 23.

[35] Long-distance bicycle riding was not new to Taylor students in the 1960s. Early in the Depression era, a freshman student, DeWitt Fowler, rode his bicycle 452 miles (90 miles per day) from Hamburg, New York, to Taylor. His motive was not exercise or adventure, but rather economic necessity. When he had pedaled as far as his uncle's home in Ohio, he had only two cents in his pocket. See *Taylor Echo*, October 6, 1931, p. 1.

[36] These transcontinental journeys continued even through the most recent period to be a major feature of the Wandering Wheels program; by 1995 Davenport himself had ridden on 35 of them, a long-distance cycling record that may be unmatched in American history.

[37] His new Taylor title became "Director of University-Church Leadership Programs."

[38] Jack Houston, *Wandering Wheels* (Grand Rapids, 1970), pp. 10-11, 33-34, 55-65, 159-60; Wandering Wheels Promotional Brochure, 1970 (Taylor University archives); *Schwinn Reporter*, June, 1971, p. 3; Barbara Stedman, *Wandering Wheels: Coast to Coast* (Nappanee, 1988), p. 5; interview with Robert W. Davenport, Winter, 1996.

[39] Houston, *Wandering Wheels*, pp. 90, 114, 135-38; Joann Neuroth, "Wandering Wheels," *Venture*, March 1967, p. 11.

[40] *Washington Post*, July 31, 1970, p. 1; *Louisville Courier-Journal*, July 24, 1970, p. 1; *Naples Daily News*, February 2, 1971, p. 10; Neuroth, "Wandering Wheels," p. 11; *Taylor Magazine*, Fall, 1967, p. 3; Wandering Wheels Promotional Brochure, 1970.

[41] *Taylor Magazine*, Autumn, 1968, p. 18.

[42] Private Indiana colleges of a size similar to Taylor today were also of a similar size early in the post-war period. For example, Taylor's enrollment of 469 in 1952 placed it in the same general category as Manchester (658), Anderson (616), Earlham (587), Hanover (578), Goshen (568), Wabash (507), Franklin (404), and Indiana Central (402). See Barnhart and Carmony, *Indiana*, II, 524; and *TUC,* 1953-54 (n.p., 1953), p. 116.

[43] See the faculty and staff sections of the college catalogs.

[44] The building currently houses the social work center.

[45] *Taylor Echo*, September 14, 1946, p. 1; "Annual Report of the President of Taylor University, 1950"; *The Taylorite*, March, 1950, p. 7; *Marion Chronicle-*

Tribune, October 8, 1950, p. 21.

[46] *Taylor Bulletin*, November, 1955, pp. 4-5; *Marion Chronicle-Tribune*, June 5, 1955, p. 28.

[47] *Taylor Magazine*, August, 1958, p. 5; *Marion Chronicle-Tribune*, November 9, 1958, p. 1.

[48] *Taylor Bulletin*, July, 1957, p. 1; *TUC*, 1959-61 (n.p., 1959), pp. 17-18 and 1963-65 (n.p., 1963), p. 22.

[49] *Taylor Magazine*, Summer, 1965, pp. 7-9, Fall, 1965, p. 12, and Winter, 1966, p. 11; *Taylor Profile*, May, 1966, p. 1 and October, 1967, p. 1.

[50] *Taylor Profile*, June, 1970, p. 1 and August, 1970, p. 1.

[51] The tenth building was the major remodeling of the Art Building on Reade Avenue to become the Ferdinand Freimuth Administration Building. The administrative offices had been housed in the basement of the library since the burning of Wright Hall in 1960. The move to the Freimuth Building not only provided for the first time in the institution's history a structure totally devoted to administrative purposes, but it also released badly needed space for the growing library collection.

[52] See William C. Ringenberg, "Milo A. Rediger and the Development of Taylor University," *Taylor Magazine*, pp. 16-18; and the Milo Rediger biography by Bob Hill, *My Book, My Poem, My Story* (Toccoa Falls, Georgia, 1983).

[53] TUTM, June 6, 1975.

Chapter Eight

THE LATE TWENTIETH CENTURY
(PART I): AN ENLARGING ACADEMIC ENVIRONMENT

The Taylor of the 1990s has been matched by earlier generations in terms of its spiritual fervor and the wholesomeness and industry of its students and faculty, but never before has the institution succeeded in combining the aforementioned traits with the current level of training and professional involvement of its faculty, breadth and quality of its academic programs, ability of its entering students, and attractiveness, functionality, and technical sophistication of its physical plant. These developments in the academic program occurred in concert with the flowering of an unusually effective student development program (a major theme of chapter nine) and a growing ability—particularly after 1985 through the person of President Jay Kesler— to communicate the Taylor story to a growing constituency (one focus of chapter ten).

Additionally, one must note that Taylor has benefited from the growing prosperity of Christian higher education in general since World War II. The secularization of American higher education which began in the late nineteenth century hit the Christian colleges with intensity from the 1920s through the 1950s, and added to the spreading secularization were the effects of the Great Depression. The recovery process for the continuing Christian colleges began in the late 1940s with the end of the depression, the end of the war, and the boon to college enrollments provided by the returning veterans with their G.I. Bill benefits. While the improvement in

> *Never before has the institution [achieved]... the current level of training and professional involvement of its faculty, [the] breadth and quality of its academic programs, [the] ability of its entering students, and [the] attractiveness, functionality, and technical sophistication of its physical plant.*

181

the quality of the continuing Christian colleges occurred gradually, the public awareness of this improvement began to grow sharply in the 1970s, partly because of the enhanced visibility of the evangelical community in general emanating from the openly-expressed faith of President Jimmy Carter (1977-81). As early as 1972 Robert Pace in his Carnegie Commission study had described the evangelical colleges as "the fastest growing group presently among Protestant colleges" and asserted that in academic quality they by then were matching the mainline Protestant colleges. Further assisting both the continuing development of and the general recognition of the evangelical colleges has been the cooperative efforts of many of them through the Christian College Consortium (begun in 1971 and comprised now of 13 colleges) and the Christian College Coalition (begun in 1976, renamed the Coalition For Christian Colleges and Universities in 1995, and numbering 90 institutions by early 1995). In both Taylor has been a very active participant. Particularly since the Kesler administration Taylor increasingly has been recognized as a leader among the colleges in these organizations.[1]

1. THE DEVELOPMENT OF THE FACULTY

During the 1970s and 1980s, Walter Randall, together with fellow scientists on the board of trustees, Matthew Welch, Richard Halfast, and Fred Stockinger, led the governing board in calling for a greater degree of faculty professionalism. A 1938 Taylor graduate, Randall had spent his career as a physiologist at St. Louis University and Loyola University, specializing in research in the nervous control of the heart during heart surgery. As chair for many years of the trustees' Educational Policies Committee (the name of this committee since 1986 has been the Academic Affairs Committee), he viewed Taylor physicist Elmer Nussbaum, with his research and grant writing skills and close mentoring relationship with his limited majors, as the ideal undergraduate faculty member. He lamented that he did not see among the faculty in general the same serious degree of commitment to research and professional involvement that Nussbaum and he embodied. Such trustee concern has been one significant factor in the growing professionalization of the faculty after 1970. When such enhanced expectations were formally implemented in the late 1970s and early 1980s, however, it was the faculty itself, with the encouragement of Dean Robert Pitts

> *Taylor has benefited from the growing prosperity of Christian higher education in general since World War II.*

and the recommendation of its own Faculty Personnel Committee, that approved both a new promotion and tenure document enhancing the emphasis upon the doctoral degree and research activity, and also a new post-tenure review system emphasizing continual professional activity. This faculty initiative was representative of its growing role in university governance.[2]

Accordingly, the percentage of the faculty holding the earned doctorate increased from 25% in 1971 to 54% in 1980 and 57% in 1994, and its involvement in research projects and the meetings of professional organizations increased significantly, especially in the 1980s under the encouragement of Dean Richard Stanislaw who promoted recognition, limited released time, and funding assistance for such activities.[3] Faculty members writing books while serving at Taylor in the last twenty-five years have included: Winfried Corduan, *Handmaid to Theology* (1981), *Philosophy of Religion*, 2nd edition (with Norman Geisler, 1988), *Mysticism: An Evangelical Option?* (1991), and *Reasonable Faith: Basic Christian Apologetics* (1993); Mark P. Cosgrove, *Mental Health: A Christian Approach* (with James Malloy, Jr., 1977), *The Essence of Human Nature* (1977), *Psychology Gone Awry* (1979), *B. F. Skinner's Behaviorism* (1982), *The Amazing Body Human* (1987), and *Counseling for Anger* 1988); Theodore M. Dorman, *The Hermeneutics of Oscar Cullmann* (1991), and *A Faith for All Seasons: Historic Christian Belief in its Classical Expression* (1995); Lee E. Erickson, *Principles of Economics Coursebook*, 2 vol. (1990, 1991); William A. Ewbank, *A Cloudburst of Math Lab Experiments*, 4 vols. (with Donald A. Buckeye and John L. Ginther, 1971); Dale Heath, *The Inherent Nature of Scripture* (1988); Larry Helyer, *Yesterday, Today, and Forever: The Continuing Relevance of the Old Testament* (1996); Paul R. House, *The Unity of the Twelve* (1990), *The Old Testament Survey* (1992), and *First and Second Kings*, vol. 8 in the *New American Commentary* (1995); Jay L. Kesler, *Is Your Marriage Worth Fighting For?* (with Joe Musser, 1989), *Energizing Your Teenager's' Faith* (1990), *Grand Parenting: The Agony and the Ecstasy* (1993), and *Challenges for the College Bound* (1994); David L. Neuhouser, *George MacDonald: Selections of His Greatest Works* (1990); William C. Ringenberg, *Taylor University: The First 125 Years* (1973), *The Christian College: A History of Protestant Higher Education in America* (1984), and *The Business of Mutual Aid: 75 Years of the Brotherhood Mutual Insurance Company* (1993); Richard J. Stanislaw, *A Dictionary of Hymnology* (1992); and Alan H. Winquist, *Scandinavians and South Africa—Their Impact on Cultural, Social and Economic Development Before 1900* (1978), and *Swedish-American*

Elmer Nussbaum

Professor

Winfried Corduan

Professor

Mark Cosgrove

Professor

Stanley Burden

Professor

Roger Jenkinson

Professor

Wally Roth

Professor

Landmarks: Where to Go and What to See (1995).

The increased professional involvement of the faculty is due in part to greater opportunity, particularly with the development of the many faith and learning integration organizations which hold special appeal for academicians in Christian colleges. Taylor faculty holding major leadership positions in state or national professional organizations in recent years have included: Stanley Burden, president, Indiana Academy of Science; Walter Campbell, president, Indiana College Personnel Association; Hazel Butz Carruth, president, Indiana College English Association; David Dickey, president, Indiana Academic Library Association; Frances Ewbank, president, Indiana College English Association; Timothy Herrmann, president, Association for Christians in Student Development; Roger Jenkinson, president, National Association of Intercollegiate Athletics, and president, Geography Educators Network of Indiana; Billie Manor, president, Indiana Association for Developmental Education; John Moore, president, Indiana Association of Biology Teachers; William Ringenberg, president, the Conference on Faith and History; Wally Roth, president of Association of Small Computer Users in Education, and president, Computing Consortium of Small Colleges; and John Wallace, president, Indiana Association of Social Work Education.

This enhanced emphasis upon professionalization meant that by the 1980s the normal expectations of a faculty member included 1) an earned doctorate, and 2) active interest and at least minimum involvement in the scholarly activities of one's academic discipline. It did not mean an institutional movement toward a "publish or perish" mentality or away from the student-centered nature of the campus. The latter focus, in fact, has increased, as will be discussed in chapter nine.

The growing professional ability and confidence of the faculty coincided with a lack of continuity of leadership at the presidential level, with the result that the faculty assumed an enlarged role in university governance. Already in the 1950s the faculty had participated in what for that period was a significant degree of involvement in institutional decision-making when Dean Rediger introduced the faculty/student/administrative staff committee structure. Yet there were limits to the Rediger idea of faculty governance; for example he was not pleased with either the change from administrative appointment to election in determining the members of the institutional committees because of the recommendation of the 1966 North Central Association accrediting team, or the enlarged faculty role in promotion and tenure decision-making beginning in the mid-1970s. Rediger's last few years in the mid1970s were less energetic ones and were followed by two relatively short presidencies (Robert Baptista, 1975-1979, and Gregg Lehman 1981-1985) that were separated by a two-year Rediger interim presidency during which he chose to provide largely symbolic leadership while delegating internal management to Gregg Lehman (general administration) and Robert Pitts (academic affairs).[4]

Baptista had spent most of his career at Wheaton College where he had been a very successful soccer coach and academic dean; however, his Taylor presidency faced difficult circumstances from the outset. The new president was limited by the fact that he was replacing a legendary figure (Rediger) who continued in the office next door as chancellor. Comparisons were inevitable, and sometimes unfair. The president, his wife Martha, and their son, Ric, regularly entertained students in their home, a practice which fit well with

This enhanced emphasis upon professionalization meant that by the 1980s the normal expectations of a faculty member included 1) an earned doctorate, and 2) active interest and at least minimum involvement in the scholarly activities of one's academic discipline.

the developing student-orientation of the campus. Baptista's skills were those of a manager rather than a visionary, and he was reluctant to pursue the aggressive capital campaign desired by the trustees. His emphasis upon program evaluation, while in many ways helpful, was sometimes threatening. Many buildings came to completion during his administration. He emphasized career planning for students and campus beautification, and he introduced the President's Associates fund-raising program and the idea of an outdoor education center. He involved the university in the many useful training, consulting, and development activities of the Council for the Advancement of Small Colleges (now known as the Council of Independent Colleges) and in the organization and early development of the Christian College Coalition, both organizations which he helped to lead.[5]

In retrospect Gregg Lehman was too young to assume the responsibilities of the Taylor presidency. With Rediger serving as the interim president, the trustees had moved slowly to replace Baptista. When they did conduct a serious presidential search, Lehman was an early candidate but withdrew from the process. Ultimately the trustees offered the position to David LeShana, president of George Fox College since 1969 and a Taylor graduate of 1953. When LeShana, after serious reflection, declined the post, the position was not offered

Robert Baptista
President

Gregg Lehman
President

William Davis
Finance Officer

to any of the other off-campus finalists, including Jay Kesler about whom the trustees expressed concern because of his lack of an earned doctorate degree. The remaining possible candidate of the original finalists was Lehman. Probably because of pressure not to delay further in relieving Rediger, and because of the disqualification for one reason or another of the other candidates, the offer was made to Lehman despite his youthfulness. He was 33 at the time he was offered the presidency and 34 when he assumed the office in July of 1981. There were fairly high expectations of Lehman in areas of fund raising, building new facilities, and leading the campus toward greater collegiality. He possessed diplomatic skills, personal charisma, and good understanding of finance but was less strong in the areas of intellectual depth, theological understanding, and general experience. Although Chairman of the Board Donald Jacobsen gave Lehman high marks at the end of the third year of his presidency, the accumulating pressures of the office became more difficult for him to handle. For personal reasons he resigned in the spring of 1985. His nearly four years saw the completion of the Smith-Hermanson Music Building and the launching of the campaign to build the $5.5 million library. Thus, the presidential leadership during the decade from 1975 to 1985, while not smooth in certain ways, nevertheless served to consolidate and strengthen the significant growth of the previous decade (1965-1975).[6]

In addition to the presidency, the development office leadership also experienced considerable lack of continuity after the early 1970s. Stability in these two offices is critical to capital fund campaigns, and such efforts were handicapped or postponed for at least a decade from the mid-1970s to the mid-1980s. In the early 1970s Development Vice-President Samuel Delcamp had introduced a promising broad-based approach to fund-raising, but in 1978 he left to assume a similar position at Fuller Theological Seminary. Noteworthy in this period in the Financial and Development Offices were the efforts of Robert Stoops who achieved much success in estate planning especially with Indiana farmers, and William Davis who served with distinction as the chief financial officer.

One of the reasons for the growth in the quality and influence of the faculty in this period is that the chief academic officers (Robert Pitts, 1973-82, 1992-93, and Richard Stanislaw, 1982-92), both served lengthy tenures and also exercised great care to hire faculty who demonstrated both scholarly achievement and vital Christian commitment. Insistence upon the latter as well as the former, the history of Christian higher education has shown, is the single most significant factor distinguishing the continuing Christian college from the institutions which have become or are in the process of becoming secularized.[7] Pitts, whose orientation was managerial, worked to systemize and democratize the personnel procedures dealing with hiring, promotion, tenure, and post-tenure development. Stanislaw reflected a marketing style and sought to increase the emphasis on the academic aspects of campus life. More recently, the current university dean, Dwight Jessup (1993-), has already established a reputation for a commitment to fairness and openness and for skill in presiding at faculty meetings.[8]

Pitts, Stanislaw, and the other hiring officials did not always find it easy to convince able scholars to move to Taylor. Some, especially minority candidates, did not find small-town life appealing. Women, except in specific areas (e.g., English, education, and student personnel) did not apply to Taylor in numbers proportionate to their representation in higher education in general.[9] Candidates in professional fields (e.g., business, computer science, and social work) often found it difficult to leave their practices. Others could not always appreciate how the moderate salary levels were impacted by the unusually generous fringe benefit package. The interview process for serious candidates was thorough and lengthy (one to two full days), and those prospects who observed the campus carefully noticed a strong sense of community, a significant degree of faculty involvement in governance, a commitment to maximum intellectual openness within the context of the religious definition of the community, and a relatively low cost of living in the area.

Slowly but steadily, faculty compensation has improved during the past twenty-five years. Trustees such as Carl Hassel and John Hershey, who worked as educational administrators, and Walter Randall regularly called for significant improvement in the faculty salary structure. Particularly startling was Hassel's comment in 1971 on the percentage (below 20%) of the Taylor budget going to faculty salaries: "Very few enterprises, either educational or industrial, operate at [so low a level]."[10] The total compensation was much better, however, as Walter Randall, chair of the trustee's Educational Policies Committee, noted in 1977, when he observed that "Taylor has the most attractive fringe-benefit package in the Christian College Consortium."[11] By the early 1990s the trustees committed themselves to bringing the salary portion of the compensation (still somewhat below average for undergraduate institutions) to above the midpoint of the schools in the Christian College Consortium. The annual salary data published by the American Association of the University Professors documents the progress suggested above. In 1970-71, of schools of baccalaureate level or

Robert Pitts
Academic Dean

Richard Stanislaw
Academic Dean

Dwight Jessup
Academic Dean

187

higher but not offering the doctorate, Taylor's total compensation package ranked at the 9 or 10 level on a scale of 10. Five years later, of schools offering only the baccalaureate, the Taylor compensation package ranked 3 or 4 on a scale of 5. The Taylor listing improved to levels of mostly 2 or 3 after 1980. The percentage of compensation devoted to fringe benefits grew from 16% in 1970-71 to 36% by 1991-92. Very few colleges matched the latter figure. Major components in the Taylor benefits package of recent years have included retirement contributions of 12% and tuition remission payments for employee dependents.[12]

One major index of faculty satisfaction is faculty longevity. The average age of the faculty, which was 40 in 1971, had become 49 by 1992

One major index of faculty satisfaction is faculty longevity. The number of faculty members with lengthy tenures at Taylor is significantly higher currently than was the case in 1970. The average age of the faculty, which was 40 in 1971, had become 49 by 1992.[13] Also many of the senior administrators in the mid-1990s were beyond the age of 55. This graying of the faculty was dramatically highlighted in the early 1990s when what had long been a very healthy faculty experienced an unusual number of major illnesses.

Perhaps it is ironic that even as the faculty experienced increasing job satisfaction they also were expected to work increasingly hard. While after the late 1970s the university officials encouraged the faculty to become increasingly active professionally off campus, they also held increasingly high expectations of them on campus for participation in university governance, student and faculty recruitment, and involvement with students outside of the classroom through counseling, advising, and providing and participating in social activities. Meanwhile with the growth of the interterm curriculum in the 1970s, the typical faculty members taught a course load which changed from the previous 12 hours per semester to 12-4-12 hours in the 4-1-4 school year. For the most part the faculty were glad to do all of these things, for they identified personally with the success of the institution. When Stephen Bedi, a graduate of the class of 1965, returned to campus in 1991 as the director of teacher education, what impressed him most was the continuing willingness of the faculty and staff to "contribute their services generously in the spirit of a missionary mentality." This, of course, was not an innovation but rather a continuation with some modification of a long historical pattern.[14]

Any commitment, of course, is limited by time and energy, and when the faculty in the early 1990s found a way constructively to reduce their commitment

Dale Heath
Professor

Phillip Kroeker
Professor

to extrainstructional activities, they did so. Acting on a recommendation from their Faculty Personnel Committee, they voted in the winter of 1994 to reduce their time commitment to committee work. This change called for fewer committees, individual faculty members to serve on no more than one committee at a time, a sharp reduction in the creation of ad hoc committees, and a reduction of faculty involvement in routine—but not major—decision-making.[15]

2. THE DEVELOPMENT OF THE PROGRAM

The faculty led by the General Education Review Committee chair Kenneth Swan adopted a new general education program in the spring of 1983. The changes were major, representing the most extensive innovations in the core curriculum since at least the 1950s. They emphasized 1) the integration of faith and learning, 2) the development of computer literacy for working and functioning in the new Information Age, and 3) the acquisition of whole-person education values and disciplines, enhanced global awareness, and basic skills. Accordingly the new Freshmen Seminar, led since its inception by Mark Cosgrove, served as an introduction to the general education program, applying Biblical perspectives to the human condition. The Senior Seminar, expanding upon the Senior Capstone course which had been introduced in 1968, sought to assist the students at the culmination of their careers in integrating the general education program as well as their major with their developing Christian world view. The restructuring of the twelve-hour religion and philosophy requirement reflected an enhanced emphasis upon the study of Christian ideas. There were new one-hour applied courses emphasizing fine arts participation and focusing upon the life-long stewardship of the body. In addition, each student chose one of many courses which developed cross-cultural understanding and appreciation. Consistent with the university's new emphasis upon the evaluation and development of program quality was the introduction of courses to develop basic student skills in public speaking, writing, mathematics, and computer science. Subsequently, the Taylor program for the development of writing proficiency in courses beyond the freshman composition experience ("Expository Writing") served as a model for other institutions in the Christian College Consortium's "Writing Across the Curriculum" project directed by English and Education Professor Mildred Chapman in the late 1980s.[16]

In the recent history of Christian higher education few ideas have received more attention than has the integration of faith and learning. This theme has been the organizing core of the Christian College Consortium and the Christian

Kenneth Swan

Professor

Mildred Chapman

Professor

Jessica Rousselow

Professor

David Neuhouser
Professor

William Ringenberg
Professor

Philip Loy
Professor

College Coalition, as well as the many professional societies organized by academic discipline both to realize this ideal and also to promote fellowship among scholars who value this approach to knowledge. Organizations of this type in which Taylor professors have regularly participated have included The American Scientific Affiliation, the Association of Christian Mathematicians, the Christian Association for Psychological Studies, the Conference on Faith and History, the Conference on Christianity and Literature, Christians in the Visual Arts, the Evangelical Philosophical Society, the Evangelical Theological Society, the Society of Christian Philosophers, the Association of Christian Librarians, the Fellowship of Christian Economists, the Christian Sociological Society, and the National Association of Christians in Social Work, the North American Association of Christian Foreign Language and Literature Faculty, the National Association of Christians in Student Development, and the Christian Coalition Chaplain's Conference.[17]

The first Taylor course to focus explicitly and entirely upon the faith and learning integration theme in an interdisciplinary manner was the Faith and Learning Seminar which was offered to a limited number of high ability juniors and seniors during the early and middle 1970s. David Neuhouser, the original promoter of the idea, developed the team-taught course with Herbert Nygren and Edward Dinse. Philip Loy, Timothy Burkholder, and Kenneth Swan participated later. Major seminar themes included the controversy between science and religion, the problem of evil and suffering in the world, and the relationship between ethics and government. The approach to the four-hour course was that of a graduate seminar with students reading twelve to fifteen books and participating in discussion based upon them. Sometimes the students interacted via the telelecture system with widely known scholars such as psychologist B.F. Skinner. The seminar served as an antecedent for the Freshmen Seminar, the Senior Seminar, the honors program and the growing curricular emphasis in general upon the integration of faith and learning. The Freshmen Seminar and the Senior Seminar courses sought to apply the faith and learning integration concept in courses taught to all students. The Freshmen Seminar, as had the Faith and Learning Seminar, sought to integrate a broad variety of academic disciplines with the Christian faith. This, however, was done at an introductory level in contrast to the Faith and Learning seminar which had admitted only high ability upperclassmen, mostly second semester seniors. The Senior Seminar was structured so that during the January Interterm for one week all seniors came together to focus upon the integration of faith and a specific theme (e.g., the Arab-Israeli conflict, the future of community). Then for the next three weeks the seniors studied in the department in which they were majoring with the focus being upon integrating their specific discipline with the Christian faith.[18]

Just as David Neuhouser had been the original promoter of the idea of the Faith and Learning Seminar, so also he provided the original impetus for the honors program. Neuhouser worked closely with William Ringenberg, who later succeeded as director, in developing the curriculum which emphasized, in addition to the integration theme, ideas and values in content, and discussion and student initiative in format. One of the most successful aspects of the program was the summer high school honors program. Each summer since 1983, typically forty students who had completed three or more years of high school but had not yet begun college work enrolled during the five-week session for six-hours of tuition-free college work.[19]

The most significant technical change in the curriculum during the last twenty-five years has been the widespread use of the computer. Among Christian colleges, Taylor was a very early entrant into this field. That fact combined with the innovative ways in which the college has been able to apply this technology has made this one of Taylor's best known programs. The first Taylor computer (an IBM 1130) and the first Taylor computer scientist (Wally Roth) both came to campus in 1967. Roth's appointment was primarily to teach the computer science classes, but he also served as the director of the computing center which provided services for the administrative offices. The center was located in the new Science Building. The first computer science course had been taught in the spring of 1967 by Taylor alumnus James Metcalfe, a Western Electric industrial engineer in Indianapolis. By the early 1970s computer science had become a department separate from mathematics; by 1978 it offered a full major. Prior to that time a student with interest in computer science could combine work in that area with mathematics or business. In 1972 Taylor received an invitation from the Lilly Endowment to enter a competition among private colleges in Indiana for receiving funding for an interdisciplinary career-oriented program. The Taylor entry, written by Stanley Burden, Metcalfe, and Roth was for a systems analysis program, and it resulted in a $320,000 grant for a three-year period. This enabled the institution to hire Leon Adkison and John Kastelein to serve as the initial professors in the program. The systems analysis curriculum has continued largely intact for two decades. Students studying in it may graduate with a B.S. degree in any academic discipline combined with the

Leon Adkinson
Professor

Timothy Diller
Professor

systems analysis component. Prior to this time students graduating from Taylor could earn either a B.A. degree with the completion of two years of a foreign language or a B.S. degree in education with the completion of the sequence of professional education courses in lieu of the language requirements. Now there was a second degree program without language requirements. During its peak period in the late 1970s, approximately 400 students were enrolled in the systems analysis program. That number now is approximately 250, with 85% of these students being majors in business or computer science. When Timothy Diller joined the faculty in 1981, the computer science program added an artificial intelligence concentration option to the major, an emphasis in an undergraduate program almost as unusual as the systems analysis program. The computer science program grew rapidly to reach a peak of about 160 majors in the late 1970s, at which time the department adopted selective admissions procedures. By the fall of 1982 the average SAT score of entering freshmen majors was over 1200. Currently the number of students majoring in computer science is approximately 100. For many years the computer science department maintained a close relationship with the Digital Equipment Corporation (DEC) whereby the company hired many Taylor graduates and provided the university, by contribution or sale at sharp discount, major laboratory equipment. Through DEC, grants from other sources, and alumni contributions, the department, led especially by the efforts of Diller, obtained external funding for the majority of its equipment.[20]   In 1977 Gus VanderMeulen, an executive at Steelcase Corporation, asked Taylor to provide computer help for the literature distribution ship Doulos, operated by the missionary organization Operation Mobilization. Later Taylor developed a close working relationship with the Wycliffe Bible Translators to provide summer training for that organization's returning missionaries. These two organizations were among the first mission organizations to use computer technology extensively. Meanwhile, John Kastelein introduced the computing assistance program (CAP) to help mission and church-related organizations in their use of computer technology. Under Kastelein's plan the computer science majors served internships in missionary settings with the experiences designed to benefit the recipient mission organization as much or more than the Taylor students. The response to the offer of assistance was overwhelming with 400 requests coming between 1979 and 1983.[21] Kastelein, who succeeded Wally Roth as director of the computing center, led the early effort to move the entire campus to the use of computer technology. During the 1970s, administrative computing at Taylor served primarily financial data-gathering purposes. Then about 1980 the center offered test scoring services for faculty and word processing services for the administrative offices. In the late 1970s a few administrative offices, beginning with that of Helen Jones in the Development Office, installed terminals, but these were merely keyboards and video screens (CRTs) connected to the mainframe. In 1981 the first microcomputers began to appear, initially in the computer science laboratories; by 1993 all administrative and secretarial offices and 80% of the faculty offices were equipped with microcomputers. In addition, there were approximately 100 student accessible computers. These microcomputers were connected to the mainframe to be able to draw from its data base, but they were also able to operate independently. Increasingly in the mid-1990s, the Taylor faculty and staff were communicating internally by electronic mail and externally by INTERNET, with the latter providing access to worldwide data base systems and computer mail.[22]

If computer science and systems analysis were the primary broad-based curricular innovations of the 1970s, environmental science, although to a lesser degree, assumed a similar role in the 1980s and 1990s. In 1980 Dean Pitts suggested to Biology Professor Richard Squiers that the college develop a program in environmental studies. What the faculty adopted originally was a program that complemented all of the majors in a manner similar to that provided by the systems analysis program, and for the next twelve years students were able to combine a major in any academic discipline with a cognate in environmental science. Thus this new program joined not only systems analysis but also teacher education, social work, and pre-nursing as Bachelor of Science programs. Students pursuing the environmental science cognate program had a choice of three career tracks: the science track, the public policy track, and the education track. The first emphasized biology and chemistry, the second political science, law and business, and the third Christian education and education. By 1994 approximately 100 students had completed the cognate program with 70% of these pursuing graduate studies in environmental science.

A major boon to the program occurred when Upland industrialist, Leland Boren, offered the institution a major incentive grant for the construction of a state-of-the-art environment science building. The Environmental Center opened for classes in the fall of 1992 as, claimed Squiers, "the best environmental science facility for undergraduate education in the United States." In the spring of 1992 the faculty adopted new majors in environmental biology and

Taylor enters the World Wide Web

On November 1, 1995, the university opened its World Wide Web site. This computer-based communications link with the general public operates through the Internet, the largest network of computers in the world. Visitors to the Taylor web site have access to a graphically-engaging system of information on admissions, academics programs, and alumni communication opportunities.
http://www.tayloru.edu

Source: *Taylor Magazine*, Spring, 1996.

Rupp Communication Arts Center

environmental chemistry. Thus, in biology and chemistry the new major replaced the cognate program although the latter continued in the other academic areas.[23]

Meanwhile professors in many of the traditional disciplines incorporated new forms of learning technology. These included videocassettes; projection screen microcomputers; a journalism computer laboratory; the Writers Workbench and Grammatik, interactive systems providing computer-based text analysis of the preliminary drafts of individual essays, particularly in the freshmen composition classes; and the sophisticated modern language laboratory.[24]

The Randall Environmental Studies Center.

In addition to the faith and learning theme, the movement toward high technology, and a growing concern with environmental stewardship, a fourth major curricular emphasis has been an embracing of multiculturalism. This has appeared in many forms as will be noted again in chapter ten; however, as relates to the curriculum the major changes have come with the new general education requirement, the dramatic increase in off-campus domestic and international study opportunities, and the introduction of the new international studies major. Since the early 1980s students have chosen from a broad variety of course offerings to meet the cross culture course requirement. These have included World Religions; the History and Geography of Asia, Africa or Latin America; Music and World Cultures; Cross-Cultural Counseling; International Business; International Economics; Intercultural Communications; Ethnic and Minority Issues; and a broad variety of international travel courses.

Taylor introduced the January Interterm as a part of its 4-1-4 calendar revision in 1969, and although many of the colleges which adopted the 4-1-4 calendar in that era have now discarded or restructured it, Taylor has chosen to retain it, in part because of how it facilitates for many students the often life-changing experience of international study. By the 1990s approximately one-third of the Taylor students were traveling overseas as a part of their undergraduate experience. Taylor's earliest off-campus programs began in the 1950s and 1960s, primarily as summer experiences, and included Elmer Nussbaum's physics program at Oak Ridge, Tennessee, Harold Snyder's biology program at the AuSable Field Station in Mancelona, Michigan, and the Spanish language programs of Carl Gongwer in the Dominican Republic and Mexico. Then came the interterm Caribbean ministry courses (see chapter nine) and the interterm transAtlantic study courses, most characteristically led by William Fry, Beulah Baker, and Kenneth Swan (English) to

The Biblical studies course in Israel has been one of the many international travel opportunities during the January term.

England, Alan Winquist (history) to Continental Europe, many Biblical studies faculty (Bible) to Israel, and Stanley Rotruck (business) to Europe. Beginning in 1989 teacher education majors could spend part of their professional (student teaching) semester in a third-world missionary school (e.g. Rift Valley Academy, Kenya; Alliance Academy, Ecuador; Faith Academy, the Philippines).[25]

Through its affiliation with the Christian College Consortium and the Christian College Coalition, Taylor students have participated in semester-long study experiences at Daystar University in Nairobi, Kenya, the American Studies Program in Washington, D.C., the Latin American Studies Program in Costa Rica, the Los Angeles Film Studies Center in Hollywood, California, and the Middle East Studies Program in Egypt. Also, the college has maintained a similar affiliation with Jerusalem University College (traditionally known as the Institute of Holy Land Studies), the Wesleyan Urban Coalition in inner-city Chicago, and the Whitefield Institute at Oxford University. Of these cooperative relationships, Taylor's earliest (since the 1970s) and most extensive participation has been with the American Studies Program (Philip Loy, local coordinator) and Jerusalem University College (Dale Heath and Larry Helyer, local coordinators). In the late 1980s Taylor developed a relationship with Singapore Youth For Christ, whereby visiting Taylor professors would teach in and direct the Taylor-in-Singapore extension program. Professors teaching in Singapore included William Fry, Beulah Baker, Jessica Rousselow, Alan Winquist, Dale Jackson, Herbert Nygren, Alice Jackson, Paul House and Winfried Corduan.

William Fry
Professor

Alan Winquist
Professor

195

One development that has resulted from the Taylor connection with Nizhni Novgorod State University has been a mentoring role by the Taylor business department for the newly developed Master of Business Administration program in the Russian University. M.B.A. programs, of course, have traditionally been associated with Western capitalist economic systems. The Taylor business department effort has been led primarily by James Coe and has featured the hosting of over 100 advanced Russian students and their professors for course work and business site visits during the summer term beginning in 1994.

Located in Nizhni Novgorod, Russia, Nizhni Novgorod University is a state-run institution offering over 27 majors and 42 areas of study to its 9,000 students.

The city of Nizhni Novgorod, which was named Gorky during the Soviet regime, has a population numbering 2 million and was the place of internal exile for dissident Andrei Sakharov. Located at the confluence of the Volga and Oka Rivers, Nizhni Novgorod is Russia's third largest city.

Stephen Hoffman

Professor

The program also provided for Taylor students to study in Singapore and for Singapore students to study in the United States. Later Christopher Bennett organized the East Asia business program, which now serves as an interterm travel course, and James Coe founded the Taylor Oxford Study program which allows select Taylor students to study in the English university, primarily following the traditional tutorial method. In 1991, in the midst of the political turmoil in Eastern Europe, Taylor developed a faculty-student exchange with Nizhni Novgorod State University in Russia. Eleven Nizhni Novgorod students were studying at Taylor when their country changed from the old U.S.S.R. to Russia. Stephen Hoffmann (political science) in 1993 became the first Taylor faculty member to teach at Nizhni Novgorod.[26]

In 1989, the Educational Policies Committee of the faculty approved a proposal originating in the history department to introduce an interdisciplinary major in international studies.[27] This Bachelor of Arts program contained a core of cross culture courses including an international travel study experience. Also it provided for a choice of ten concentration area options: Spanish language and literature, French language and literature, world literature, the Christian world mission, international and comparative politics, international economics, comparative systems, the non-Western world, the Western world, and Middle East studies. The program grew rapidly, numbering 45 majors by 1993.[28]

Gradually the university provided greater flexibility in the curriculum, making it possible for departments to offer courses on specialized topics without those courses becoming part of the permanent curriculum and for students to enroll in independent study experiences. Also, internships became increasingly common, especially in the professional disciplines.

The summer school has operated continuously since its reinstatement in 1968. It has always featured nontraditional more than traditional curricular structures. In addition to the aforementioned independent study and internship or practicum courses, some students enrolled in off-campus courses whose locations provided distinctive learning environments. These included advanced Spanish study in the Caribbean or Central America (led most recently by Richard Dixon), and botany in Northern Michigan. For years the college program of the AuSable Field Station in Michigan served primarily Taylor students not only through the summer program but also in providing the regular year laboratory experience for 1300 enrollees (1973-82) in the Environment and Man class. During the 1979-81 period the operations of AuSable became more broadly based. Taylor still maintains an affiliation with what is now the AuSable Institute of

Environmental Studies, and all biology majors except the premedical students are required to complete at least six hours in the AuSable or a similar field program. Gordon Aeschliman, editor of *Green Cross*, a Christian environmental quarterly, describes the Ausable Institute as "one of the leading Christian environmental organizations in the United States." The most frequent Taylor instructors in the AuSable program, in addition to founder Harold Snyder, have been Stanley Burden, Timothy Burkholder, and George Harrison. Also Robert Pitts served on the AuSable Board of Directors from 1973 to 1985.

Another major recent summer session innovation in the Science Division has been the research training program in which high-ability students participate meaningfully in faculty research projects often coauthoring papers, reports, and articles based upon the research. Although for a generation Taylor scientists had worked with students on such projects, it was in 1989 that the program formally became established when funded by a combination of Taylor monies, a matching grant from the Lilly Endowment, and Walter Randall's grant from the National Institutes of Health. Randall, a long-time trustee, had retired from the Loyola University Medical School in 1987, at which time he moved his residence and research base to Upland. Beginning then in the summer of 1989, selected students were able to work full-time with stipends during the eight week summer session. Major recent sources of program financing have included a fund which Randall and his wife endowed prior to his death in August, 1993, together with a major National Institutes of Health grant which Burkholder received in 1992. In the summer of 1991, the cooperative faculty/student research program extended to the social science division. The science research training program received a major boost in the fall of 1994 with the appointment of Lockhead Corporation space scientist Henry Voss as a research professor and the program director. During the 1994-95 year 20 students worked part-time— mostly on a satellite instrument design project for the National Aeronautics and Space Administration, and a similar number worked full-time for much of the summer of 1995. Most of the current student research projects are in the areas of space science, microelectronics, heart physiology, and environmental science.

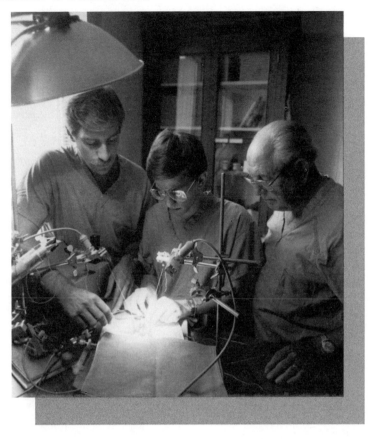

Walter Randall brought his National Institutes of Health-funded research on the para-sympathetic function of the brain and heart to Taylor students to provide them with participatory learning experiences.

In 1995 the National Science Foundation awarded Taylor a grant in cooperation with Stanford University for a space science project on which Voss was one of the principal investigators.[29]

The summer high school honors program, increasingly an effective student marketing tool for the institution, has been enthusiastically promoted and partially administered by the Admissions Office. Typically the high-ability students in this program have responded ably and with delight to the novelty of their first collegiate experience. The students enrolled in a section of a two-hour integrated seminar (most typically God, Humanity, and Society taught by William Ringenberg) and then choose the balance of their work from such introductory general education offerings as English composition, world history, psychology, Biblical literature, computer science or calculus.[30]

Other notable academic developments during the past twenty-five years include the introduction of the university's first Associate of Arts programs, the achievement of professional accreditation by two departments whose disciplines offer that recognition, and the addition of several new majors. In 1975 the college introduced, partly as an experimental marketing measure, Associate of Arts programs in management information systems and early childhood education. While these programs have not attracted a large number of students, they have continued to the present and have been joined by additional two-year programs in liberal arts and business administration. The National Association of Schools of Music awarded full accreditation to the Taylor music program in 1975-76 while the Council on Social Work Education gave similar recognition to the Taylor social work program in March of 1981. New majors added since 1970 include several previously discussed: computer science (with tracks now in business information systems, scientific programming, and artificial intelligence); biology with an environmental science track; chemistry with an environmental science track; and international studies. Also new in the modern period are accounting (1978), mass communications (1978), theatre arts (1983), recreational leadership (1984), English with a writing concentration (1989), and athletic training (1994). Since 1979, a student has been able to design an individual goal-oriented major from the existing curriculum.[31]

Departments showing significant growth in this period in addition to the aforementioned computer science, system analysis, and environmental science, have included psychology, business and accounting, mass communications, and history (including international studies). In 1970-71, the majors with the largest number of students respectively were elementary education, physical education, biology, music, business, mathematics, English, social studies, psychology, and art. By the early 1980s, the order of the largest ten majors was business, elementary education, information sciences, psychology, biology, Christian education, accounting, social work, English, mass communications, and political science. By 1993-94, the leaders in this order were elementary education, business, psychology, computer science, English, biology, Christian education, history, accounting, and mathematics.[32]

3. THE DEVELOPMENT OF THE PHYSICAL PLANT

Parallel to and supportive of the growth in the academic program since the early 1970s has been the increase in the quantity and quality of the university buildings and the aesthetic appeal of the campus in general. Of the 24 buildings listed in the 1994-96 university catalog, 17 have been built or extensively restyled since 1970. Even more remarkable for an institution that has operated continuously on its present site for over a century, no current building existed in its present form in 1965.[33] The new or newly designed post-1970 buildings include Gerig Hall (1971),

Of the 24 buildings listed in the 1994-96 university catalog, 17 have been built or extensively restyled since 1970.

Hodson Dining Commons (1972), Freimuth Administration Building (remodeled 1972), the Student Union (remodeled 1973), Fairlane Village (acquired 1970), English Hall (1975), Haakonsen Health Center (1975), Odle Gymnasium (1975), Rediger Chapel/Auditorium (remodeled 1976), Smith Hermanson Music Center (1983), Zondervan Library (1986), Helena Memorial Hall (remodeled 1987), Ayres Alumni Memorial Building (modified 1987), Bergwall Hall (1989), West Village (1989), Swallow-Robin Hall (remodeled 1990), Randall Environmental Studies Center (1992), Rupp Communication Arts Center (1994), Boyd Physical Plant and Service Center (replaced 1995), and Sickler Hall (remodeled 1995).[34]

Gerig Residence Hall and Hodson Dining Commons were the first two buildings to join the campus woods and the campus lake in the southwest corner of the outer rim of the main 160 acre campus.[35] The trustees renamed what had been South Hall for Lester Gerig in 1986 and the dining commons for Arthur Hodson in 1978. Gerig, for many years president of Mutual Security Life Insurance Company of Fort Wayne, was a member of the Taylor Board of Trustees from 1955 to 1989. He served as board chairman from 1964 to 1981, during which time he was known for his organizational skills, frequent presence on campus, and close working relationship with President Rediger. Hodson, a

former Taylor student, was a long-time president of the Upland bank and a Taylor trustee from 1954 to 1964.[36]

The completion of the dining commons during the 1971-72 school year allowed the old dome-shaped dining commons adjacent to Morris Hall to be remodeled as a two-level student union containing book store, grill, student activities offices, and recreational areas. Many of these functions had taken place previously in the old turn-of-the-century wooden building at the northeast corner of campus; during its demolition in 1973, Taylor editor Will Cleveland noted nostalgically, "The old post office and grill will soon join the sunken gardens, the 'Ad' building and 'Hector's Hut'[37] in the land of fond memory."[38]

Continuing the pattern whereby the construction of many new buildings in the late 1960s and early 1970s allowed some of the older buildings to be remodeled to meet other needs, the college converted the Art Building to the Ferdinand Freimuth Administration Building in 1972. With the conversion came the addition of a new east wing for the student development department. Freimuth was a Fort Wayne stockbroker who helped to underwrite the cost of the project. The newly remodeled building allowed the administrative offices, which had been located in the basement level of the Ayres Building, to have their first adequate home since the 1960 fire destroyed the historic Wright Administration Building.[39]

Other than the Wright Hall fire, no passing of a campus building caused as much trauma as the demolition of classic Magee-Campbell-Wisconsin (MCW) Dormitory in 1975. During the previous half century, perhaps the majority of Taylor students had called it their home, and for many of these students, it also had served as dining commons, infirmary, and a major social center. But it had to come down. The college's architectural engineering consultants said it had become dangerous. Made mostly of wood, it had obsolete and hazardous wiring; thus a major renovation, particularly of a building its size, was not possible. When in the fall of 1975, English Hall for women had replaced it, Dean of Students Thomas Beers could remark, "At last, I am able to sleep soundly."

Actually, it was a combination of English Hall (227 students) and the Haakonsen Health Center that replaced the MCW dormitory including its infirmary wing. Both new structures were built on the south campus next to what is now Gerig Hall, with English Hall containing the same Gerig Hall design of multiple-room suite complexes within the traditional floor plan. English Hall took its name from Mary Tower English of Fort Wayne who had given approximately $250,000 to Taylor between 1968 and 1975. The health center was named for long-time campus nurse Lilly Haakonsen.[40]

By the 1970s, Maytag Gymnasium was no longer adequate to meet the athletic and recreational needs of a student body which had grown over fourfold during the nearly half-century since it opened in 1930. Furthermore, the facility had never provided a satisfactory environment for the thrice-weekly chapel services, although it had served as the meeting house for chapel since 1960 when the college officials abandoned their effort to continue crowding the student body into the small, although venerable, Shreiner Auditorium. Accordingly, the university officials sought to solve two problems with one plan by first building a new gymnasium, and then remodeling the old one into a chapel/auditorium. The new facilities assumed the names of the best-known figures in Taylor's postwar era: Don Odle, long-time basketball coach, and Milo Rediger, long-time dean and president. The cost for the two projects was $1,750,000. Odle Gymnasium was completed first, and the long-standing practice of holding basketball games and chapel services in the same auditorium continued for most of another year, albeit in the new facility

while Maytag Gymnasium was being transformed into Rediger Chapel/Auditorium (1500 to 1600 seating capacity). The Rediger building opened for the last chapel of the 1975-76 school year, the traditional dedication service for students serving as short-term missionaries and in other summer-of-service ministries.[41]

The two major new facilities to appear in the 1980s, the Smith-Hermanson Music Center and the Zondervan Library, were built in the large, open central-campus area between the major classroom buildings and the Rediger Chapel/Auditorium. The trustees named the music facility for major benefactor Nellie Scudder Smith of Tipton, Indiana, and music educators Edward and Louella Hermanson. The 23,000 square foot structure included a 250-seat recital hall that was named for Hazel Butz Carruth, a 29-year member of the English department.[42]

With the construction of the new music center and library building, both the music department and especially the library changed from being probably the least adequately housed Taylor departments to becoming the campus showpieces. Following the January 20, 1972, fire in the Helena Building, the music

department relocated from its traditional home to modular units on Reade Avenue adjacent to what was in the process of becoming the Freimuth Administration Building.[43] Already in the middle 1970s, the Educational Policies Committee of the Trustees was expressing concern that "the library may be a potential

The Smith-Hermanson Music Center.

problem in the North Central [Accreditation Association] review." The trustee concern about the library focused on its space limitations. Between 1950 when the Ayres Library was built and the 1970s, the student body had grown from 600 to 1500 and the library volumes had increased from 25,000 to 125,000. But the library size remained unchanged at 16,840 square feet. The serious planning for the new library began in 1983. When President Lehman called for a state-of-the-art structure, Library Director David Dickey, who had an unusually large role in the planning process, asked for and received a building that was architecturally delightful and technically advanced. The 61,000 square foot facility was built with a capacity for 210,000 volumes and a natural expansion to the west. It also housed the learning support center, the university archives, and a walk-through galleria that served as a major informal and formal social center. Dwight Mikkelson, the first Taylor faculty member to serve primarily as an archivist, relocated the archives holdings from the Ayres Building to an 1,880 square foot complex in the lower east section of the new facility where he preserved primarily internal institutional records but also such external collections as the Elwood H. "Bud" Hillis Congressional records,[44] the Alfred Backus and William Taylor collections of early Methodism, and the John C. Wengatz and Mabel T. Michel collections of African artifacts. The university officials named the galleria in honor of Ted and Dorothy Weaver Engstrom, graduates of the class of 1938. Ted Engstrom, prominent evangelical leader and author, had served not only as president of Youth for Christ International and president of World Vision (see chapter six) but also as a Taylor trustee and board chairman. The trustees named the library for Zondervan Publishing Corporation President Pat Zondervan and his wife, Mary, who contributed over $1 million to the project.[45]

The Zondervan building was designed to accommodate well the technology of the new information age. Already in the middle 1970s the library had joined the Ohio College Library Center (OCLC) computer-based interactive network system which initially provided for cataloging and then interlibrary loan functions. By the mid-1980s, according to Librarian Dickey, "The entire world[46] knew of our holdings and could access them through our interlibrary loan system." Before the Taylor connection with OCLC, the library loaned beyond the campus less than 20 volumes a year;

The Zondervan Library.

now through the interlibrary system it both lends and borrows over 1,000 volumes per year. At its opening in 1986, the Zondervan facility was the first private college library in Indiana to operate an interactive on-line catalog and circulation system. Subsequently, through the Canadian-based GEAC network, Taylor and ten other private college and public libraries in central Indiana linked together through an online system which showed users in each library the holdings and availability status of the collections in all eleven libraries. In the early 1990s, Taylor staff and graduates provided much of the leadership for creating a new networking system called PALNI (Private Library Network of Indiana). With 24 private college and seminary members, it became the largest consortium of libraries in the nation cooperating to share the same system. A Lilly Endowment grant of nearly $5 million allowed the libraries, beginning in the fall of 1994, not only to share their resources, but also to employ the latest technology in a rapidly changing field. The most significant of the data base retrieval systems available in the Zondervan Library in the 1990s include DIALOG (introduced in 1983) WILSEARCH (introduced in 1990), and INTERNET (introduced in 1994).[47]

In August, 1986 fire struck the Helena Building for the second time in fifteen years.[48] This arson-related tragedy brought resolution to the question of what to do with the recently vacated Ayres Building. The art department and the

Little Theater relocated to Ayres from the heavily damaged Helena Building. As he did later during the debate on what to do with Swallow Robin Dormitory, President Kesler, with the active encouragement of trustee Advancement Committee chair Richard Russell, successfully argued that as the campus was so short on physical reminders of its history, tradition demanded that the institution seek to restore old traditional buildings like Helena even when it would be more cost effective to dismantle them and build new structures. Essentially, the renovated Helena became a second administration building, both relieving the space pressures in the Freimuth Building and creating a new home for the Admissions Office and the Office of the President. In attractive modern facilities these offices could now court prospective students in a manner reflecting the institution's newly aggressive approach to student recruitment.[49]

Helena Memorial Hall.

The steadily growing student enrollment and the largely residential nature of the college required the renovation and replacement of existing living units and the building of new ones. In 1970, the university purchased the red brick, modern construction Fairlane Village apartments (90 students), from contractor Edward Hermanson. These north-of-campus units for married students and upperclass single students replaced the series of wooden buildings collectively also known as Fairlane Village which the college had brought to the same north-of-campus location from Fort Atterbury after World War II. In 1986 the university closed Swallow Robin Dormitory for the same reason that it had razed MCW Dormitory a decade earlier, namely it could no longer meet modern fire safety standards. Four years and $1.2 million later, Swallow Robin reopened essentially as a new building; however, it retained the style and character of the old one. The construction of Bergwall Hall (181 students and named for 1950s president, Evan Bergwall) and the addition of the West Village (west of Odle Gymnasium) mobile units (91 students) in the late 1980s eased the demand for on-campus housing. Bergwall Hall, located between the campus woods and the dining commons with a walkway connecting it to the latter, was designed to serve as a living unit for conferees in the summer as well as a student residence during the school year. This double purpose combined with its style and appearance led the students to label it the "Holidorm."[50]

In the early 1990s as a result of a major capital campaign, the university for the first time in its history was able to construct buildings—the Randall Environmental Science Center and the Rupp Communication Arts Center—with the funds for their cost and maintenance already identified. In the late 1970s, the biology faculty had developed an arboretum on 50 acres of the 80 acre plot west of the main campus, and the Randall Center, a $3.6 million, 19,000 square foot, high-tech rustic structure, was built on this environmental education and research site. The building took the name of Trustee and Research Professor Walter Randall and his wife, Gwen. A $500,000 grant—the largest foundation grant in the history of the university—from the Lilly Endowment stimulated the fund-raising effort for the Rupp Center, a $5.2 million, 45,000 square foot building that includes a 300-seat theatre and arguably the finest and most high-tech facilities on campus. The center took the name of benefactors Ora and Herma Rupp of Archbold, Ohio. The trustees named the theatre for benefactors Elizabeth and William Mitchell of Fort Wayne, the daughter and son-in-law of Mary Tower English for whom English Hall is named. When the communication arts department relocated from Sickler Hall (and elsewhere) to the Rupp Center, the university remodeled the former structure—which was the oldest existing campus building—to house the William Taylor

The TV control room in the Rupp Communication Arts Center.

Foundation which the institution had revitalized in the 1980s as the Development Office's planned giving center.[51]

In addition to Gerig Hall and the Hodson Dining Commons, other buildings in the period since 1970 to receive a specific name or an altered name years after their original construction include Olson Hall, the Reade Memorial Liberal Arts Center, and the Nussbaum Science Building. East Hall assumed the name of retired History Professor and Registrar Grace Olson in 1974. Five years later (1979), the main classroom building, the Liberal Arts Building, was renamed the Reade Memorial Liberal Arts Center in honor of the major institutional leader during the late Fort Wayne and early Upland periods. In 1984, the year preceding the retirement of Physics Professor and Science Division leader Elmer Nussbaum, the university named the Science Building for him.[52]

Parallel with the improvements in the campus buildings came an explicit commitment to campus beautification in general. Reflective of this new emphasis was the change in name of what had been traditionally the maintenance department to the department of buildings and grounds. President Rediger hired landscaper J. D. Miller as the first superintendent of grounds, and many new trees began to appear in the campus open spaces. President Baptista initiated the creation of little hills as aesthetic breaks in the flat land along the north central part of the new major circular drive through the heart of campus. Paul Lightfoot with a graduate degree in botany succeeded as the campus landscaper in the early 1980s and demonstrated skill, not only in growing attractive flower beds but also in raising funds for his many projects of campus beautification. When Daryl Yost became provost in 1985, he embraced and expanded these earlier efforts. Influenced by the idea of Ernest Boyer of the Carnegie Commission that the physical appearance of the campus is highly important in recruiting students, Yost's efforts resulted in many high quality physical improvements: a new strategically located major entrance to the campus, additional and enlarged parking lots and sidewalks, a standardized campus-wide lighting system, creative and timely painting, attractive dispensers, efficient and hidden-from-view refuse systems, and well-designed campus signs and historical markers. Also appearing on the heretofore primarily functional campus were large prominently located works of architectural and sculptural symbolism. Geographically and symbolically the most central of these was the Rice Bell Tower symbolizing with its twin spires the academic and spiritual emphases of the college (see the book cover and accompanying narrative). Multiple times daily from the tower came the sounds of the Gentile Carillon which chimed each hour and broadcasted hymns, anthems, and the Taylor song as played by Frederick Schulze, chapel organist since the opening of the Rediger Chapel/Auditorium in 1976. Also Art Professor Craig Moore obtained the gift to Taylor of three pieces of large outdoor sculpture from the 1988 Sculpture Chicago Project. Consistent with the growing emphasis upon visual reminders of its historical tradition was the decision of the university to commission as a

Parallel with the improvements in the campus buildings came an explicit commitment to campus beautification in general.

part of its sesquicentennial celebration a series of three statues of Taylor's most famous student, Sammy Morris. Anderson University sculptor Kenneth Ryden designed and created the $133,000 cast bronze works which in 1995 were placed southeast of the new Rupp Center in the central campus plaza known as the Richard H. Schmitz Memorial Sculpture and Park.[53]

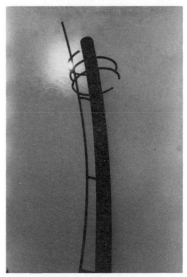

Noteworthy developments in the outdoor athletic facilities included the construction of modern-design facilities for track and field (1966) and tennis (1990) and the building of the 3,500 seat Wheeler Memorial Football Stadium (1981) between Odle Gymnasium and the Field House. Alumnus John and Jodi Wheeler were the major benefactors in the construction of the stadium to honor their son Jim, a popular and talented student in the late 1970s. [54]

The Hurl

The Flexing of Florida, Part II

Developments in the late 1980s on land tracts to the east and south of the traditional 160 acre campus also have been of significance for the university. Taylor benefactor Leland Boren and his wife, Taylor trustee LaRita Boren, in 1986 built their new Avis Corporation (a holding company for twelve industries) Headquarters Building directly across the highway from the main Taylor campus entrance. To design the $3,500,000 structure, they employed Leroy Troyer and Associates of Mishawaka, Indiana, the same architectural firm that planned the Zondervan Library. The idea was to create a structure which would blend in with the red brick architecture of the Taylor buildings. A year later, retired basketball coach Don Odle, trustee Paul Gentile, and their wives donated to the university the 40-acre plot adjacent to the campus to the south.[55]

Such were the developments in the academic program and its support structure during the sixth and most recent quarter-century in the history of the institution. The formal studies, of course, operated in a larger milieu that included the broad range of activities called the cocurriculum and the general campus ethos and sense of community which encompassed the entire program. These latter aspects of the recent Taylor past are the subject of the next chapter.

The Space Grip

[1] See "The Reconstruction of Christian Higher Education," chapter six in William C. Ringenberg, *The Christian College: a History of Protestant Higher Education in America* (Grand Rapids, 1984); *The News* (of the Coalition for Christian Colleges and Universities), March, 1995, p. 1.

[2] Interview with Walter Randall, Summer, 1993; interview with Robert D. Pitts, Summer, 1994, and Fall, 1995; interview with Robert C. Gilkison, Fall, 1994; TUTM, May 16, 1986; MS Minutes of the Taylor University Faculty Meetings, March 10, 1977, April 26, 1979, February 9, 1984 (Taylor University Archives). Hereafter all references to the above faculty records will appear as TUFM.

[3] *TUC*, 1971-73, pp. 97-105, 1994-96, pp. 112-17; MS Annual Report of the Office of Academic Affairs, 1979-80 and 1992-93; letter, Richard J. Stanislaw to author, September 15, 1993; TUTM, October 15, 1982.

[4] TUTM, June 2, 1979; interview with R. Philip Loy, Summer, 1992.

[5] TUTM, June 6, 1975, January 23, 1976, June 3, 1976, January 20, 1978, May 19, 1978, May 7, 1979, May 17-18, 1979. MS Annual Report of the President of Taylor University, 1978-79; interviews with Charles R. Jaggers and Thomas G. Jones, Summer, 1992; interview with Robert C. Baptista, Fall, 1994; letter, Robert C. Baptista to author, November 11, 1994. Also see Bob and Martha Baptista, *Ric* (Chicago, 1981).

[6] TUTM, December 13, 1980, January 7, 1981, March 7, 1981, May 7, 1981, May 25, 1984, February 7, 1985; interviews with Charles R. Jaggers and Thomas G. Jones, Summer, 1992.

[7] See William C. Ringenberg, "The Marks of A Christian College," *Christianity Today*, November 2, 1979, pp. 26-28; George M. Marsden and Bradley J. Longfield, eds., *The Secularization of the Academy* (New York, 1992); and George M. Marsden, *The Soul of the American University: From Protestant Establishment to Established Nonbelief* (New York, 1994).

[8] Interview with Robert D. Pitts, Summer, 1992, and Fall, 1995; letter, Richard J. Stanislaw to author, September 15, 1993.

[9] Women faculty members comprised between 13 and 25 percent of the faculty in the recent period. The percentage is higher when the data includes the student development staff and other nonclassroom faculty. See *Academe*, August 1981, pp. 250-51, April-March, 1985, pp. 32-33, March-April, 1991, pp. 46-47; MS Annual Report of the Taylor Office of Academic Affairs, 1992-93.

[10] TUTM, October 7, 1971.

[11] TUTM, May 27, 1977.

[12] TUTM, October 20, 1988, February 3, 1989 and October 18, 1991; *AAUP Bulletin*, Summer, 1971, pp. 254-55 and Summer, 1976, pp. 236-37; *Academe*, August, 1981, pp. 250-51, March-April, 1986, pp. 28-29, March-April, 1992, pp. 44-45; March-April, 1993, pp. 44-45; March-April, 1995, pp. 10, 42-43.

[13] MS Faculty Contract List, 1971-72; MS Annual Report of the Taylor Office of Academic Affairs, 1992-93.

[14] Interview with Stephen S. Bedi, Summer, 1992.

[15] TUFM, February 10, 1994.

[16] TUFM, March 3, 1983; *Taylor Magazine*, Fall, 1983/Winter, 1984, pp. 8-12, *TUC*, 1950, pp. 39-40 and 1954-55, pp. 39-40; interview with Kenneth D. Swan, Fall, 1995.

[17] See Ringenberg, *The Christian College*, pp. 199-200, 204-07.

[18] Interviews with David L. Neuhouser and E. Herbert Nygren, Summer, 1992; TUFM, March 3, 1983.

[19] Interview with David L. Neuhouser, Summer, 1992; TUFM, December 8, 1977; MS Annual Report of the Director of the Taylor University Honors Program, 1992-93; *Taylor Magazine*, Summer, 1981, pp.12-13.

[20] Interview with R. Waldo Roth, Summer, 1992; interview with Stanley L. Burden, Summer, 1992; *Taylor Magazine*, Winter, 1985, p. 17.

[21] Interview with R. Waldo Roth, Summer, 1992.

[22] Interview with Robert D. Hodge, Summer, 1993.

[23] Interviews with E. Richard Squiers, Summer, 1992 and Summer, 1994; *Taylor Magazine*, Summer, 1991, p. 4.

[24] Interview with William A. Fry, Summer, 1994; interview with Janet C. Loy, Summer, 1994.

[25] *TUC*, 1968-69, p. 6; *Taylor Magazine*, Spring, 1989, pp. 7-8, Fall, 1989, p. 16, Fall, 1991, p. 8; TUTM, May 23, 1991; interview with Steven S. Bedi, Summer, 1995.

[26] *TUC*, 1992-94, pp. 10-12 and 1994-96, pp. 7-9; *Taylor Magazine*, Autumn, 1991, p. 5; interview with Robert Pitts, Fall, 1995.

[27] This action stood without the vote of the full faculty because the faculty had voted in 1977 that thereafter the actions of university committees stood as announced unless the originating committee, the vice-president for academic affairs, or three faculty members request that the issue have a subsequent hearing and action at the faculty meeting. This action, one of efficiency, reflected the growing complexity of university business. See TUFM, September 8, 1977.

[28] MS Minutes of the Taylor University Educational Policies Committee meetings, November 2, 1989; MS Student Registration Statistical Report, Fall, 1993.

[29] Interview with Harold Z. Snyder, Winter, 1995; interview with Timothy J. Burkholder, Summer, 1994; Gordon Aeschliman, "Editorial," *Green Cross*, Fall, 1994, p. 5; *Taylor Magazine*, Fall, 1979/Winter, 1980, pp. 11-13; interviews with Stanley L. Burden, Summer, 1992, and Spring, 1995; interview with Walter Randall, Summer, 1993; Walter C. Randall and Stanley L. Burden, "A Faculty Research and Training Program for Undergraduates in the Sciences," *American Journal of Physiology*, 263, 1992; *Taylor Magazine*, Spring, 1988, p. 2; interview with Stephen C. Messer, Summer, 1994; interview with Henry D. Voss, Summer, 1995.

[30] MS Annual Report of the Director of the Taylor Honors Program, 1992-93.

[31] MS Annual Report of the President of Taylor University, 1975-76, and 1980-81; TUFM, January 12, 1978 and February 8, 1979; interview with Oliver F. Hubbard, Winter, 1995.

[32] MS Student Registration Statistical Reports, Fall, 1970, Fall, 1981, and Fall, 1993.

[33] Morris Hall assumed a new red brick exterior in 1969, thus matching the developing campus architectural pattern; however, it changed little on the interior.

[34] *TUC*, 1994-96, pp. 9-11; *Taylor Magazine*, Spring, 1973, 20-21, Summer, 1983, p. 2; *Taylor Echo*, April 14, 1972, p. 1.

[35] See Chapter 7.

[36] TUTM, May 22, 1986; *Taylor Magazine*, Spring/Summer, 1978, pp. 10-11.

[37] Named for the mythical Trojan warrior, Hector's Hut was a short-lived student center located in the old Reade Avenue greenhouse which the biology department had vacated following the construction of the new science building in the late 1960s.

[38] *Taylor Magazine*, Spring, 1973, pp. 20-21.

[39] *Taylor Magazine*, Summer, 1972, pp. 20-21.

[40] TUTM, August 27, 1975; October 16, 1975; *Taylor Magazine*, Fall, 1975, pp. 3-4.

[41] TUTM, October 16, 1975; *Taylor Magazine*, Spring, 1976, p. 10.

[42] TUTM, May 22, 1981; *Taylor Magazine*, Winter, 1979, p. 8 and Fall/Winter, 1982, p. 26.

[43] These units now house the post office and the university press.

[44] Congressman Hillis is the maternal grandson and namesake of former Taylor trustee and automobile inventor Elwood Haynes. See chapter five.

[45] *Taylor Magazine*, Winter, 1972, pp. 23-24, Summer, 1972, pp. 20-21, Fall, 1986, p. 15, 23; TUTM, June 4, 1976, May 18, 1979; letter, Jay L. Kesler to John McDougall, December 10, 1985; interview with David C. Dickey, Summer, 1993; interview with Dwight L. Mikkelson, Summer, 1993. Also see Owen, *Engstrom.*

[46] The OCLC system started at Ohio State University and has become the largest interlibrary network in the world.

[47] Interview with David C. Dickey, Summer, 1993; interview with Robert D. Hodge, Summer, 1993; *Taylor Information Resources Newsletter*, February/March, 1994, p. 1; *Taylor Echo*, November 11, 1994, pp 1-2.

[48] Another recent campus fire—this one of uncertain origin—destroyed two of the three buildings at the Ralph C. Boyd Buildings and Grounds Complex on the west 80-acre section of campus on November 11, 1993. The main building was rebuilt in 1994 and occupied again in 1995. See TUFM, November 11, 1993; *Taylor Magazine*, Winter, 1994, p. 3, and Winter, 1995, p. 3.

[49] *Taylor Magazine*, Fall, 1986, p. 22, and Summer, 1988, p. 9; interview with Jay Kesler, Fall, 1995.

[50] Letter, Timothy W. Herrmann to author, September 28, 1993; interview with Denise A. Bakerink, Summer, 1994; TUTM October 25, 1985, May 20, 1988, May 18, 1989; *Taylor Magazine*, Fall, 1988, p. 8, Winter, 1989, p. 56, Summer, 1990, pp. 8-9.

[51] *Taylor Magazine*, Spring, 1990, pp. 2-5, Summer, 1991, p. 4, Winter, 1995, pp. 11-23; interview with E. Richard Squiers, Summer, 1992; TUTM, May 19, 1978, January 30-31, 1992, p. 3, May 20-21, 1993, pp. 5-6; January 27, 1994, p. 5; May 19-20, 1994, p. 7; letter, V. Donald Jacobsen to Milo A. Rediger, June 7, 1988; interview with Robert Pitts, Summer, 1995.

[52] *Taylor Echo*, April 26, 1974, p. 1; *Taylor Magazine*, Winter, 1978, p. 27,

Fall/Winter, 1979-80, p. 21, Fall, 1984, p. 15.

[53] *Taylor Magazine*, Fall, 1986, p. 16, Summer, 1988, p. 8; interview with Daryl R. Yost, Summer, 1992; TUTM October 21, 1988, November 4, 1988, May 18, 1989, February 14, 1991; interview with Craig W. Moore, Summer, 1994; interview with Ray E. Bullock, Summer, 1994; interview with Frederick B. Shulze, Summer, 1995.

[54] Letter, Gregg O. Lehman to the Taylor University Board of Trustees, June 20, 1980; TUTM June 27, 1980, *Taylor Magazine*, Fall/Winter, 197980, pp. 6-7; interview with Joe W. Romine, Summer, 1992; interview with George A. Glass, Summer, 1994. On Jim Wheeler, see Bob Hill, *Jimmy: He Touched Our Lives* (Lilburn, Georgia, 1981).

[55] *Taylor Magazine*, Winter, 1987, p. 14, Spring, 1988, p. 10; interview with Leland E. and LaRita R. Boren, Summer, 1993.

Chapter Nine

THE LATE TWENTIETH CENTURY
(PART II): WHOLE PERSON EDUCATION

U niversities will stress development of the whole student. They will redesign the total university environment to promote that development." Thus wrote futurologist, Marvin Cetron, in his recent essay describing what he envisions as the developing trends in American society.[1] What Cetron sees as a wave of the future, Taylor, to a large degree already has been experiencing as the major emphasis of its recent past. The university has always sought to nurture both the spiritual and intellectual development of the students, but since the late 1960s there also has been a focused design for facilitating their social and psychological development as well. This has happened partly through the commitment of significant institutional resources to the student development program, partly by convincing the faculty to see themselves as de facto student development staff members ("holding their [the students'] hands while stretching their minds"), and partly by the development of a general campus ethos of pervasive friendliness.

> *The university has always sought to nurture both the spiritual and intellectual development of the students, but since the late 1960s there also has been a focused design for facilitating their social and psychological development as well.*

1. A STUDENT CENTERED CAMPUS

Already in the late 1980s, Provost Daryl Yost could say, "Taylor has one of the most high tech campuses in the Christian College Coalition." Taylor's commitment to "high tech," however, has not limited its even greater commitment to "high touch,"[2] undoubtedly in part because the latter predated the full-blown appearance of the information age.[3]

It was Milo Rediger who first introduced and articulated the modern Taylor philosophy of a student-centered college. After World War II, while dean of students as well as academic dean, he initiated the effort to achieve student representation on the institutional committees and to give decision-making authority to the student government organization. He believed that the university needed to view the students as whole people participating in the decision-making process (see chapter seven). Then in the later 1960s as president, and in cooperation with Dean of Students Samuel Delcamp, he began the effort to bring greater professionalization to the Office of Student Affairs by hiring as residence hall directors only M.A. trained applicants who would become regular members of the faculty. To bring further dignity to the student development program, the trustees in the mid-1970s voted to give vice-presidential rank to the dean of students and to construct improved living quarters for the directors of the three larger, older residence halls. These townhouses were located immediately adjacent to but separate from the halls.

Charles Griffin, vice-president for student development, 1969-1973, more than any other person, gave major emphasis to the counseling mode of student development that to a large extent continues to the present. He believed strongly in the need to help people with problems as opposed to too easily suspending them from college, and it was to further implement this counseling emphasis that the university, during his tenure, introduced the personnel assistant program whereby paid student assistants (personnel assistants or PAs) on each residence hall floor assumed a larger role than that of the previous floor leaders. Griffin and Charles Nies worked as part-time therapists in the new counseling center, and Robert Haubold became the university's first full-time counselor in 1981.[4] This enlarged institutional commitment to demonstrating personal interest in the students and helping them as necessary with their personal problems has extended beyond the student development staff to include the classroom faculty with the latter assuming a larger degree of extra-classroom personal interaction with students. This undoubtedly is one of the major reasons for the high rate of retention in recent years.[5] There is an unwritten community expectation that the faculty and staff will develop strong supportive relationships with the students.[6]

Other innovations of note in the 1970s and early 1980s included the modern orientation program (PROBE) introduced by Walter Campbell; the student chaplaincy program, with its residence hall system of discipleship coordinators (DCs), introduced by campus Chaplain William Hill; and the student leadership program developed by Lowell Haines. Haines built upon the Taylor leadership program to organize in 1980 and host thereafter the annual meetings of the National Student Leadership Conference for Christian college students and student development officers. Taylor's leadership role in these conferences and other student development activities for small Christian colleges helped to focus attention on how advanced the Taylor student development program had

Members of a PROBE group participate in a community clean-up project.

become, with the result that by the 1980s many Christian colleges came to view the Taylor program as a model.[7]

Charles Jaggers administered the student development program from 1979 to 1985. His primary contributions were to organize and systematize the program and to articulate the theoretical framework for it. He developed job descriptions and systems of evaluation; authored the position paper "A Student Development Point of View for Taylor University"; and, with Stanley Burden, William Hill and Nancy Cicero, led in the creation of the current Life Together Statement which reflects the supportive, counseling orientation which has come to characterize both the department and the institution as a whole. Jaggers also led in the relocation of the Student Affairs Office from the east wing of the Freimuth Building and elsewhere into the newly-named and well-furnished Center for Student Development on the ground floor of the Rediger Chapel/ Auditorium. Jaggers believed that the new center helped to identify symbolically the significance of the student development services at Taylor.[8]

Not all in the Taylor community agreed with the extent of the institutional commitment to the student development program. Reflecting this sentiment, the 1986 reaccredidation team from the North Central Association stated, as paraphrased in a report to the trustees, that "Taylor has a Cadillac student development program and could probably get by with less." Nevertheless, with student satisfaction and retention ranking very high, few at Taylor were willing to call for a significant decrease in emphasis in what unquestionably had become one significant component in the achievement of that satisfaction.[9]

Charles Jaggers
Student Development

Walter Campbell
Student Development

Coalition for Christian Colleges and Universities

Membership List, 1995

2. THE BASIS OF COMMUNITY

The modern Taylor University is a voluntary, intellectually open, evangelical, transdenominational institution and community that exists primarily for educating young developing adults. It educates young men and women in the liberal arts, humane and critical thinking, and vocational preparation, all with the conviction that the Christian world view is the key to human understanding and experience.

The traditional identity of Taylor as a "common man" Methodist College continued until the post-World War II era when Taylor began to attract an increasing number of students from a wider variety of religious traditions. Since 1970 the institution has departed even further from its original Methodist orientation. Today the Biblical Studies, Christian Education, and Philosophy faculty evidence little Wesleyan/Arminian orientation and the university in general trains very few candidates for the Methodist ministry. The report of the institution's marketing consultants in the late 1980s described the trustee board as "weak on Methodist representation." Also, like many other "continuing Christian" colleges that survived the secularization movement in higher education, Taylor began to see as its institutional allies the many evangelical colleges from a broad range of denominational traditions (including the members of the Christian College Consortium and the Christian College Coalition or the Coalition for Christian Colleges and Universities, as the latter organization is now known). Among these colleges the ones with which the general public most frequently compares Taylor include Asbury College, Wheaton College, Calvin College, Gordon College, Messiah College, Bethel College (Minnesota), Westmont College, Huntington College, Anderson University, Indiana Wesleyan University, Goshen College, and Bethel (Indiana) College. Throughout much of the twentieth century Taylor identified with the Holiness Methodist tradition of Asbury. Taylor and Wheaton have become probably the two most widely recognized transdenominational, evangelical liberal arts colleges in the Midwest. No college has influenced Taylor and the other evangelical colleges in their modern focus upon the integration of faith and learning more than has Calvin. Huntington, Anderson, and Indiana Wesleyan are small, evangelical Indiana colleges in the same or immediately neighboring counties with Taylor. While Taylor is not an Indiana Mennonite college like Goshen, it nevertheless in recent years has possessed more than normal Mennonite representation among its personnel and constituency as reflected in the fact that four of its recent buildings carry such obviously Mennonite names as Rediger, Gerig, Nussbaum, and Rupp. Following the 1992 merger with Summit Christian College, Taylor and Bethel increasingly became competitors for the support of the Missionary Church denomination. The colleges which Taylor most closely identifies with are those anywhere that seek 1) to balance evangelical commitment with intellectual openness, 2) to achieve academic excellence without a spirit of elitism, 3) to transcend the limitations of denominational parochialism, and 4) to create an environment of mutual support and institutional community.

While the modern Taylor seeks to identify with and serve evangelical Christians from a broad range of backgrounds, its current constituency base continues to be primarily Baptist, Methodist, Independent, and small pietistic types of denominations. This transdenominational nature has probably been an advantage to institutional growth. Historically, denominational affiliation for a college has afforded the advantage of providing an enrollment and financial support base but the disadvantage of discouraging the growth of the base beyond the primary group. Currently, with President Kesler's appeal to a broad range of evangelical groups, the advantage appears to be with independence. Few observers of higher education realize how uncommon it is for a liberal arts college to be unrelated to a specific denomination yet clearly identified with the evangelical Christian community in general. For example, within the Coalition for Christian Colleges and Universities, only 17 of 90 schools share this identity with Taylor.[10]

Colleges, churches and other institutions which identify themselves as evangelical Protestant differ in the degree to which they tolerate and even welcome a broad range of perspectives on sensitive issues.[11] Taylor encourages its students to be continually open in their search for truth, which it sees as synonymous with a continual search for God. This is not to suggest that a person cannot hold with deep conviction to a meaningful belief system, but that one always humbly seeks to know better the ways and mind of the Creator and His creation. For the institution to identify itself as evangelical Protestant is to define limits, but it views these limits less as a test for truth than as a basis for membership in its voluntary community. President Kesler in his inaugural address spoke eloquently of the value of intellectual diversity among its faculty:

"Faculty are the embodiment of learning expressed in incarnational terms. They are models of what the educated person should look like.... As in all of life, there is diversity, even strongly held and argued differences. It is precisely in this diverse expression of truth that the value of learning is exposed.

"Indoctrination allows no contrary opinion. Educated people learn to research and think before they decide. Exposure to equally diligent people with equally noble motives holding fast to differing degrees of certainty produces humility....

Malone College
The Master's College
Messiah College
MidAmerica Nazarene
    College
Milligan College
Mississippi College
Montreat College
Mount Vernon Nazarene
    College
North Park College
Northwest Christian College
Northwest College
Northwest Nazarene College
Northwestern College (IA)
Northwestern College (MN)
Nyack College
Oklahoma Baptist University
Olivet Nazarene University
Pacific Christian College
Palm Beach Atlantic College
Point Loma Nazarene
    College
Redeemer College
Roberts Wesleyan College
Seattle Pacific University
Simpson College
Southern California College
Southern Nazarene
    University
Southern Wesleyan
    University
Southwest Baptist University
Spring Arbor College
Sterling College
Tabor College
Taylor University
Trevecca Nazarene College
Trinity Christian College
Trinity International University
Trinity Western University
Union University
University of Sioux Falls
Warner Pacific College
Warner Southern College
Western Baptist College
Westmont College
Wheaton College
Whitworth College
Williams Baptist College

Faculty are the embodiment of learning expressed in incarnational terms. They are models of what the educated person should look like.... As in all of life, there is diversity, even strongly held and argued differences. It is precisely in this diverse expression of truth that the value of learning is exposed. Indoctrination allows no contrary opinion. Educated people learn to research and think before they decide. Exposure to equally diligent people with equally noble motives holding fast to differing degrees of certainty produces humility.... It is in disagreement and stress that true learning exhibits its value.

–Jay Kesler

It is in disagreement and stress that true learning exhibits its value."[12]

Consistent with Kesler's thinking, the institution in recent years has refused to embrace a single theological system, a single acceptable view on what it considers to be secondary theological issues, or a single view on such controversial social issues as war and peace, political philosophy, the role of women in the church, and the role of the government in the abortion issue. In the early 1990s Kesler had the occasion to represent the institution in discussions on two of these social issues. President Bill Clinton, who often identified with the evangelical movement, had received much criticism from many evangelicals for the social views which he expressed in his administration. When he desired to meet with a group of evangelical leaders who had not been among those attacking him, President Kesler was one of twelve such leaders invited to the White House for an informal breakfast meeting. President Clinton and his wife Hillary identified as their goals for the meeting: (1) to hear advice on how they might develop their personal spiritual experience and (2) to learn how they might "build bridges" to the evangelical movement. Kesler's personal advice to the president was to "resist the temptation to put all evangelicals in the same bag. Not all of us share the same opinions as the extreme religious right-wing. Everyday I hear things said by evangelicals that embarrass me. I spend a lot of time getting shot down myself." Later, Kesler noted that "I just attempted to communicate that there are evangelicals who understand the

President Kesler joins President Clinton in an informal White House meeting.

complexity of moral issues and the political realities of attempting to govern in a diverse, pluralistic society. We need to reach across partisan labels and seek understanding as Christian brothers and sisters with diverse political views. My prayer is that he would feel that we, as Christians, are capable of being civil and of Christian brotherhood, despite some pointed and different views."[13] Also in the early 1990s, the university came under attack from the leaders of the Northeast Indiana branch of the political action organization Operation Rescue when the latter discovered that not all of the Taylor faculty held views that it believed to be acceptable. Kesler recalled that earlier in his career, Billy Graham had advised him: "Don't answer your critics." However, in this case he chose to become involved in dialogue with them because, as he suggested, he did not want to appear to be trivializing this important issue. Essentially Kesler sought to uphold the sacredness of life even while being very careful to avoid unnecessarily circumscribing diversity. Such criticism by outside individuals of thoughts expressed by Taylor professors or other spokespersons has not been common in the history of the institution in part because of Taylor's long standing freedom from control by any denominational organization.[14]

For many decades the university has operated with the general philosophy that it should provide an adult environment and a trusting atmosphere, with expectations that the mostly 18-22 year-old students will grow into adulthood within the system while being allowed to make choices and even mistakes. One of the most significant applications of this philosophy has been in the operation of the chapel program. The university views the spiritual and educational development provided by the chapel services as one important component in the "whole person" education of the students. The institution has worked very carefully to structure the chapel programming and the entire environment surrounding the experience so that the students view chapel as something that they want to do rather than something that they have to do. It defines attendance at the

Sociologist and activist Tony Campolo speaks to the students.

services as expected rather than required; for the most part, this approach works as long as the students see the programs as spiritual experiences rather than as general assemblies and as long as the style and quality of the programming appeal to the majority. Most students attend chapel most of the time, and, typically, the auditorium is mostly full.[15]

The current document identifying behavioral standards for students was adopted by the faculty and trustees in 1982, and it sought as much as possible to place the rules for community life in the context of a "statement of mutual love, concern, and reconciliation." Major ideas in the document include "tolerating one another," "burdenbearing," "speaking the truth in love," and "reconciliation, restoration, and restitution." Furthermore, the document sought to distinguish clearly between "behavior...expressly prohibited in Scripture" (e.g., theft, lying, dishonesty, gossip, slander, back-biting, profanity, vulgarity, sexual promiscuity, drunkenness, immodesty of dress, and occult practices) and other "university expectations" (e.g., refraining from use of tobacco, alcoholic beverages, and illegal drugs, gambling, social dancing, pornography, and racial and other forms of discrimination). Of these standards, one receiving much discussion in recent years has been that of dancing. In 1984, the trustees approved a proposal to permit square dancing. Recent student surveys show that a significant minority of students would also favor allowing social dancing.[16]

3. BEYOND THE CLASSROOM

The 1893 relocation of Taylor to Upland had created a rural and, after the turn-of-the-century years, largely residential campus. Consequently, the twentieth century institution increasingly focused upon creating a sense of community and providing a broad range of cocurricular activities. While the number of available activities has increased since 1970, more noteworthy has been the larger degree of their organization and coordination.

The 1992-93 members of Second West Olson Hall.

The basic center for student social development and activity has continued to be the residential living units. The student development staff has strongly called for housing the maximum number of students in on-campus residence halls because of how this arrangement facilitates the peer mentoring of lower-division students by upper-division students, the social and spiritual maturation process, interpersonal bonding experiences, and the influencing of student behavior. Counter pressures included the desire of the education and other departments to place advanced students in off-campus internship programs and the increased pressure to

222

accommodate the growing number of students applying to Taylor—and to experience the increased financial security associated with the additional tuition income which they would provide—even though their acceptance meant housing more students off campus. The housing debate reached a peak in the 1980s. The trustees regularly heard the concerns of Student Development Vice-President Lowell Haines and others, and in the late 1980s, the President's planning council recommended an enrollment cap of 1,625 including 130 commuters and 45 off campus residents. In 1970, the university had purchased the Fairlane Apartments to use as an alternate form of housing for married students, international students, student teachers, and other students with special housing needs. Less acceptable to the student development staff was the placing of students in privately owned off-campus apartments such as Delta Apartments and Casa Patricia Apartments. The housing problem was compounded by the closing of Swallow Robin Residence Hall in 1986, but then largely relieved by the reopening of the new Swallow Robin in 1990 and especially the opening of Evan Bergwall Hall in 1989. By 1994, the students were housed as follows: central campus residence units, 1,414; Fairlane Village, 90; privately owned apartment units adjacent to campus, 100; and commuters and off-campus residents, 180.[17]

Years later, former students remember their residence hall experience with an affection usually matched only with that for the professors and fellow students in their major area of study.

Years later, former students remember their residence hall experience with an affection usually matched only with that for the professors and fellow students in their major area of study. Alumni Director George Glass reports that in his many discussions with alumni, second only to their inquiries about the current spiritual status of the university are their inquiries about the current state of living in their former residence hall. Taylor residential life has become increasingly structured. Timothy Herrmann, a long-time student development officer, views the personnel assistants (PAs) as the "backbone of the residence life program." The PAs counsel, organize activities, administer hall rules, and unlock doors. Paid for their services, they serve under the leadership of the residence hall director. Currently, each month they organize a broad variety of activities including two spiritual activities (often involving faculty members) and two social activities (often planned with a living unit in an opposite-sex hall). Social activities, including "pick-a-date" outings, involve an enhanced effort to provide natural social interaction between the male and female students.

Also important in the residence hall activities structure is the network of discipleship coordinators. Each living unit has at least one discipleship coordinator (DC) to lead small prayer and support groups. In the spring of 1994, up to 1,200 students participated in these groups. Also, much of the reason for the popularity of the intramural athletic program stems from its organization into teams by living units.[18]

Currently, the residence hall personnel assistants (60 students) and the discipleship coordinators (45 students) are two of the largest groups in the Taylor leadership program. Other groups include the freshman orientation (PROBE) leaders (60 students), the Development Office student ambassadors (14 students), the Taylor Student Organization officers (12 students), the Taylor World Outreach program leaders (12 students), and the career development assistants (10 students).

Steve Roggenbaum ('93) carries a new friend on a TWO trip.

Each year the university offers two one-hour Leadership Development courses to the approximately 200 students who are serving for the first time in one of the up to 400 leadership positions. The student development staff hopes that a majority of the students will participate in one or more of the leadership experiences during their Taylor career.[19]

The Taylor World Outreach (TWO), begun in the 1960s to recognize, encourage, and coordinate student participation in summer missions activity (see chapter 7), continued throughout the post-1970 period as the umbrella organization to promote and administer the campus, community, national, and international student ministry programs. By the mid-1990s, approximately one-half of the students participated regularly and up to three-fourths participated occasionally in one or more of the TWO programs; thus, outreach ministry joined with small-group fellowship and intramural athletics as the cocurricular activities involving the largest number of students. The eight student-led divisions of TWO and the number of student participants in each of these during the 1993-94 year included (1) Community Outreach (e.g. Youth for Christ, church, children's home, nursing home, veterans' hospital, disadvantaged youth, Big Brother/Big Sister ministries), 579 students; (2) Taylor

Christian Artists (e.g. music and performing arts groups), 55 students; (3) World Christian Fellowship (e.g. spring and summer short-term missions projects, Grant County Rescue Mission, flood relief), 193 students; (4) World Opportunities Week (plan and administer the fall international missions emphasis week), 15 students; (5) Youth Conference (plan and administer the traditional—since 1934—on-campus, spring weekend religious retreat for high school youth), 350 students; (6) Discipleship Coordinators, 45 students; (7) Habitat for Humanity (house construction projects for needy citizens), 100 students; and (8) Lighthouse (January interterm cross-cultural ministry experiences), 46 students. Lighthouse was the name of the original interterm missions teams to the Bahamian Islands led by Christian Education Professor Ruth Ann Breuninger and her upperclass majors beginning in 1972. More recently, the term has become a generic one to describe all of the January missions trips which in recent years have been organized by Charles Gifford, campus pastor. In 1993, 1994, and 1995 student teams ministered in the Bahamas, Haiti, India, Mexico, Singapore, Venezuela, and Zimbabwe.[20]

A performance of Amadeus in the Little Theatre in 1988.

Student involvement in arts activities was enhanced by (1) the construction of the first two buildings (music and communications arts) of the large fine arts complex and (2) the new general education program of 1984. The student newspaper (*The Echo*) and the yearbook (whose name had changed in 1963 from the *Gem* to the *Ilium*)[21] both continued throughout the most recent period as did the Trojan Players, the theater group which, following the 1972 fire that destroyed its traditional stage in Shreiner Auditorium, converted to an intimate "little theater" format. Oliver Hubbard and Jessica Rousselow have directed most of the dramatic productions since 1970. The Taylor radio station WTUC began broadcasting to student residence hall rooms by transmitter in 1970 and by cable in 1985. That same year the campus radio station became one of eight channels of a television cable system which began broadcasting three network stations, one educational station, two campus-based channels for presenting course-related materials and student programing, and an educational (public) FM radio station. The system added satellite-fed news and sports channels in 1990. Then in the fall of 1995 WTUC became WTUR, a student-operated and youth-oriented FM station with

Taylor's new radio station.

225

a broadcasting radius of 20 miles from the transmitter located three miles south of campus. In 1966, Dale Jackson reintroduced intercollegiate debate to Taylor; however, this activity continued only until 1971. The Concert Chorale (with its emphasis upon sacred classics and under the direction of Philip Kroeker since

The Concert Chorale and the Fort Wayne Philharmonic Orchestra have joined together several times in the 1990s to perform Handel's *Messiah*.

the early 1970s) and the Symphonic Band (with its classic band repertoire and currently under the direction of Albert Harrison) have been the primary musical ensembles to operate continuously since 1970. These ensembles and two others introduced in the early 1980s, the Taylor Ringers (founded and directed since 1982 by Richard Parker) and the Taylor Sounds (a sixteen-member choral group with a broad repertoire) currently are the major off-campus touring groups. The 1984 general education requirement calling for all students to complete a one-hour participation-in-the-arts experience led to a sharp increase in the number of ensembles. The current catalog identifies six choral and ten instrumental groups.[22]

The Taylor athletic program in the 1970s continued its 1960s dominance in the minor sports for men and introduced its modern intercollegiate program for women. The 1980s witnessed the emergence of the men's basketball program as a national power and the beginning of a decade-long experience of instability in conference relationships. From the mid-1960s to the late 1970s, the Taylor men won the conference all-sports trophy in 13 of 14 years, being especially strong in golf (coached by Don Odle), cross country and track (coached by George Glass), wrestling (coached by Thomas Jarman and Dana Sorensen), and tennis (coached by Dale Wenger, Robert Blume, and Sheldon Bassett). The home course winning streak of the golf team reached 117 matches in the late 1970s. Intercollegiate athletics for women offered only basketball, begun during the 1946-47 season, until adding field hockey in 1966, volleyball in the spring of 1970, lacrosse, tennis, and track in 1970-71, and softball in 1974. With the development in the 1970s of high school sports for girls, the women athletes came to college with advanced skill levels and program expectations. Consequently, not only the number of sports but also the size of schedules and length of seasons expanded. The 1984 women's track team led by coach Ruth

Ozmun and multiple-event winner Lori Shephard won the National Christian College Athletic Association (NCCAA) track meet. Similarly, the women's volleyball team produced NCCAA championships under coach Karen Traut in 1989, 1990, and 1991. Also, the men's track team won NCCAA titles in 1985 (under George Glass), 1986 (under Joe Romine), and 1995 (under Christopher Coy). A major program evaluation in 1984 resulted in the dropping of field hockey and wrestling and the introduction of women's cross country (coached by Ray Bullock) and men's soccer (coached primarily by Joe Lund). The Equestrian Club (sponsored by Brian Christy and Janet Loy) also began in the early 1980s.[23]

The men's basketball team coached by Paul Patterson since 1979, completed the 1993-94 year with its tenth consecutive season of 25 or more wins, a feat matched on the collegiate level only by UCLA (1967-76), UNLV (1983-92), and David Lipscomb University (1984-1994). Although the 1993-94 team expanded the multi-season home court winning streak—which ended at 45 in February, 1995—and entered the National Association of Intercollegiate Athletics (NAIA) Division II playoffs with the number one national ranking, Patterson's most successful team was probably the 1990-91 unit which, with its 34-4 record—an Indiana collegiate record for total wins in a season—and final four appearance in the NAIA Division I playoffs, earned Patterson National Coach of the Year honors. Players of note during this decade included All-American selections Ralph Gee in 1987, David Wayne in 1992, and Steve Mozingo in 1994, as well as Jim Bushur, who established Taylor season (702 points) and career (2,213 points) scoring records.[24]

Paul Patterson

Basketball Coach

Natalie Steele: All-American honoree in two sports.

James Njoroge: Multiple-time All-American selectee.

Individual NAIA national champions in this period, in addition to Phil Captain (steeplechase) and Ralph Foote (cross country) in 1969 (see chapter seven) included Glen Guerin, Lori Shephard, and James (Murage) Njoroge. Guerin is Taylor's only athlete to become an individual national champion in two different years (wrestling, 1976 and 1977), and he was named the outstanding wrestler at the national meet in 1976. Trackster Shephard won the high jump in 1982 to become Taylor's first woman national champion. Njoroge not only won two events (the 800 meters and mile runs) at the 1996 indoor track and field national meet, but he set an NAIA record in each race in the process of being named the meet's outstanding runner.

NAIA All-American selections in addition to the above basketball players and national winners were Dana Sorensen (1972), Cecil Bergen (1975 and 1976), Steve Muterspaw (1976), Bob LaFollette (1978 and 1980), and Jay Tyree (1979) in wrestling; Brad Ludwig (1972), Larry Brown (1981), Mark Cornfield (1984 and 1985), Amy Boothe (1992), and James Njoroge (1994 and 1995) in track; Mark Cornfield (1985), James Njoroge (1994 and 1995) and Tony Newman (1995) in indoor track; Steve Gradeless (1975 and 1976) and James Njoroge (1993 and 1994) in cross-country; Ken O'Brien (1968) in baseball; Natalie Steele (1995 and 1996) and Steve Wit (1996) in basketball; Natalie Steele (1995) in volleyball; Don Faimon (1977) and Terry Schaumleffel (1979) in golf; and Gordon Pritz (1975 and 1976), Wade Russell (1985), Tim Shapley (1989), Casey Sparrow (1992), Doug Bonura (1993 and 1994) and John J. Guedet (1995) in football. Long distance runner Njoroge, an international student from Kenya who enrolled in Taylor in 1993, earned All-American honors in nine events during his first eight collegiate sports seasons. Steele became Taylor's first woman athlete to win All-American honors in two sports. Wide-receiver Bonura's selection in 1993 came after his 1610 yards receiving became the second highest season total in NAIA Division II history.

Taylor participated in the Hoosier College Conference (primarily with long-time rivals Anderson, Earlham, Franklin, Indiana Central, Hanover, and Manchester) until 1970 at which time it became a member of the new Hoosier-Buckeye Collegiate Conference (HBCC) which joined five members from the old conference, (Anderson, Earlham, Hanover, Manchester, and Taylor) with four colleges from western Ohio (Bluffton, Defiance, Findlay, and Wilmington). In the early 1980s, the Development Office under new Vice-President Gerald Oliver introduced a method of raising money to help individual students. The Taylor officials believed that such awards ("sponsorships") were consistent with the HBCC guidelines prohibiting athletic scholarships as they provided no advantage or disadvantage for athletes. The conference governing board, however, viewed this aid program differently, and the institution elected to withdraw from the conference. The conference itself disbanded in 1985; however, continuing conversations resulted in Taylor becoming a founding member of a reorganized conference, the Indiana Collegiate Athletic Conference (ICAC) which came into existence in 1988 when a nucleus of colleges with which Taylor had been traditionally aligned (Anderson, Franklin, Hanover and Manchester) joined with three other private Indiana institutions (Depauw, Rose Hulman, and Wabash). Not all of the ICAC colleges held membership with the same national organization, and when they organized as a conference they agreed that after a three-year period they would determine whether the conference members would all align with the NAIA, all align with the National Collegiate Athletic Association (NCAA) Division III, or continue to operate as before with colleges in each category. When, in 1991, the conference schools voted by a 6-2 margin to have all of its members affiliate with the NCAA Division III, Taylor, preferring to continue its tradition with the NAIA, chose to withdraw from the conference. Thus, again in 1992, Taylor returned to independent status until the mid-1990s when for all men's and women's sports, except football, it joined with the Mid-Central Conference (other members: Bethel College, Goshen College, Grace College, Huntington College, Marian College, St. Francis College and Indiana Wesleyan University), an organization of Indiana colleges with scholarship offerings and an NAIA affiliation. At the same time

The Taylor football Trojans.

the football team began competing in a separate conference, the Mid-States Football Association.[25]

For many years, the Taylor intramural athletic program has been one of the most popular student activities. Its broad appeal is explained partly by the institution's highly residential nature and its rural location where students are somewhat isolated from off-campus recreational opportunities. Furthermore, the program is well organized—particularly so in recent years under Professor James Law and the recreation leadership majors. In 1991-92, 1,100 of the 1,700 students participated in one or more of the intramural activities. When one adds the 300 students competing in intercollegiate athletics, this means that a large majority of the Taylor students participate in organized athletic programs. Ironically, with this high degree of participation in athletics, the high quality of the Taylor physical plant in general and the major institutional commitment to cocurricular programming, the school's indoor athletic facilities are below average for institutions of similar size and reputation. Consequently, the Taylor intramural program involves more people participating with less facilities than is the case in most colleges. Likely, this situation will be remedied in the near future—perhaps before the turn of the century—by the construction of a student recreational center.[26]

Taylor's first NCCAA volleyball championship team.

Jack King

Athletics and Development

Taylor's role in the promotion of athletic evangelism, while continuing in recent years, nevertheless has become a less unique and less publicized characteristic of the school than was the case in the decades after World War II (see chapter seven). Taylor students still participate in athletic missions. In fact, probably more Taylor athletes served on overseas mission tours during the early 1990s than participated on all of the 1952-1965 basketball tours led by Coach Odle. Recent athletic missionaries from Taylor have included the women's volleyball and tennis teams and the men's basketball, tennis, soccer and baseball teams as well as individuals on teams comprised of athletes from multiple colleges. Also, Bob Davenport's Wandering Wheels program has continued to lead long-distance bicycle trips to the present; however, Taylor ended its affiliation with the organization in 1989 after the university's insurance carrier and legal counsel advised that the bicycle program exposed the university to an excessive level of legal liability. In 1970 Davenport's organization added a "Possum Bus" (a mobile retreat vehicle) ministry, and a decade later it constructed a modern retreat center which has hosted many church youth groups. With these most recent services, Wandering Wheels continues to serve as a travel service and rental facility for Taylor groups.

Probably Taylor's greatest contribution to athletic evangelism has been the example that it provided for the many programs that followed its efforts. Both Odle and Davenport served as pioneers to launch innovative Christian ministry programs which then became widely imitated by other organizations. Jack King, former Taylor baseball coach and currently a member of the development staff, identifies Odle as the "father of overseas sports evangelism." King, himself, left his position at Taylor to serve with Sports Ambassadors, the athletic evangelism arm of Overseas Crusades and the organization which most directly continued

Odle's Venture for Victory program. Later, King organized and led teams of undergraduate athlete-evangelists in overseas efforts for Athletes in Action, an agency of Campus Crusade for Christ and an organization which with the Fellowship of Christian Athletes has become one of the two most widely recognized of the over 100 American-based organizations to minister to athletes and/or lead efforts by Christian athletes to provide ministry to those who attend their athletic events.[27]

4. A MODERN STUDENT PROFILE

The Taylor students of the mid-1990s are much like the Taylor students of 1970; however, there are some slight differences between the two groups. The modern students come to college with slightly higher high school scores; they are more likely to have graduated from a parochial high school; they are less likely to be Methodist in church preference; they are more likely to come from the South; they are less likely to be middle middle class and more likely to

Graduation Day!

be either upper middle class or lower middle class in economic background; they are much more widely traveled; they are more conservative in religious and social ideas and practices; and they hold higher expectations that the university will provide a broad range of personal services for them.

The entering freshman class of 1993 came to college with an average SAT (or converted ACT) score of 1102 and GPA of 3.50 (compared to 956 and 3.3 in 1987). The percentage graduating in the top 20% of their high school class was 66% and in the top 40% was 88% (compared to 44% and 71% respectively in 1980).[28]

The Taylor students continue to come from the low-church, evangelical Protestant tradition. Although the United Methodist Church still remains the specific denomination with the single largest number of students, its current enrollment at Taylor (131) represents a sharp drop from 1970 (254); this decline is even more significant for the traditionally Methodist college when one notes that the student body grew by 400 students (approximately 30%) in this period. The Presbyterians are the only mainline denomination with significant representation at Taylor to show a sharp increase (60 to 115) since 1970. The numbers of American (Northern) Baptists (74) and Lutherans (24) are little changed. In addition to the Presbyterians, denominations or church groups to show noteworthy increases in representation in the registration data between 1970 and 1993 include Assemblies of God (not identified to 31), Bible churches (not identified to 56), the Christian Church (42 to 70), the Evangelical Free Church (44 to 105), nondenominational (not identified to 213), and the Wesleyan Church (12 to 44). The cluster of categories including 1) Baptists other than American Baptists (265), 2) independent (144), 3) nondenominational, 4) other (groups not included in the 30 specifically defined categories of the registration data (195), and 5) Bible churches represent nearly one-half of the 1993 students. In summary, the Taylor students come from a broad variety of evangelical Protestant churches including primarily Baptist, Methodist, Presbyterian, many small denominations (e.g., Brethren, Mennonite, Missionary, Christian and Missionary Alliance), and a growing number of independent or congregationally based churches.

Both in 1970 and the mid-1990s, it generally has been true that one-third of the students come from Indiana, one-third come from the three adjacent states of Ohio, Michigan, and Illinois, and one-third come from the other states. The 34% from Indiana rose to 46% in 1986, however, just before the full impact of the Kesler administration and the implementation of the new admissions guidelines following a major marketing study (see Chapter 10). The most significant demographic changes between 1970 and 1993 have been the increase in students from the South and the decrease in students coming from the Middle Atlantic states. For example, the representation from the southern states grew in Florida (18 to 32), Kentucky (6 to 15), Maryland (8 to 22), North Carolina (3 to 22), Tennessee (3 to 20), Texas (1 to 13), and Virginia (3 to 25), while it fell in New Jersey (70 to 29), New York (49 to 33) and Pennsylvania (105 to 57). Factors in these changes undoubtedly included the enhanced Taylor Admissions Office recruitment effort in the South and the growing prominence of Messiah College (Pennsylvania) in the East.[29]

One long-standing characteristic of Taylor students that continues with marked intensity to the present is their reputation for being unusually friendly.

The Taylor Office of Student Development conducted student life surveys in the mid1970s and annually since 1983. The surveys show that the college continues to serve a single (98%) immediate post-high school (usually 96% in the age bracket of 17-22), mostly residential (approximately 80%), clientele of professing Christians (99%). In recent years, over 20% of the students have come from Christian high schools and approximately 10% have divorced parents. Also in recent years according to the surveys, approximately 82% attend church once or more per week, 80% attend chapel frequently, and 60% "had regular personal Bible study and prayer." The data shows that in their social practices the contemporary students are more conservative than were their counterparts of the mid-1970s. The percentage in each period reporting that during the school year just ended they "never" participated in specific activities is as follows (the data for the earlier period is listed first and that for the more recent period is second): drinking alcoholic beverages (63% to 80%), using tobacco (78% to 91%), using illegal drugs (90% to 99%), gambling (82% to 92%), stealing (86% to 95%), cheating (66% to 86%), engaging in premarital sexual intercourse (82% to 94%), and dancing (48% to 65%). In two areas there has developed greater freedom between male and female students, namely a greater willingness to support the idea of women initiating relationships with men (51% to 80%) and of dating partners discussing their convictions about sexual morality (87% to 99%). Within the last decade the students have increasingly viewed the Taylor environment as "supportive of...spiritual growth" (from 82% in 1985 to 94% in 1992).[30]

Organized chaos: over 500 Taylor students celebrated the 1996 leap year by leapfrogging around the campus loop.

One long-standing characteristic of Taylor students that continues with marked intensity to the present is their reputation for being unusually friendly. It is doubtful that this trait developed from a planned policy initiated by a well-meaning leader; more likely it evolved largely of its own initiative. Once the pattern began, prospective students who especially valued this characteristic when they observed it during campus visits then chose to enroll and thus helped to perpetuate this campus phenomenon. Perhaps this pattern of unusual friendliness developed as early as the period when the college was serving primarily young men and women from the common classes of Methodism. Such people were known for their exuberant fellowship and egalitarianism in the context of a family environment.[31]

In recent years, a discussion has developed over what in the Taylor experience

233

most influences the Taylor students. Psychologist Joe Lund spent a 1992 sabbatical studying faculty and student perceptions of the Taylor experience. Unlike President Kesler, who has always emphasized that the faculty are the heart of the Taylor program, Lund concluded that the students were less influenced by the faculty or programs than by other students. Higher education researcher Alexander Astin in his study of students in 200 colleges and universities reached conclusions similar to those of Lund, noting that "the single most powerful source of influence in the undergraduate academic and personal development is the peer group." Astin, of course, studied primarily secular students in secular colleges where there was no overall philosophical framework unifying the educational experience. At Taylor, by contrast, undoubtedly what is a larger influence than any one element alone—students, faculty or programs— is the combined effect of these three elements working together to reinforce the central institutional conviction—and the campus ethos that results from it— that our purpose as humans is to know and enjoy God and His creation. Likely what Taylor students receive most from each other is a sense of emotional bonding that often results from shared experiences involving meaningful interaction.[32]

While most of the modern students are very pleased with their Taylor experience, they repeatedly cite two deficiencies, namely the dating environment and the facilities for student activities. Many women, noting the slightly disadvantageous male:female ratio (48:52 in 1993) to begin with, lament that many of the men are not as aggressive in seeking dating opportunities as they would like for them to be. Also many students, emphasizing the major importance of student activities for a residential yet rural, somewhat isolated campus, find the existing facilities—particularly the gymnasium and student center—as inadequate for meeting their purposes.[33]

This ends the two-chapter survey of most of the broad university developments since the publication of the first edition of the Taylor history in the early 1970s. What remains for the next chapter is a more focused description of the Kesler era (i.e., the period since 1985) and its effort to provide the institution with a larger image, constituency, vision, and base.

[1] Marvin Cetron, "An American Renaissance: Seventy-four Trends That Will Affect America's Future—And Yours," *The Futurist*, March/April, 1994, insert p. 6, taken from the author's book *American Renaissance*, second edition, (New York, 1994).

[2] For the introduction of these phrases into the modern vocabulary as well a discussion of the societal developments which they represent, see John Naisbitt, *Megatrends: Ten New Directions Transforming Our Lives* (New York, 1982), chapter two.

[3] TUTM, May 9, 1988; interview with Robert D. Hodge, Summer, 1993.

[4] In the same year that the college employed its first full-time counseling therapist, it also added its first full-time physician, James O. Oliver. Five years later, in 1986, a second medical doctor, David H. Brewer, joined the Health Center practice; and both physicians served community clients as well as student patients. See TUTM October 16, 1981, February 13, 1986.

[5] Illustrative of Taylor's high retention in recent years are the following: of the students eligible to return in the fall of 1991, 94% actually did; also, of the freshman class entering in the fall of 1988, 73% had graduated by 1994. Daryl Yost stated in 1994 that Taylor's consistent year-to-year retention rate of approximately 90% places it in the top 5% of American colleges and universities. See TUTM, May 23, 1991; *Taylor University Fact Book*, October, 1994, Office of Research and Planning, p. 34; *Taylor Echo*, September 9, 1994, p. 1.

[6] Interview with Charles R. Jaggers, Summer, 1992; interview with Walter E. Campbell, Summer, 1992; TUTM, June 4, 1976.

[7] Interview with Charles R. Jaggers, Summer, 1992; interview with Walter E. Campbell, Summer, 1992; TUTM, October 23, 1980.

[8] Interview with Charles R. Jaggers, Summer, 1992; interview with Walter E. Campbell, Summer, 1992.

[9] TUTM, February 6, 1988.

[10] William C. Ringenberg, "Seven Score Years and Beyond: A Personal View of the Taylor Heritage," *Taylor Magazine*, Fall, 1986, pp. 9, 12; interview with Paul R. House, Summer, 1994; MS Taylor University Master Marketing Plan, January 30, 1987; *TUC*, 1994-96, p. 6; *The Christian College Coalition Resource Guide for Christian Higher Education* (Washington, D.C., 1994), pp. 8-10.

[11] See Ringenberg, *The Christian College*, pp. 216-17.

[12] Jay L. Kesler, "Five Smooth Stones," *Taylor University Magazine*, Winter, 1987, pp. 12-13.

[13] See TUFM, November 11, 1993; *Taylor Echo*, October 22, 1993; "Clinton Meets Evangelicals," *Christianity Today*, November 22, 1993, p. 51.

[14] TUFM, February 11, 1993.

[15] Interview with Charles Jaggers, Spring, 1992; TUTM, October 23, 1980.

[16] TUTM, October 22, 1976; January 26, 1980; May 25, 1984; "President's Annual Report," 1977-78, p. 2; 1981, p. 10; *Taylor Magazine*, Fall/Winter, 1982, pp. 27-29; "Life Together Covenant: Expectations and Responsibilities for Community Life at Taylor University," October, 1993 edition.

[17] TUTM, January 26, 1980, May 23, 1980, January 31, 1981, May 23, 1986; interview with Timothy W. Herrmann, Summer, 1993; interview with Denise A. Bakerink, Spring, 1994; letter, Timothy W. Herrmann to author, September 28, 1993; *TUC*, 1994-96, pp. 9, 11.

[18] Interview with George A. Glass, Summer, 1992; interview with Walter E. Campbell, Summer, 1994; interview with Charles R. Jaggers, Summer, 1992; *Taylor Magazine*, Fall, 1988, p. 7.

[19] Interview with Stephen Beers, Summer, 1994; interview with Walter E. Campbell, Summer, 1994.

[20] Interview with Mary Rayburn, Summer, 1994; Lois Whiteman Schoenals, "A Light Shines In Nassau," *Taylor Magazine*, Spring, 1972, pp. 10-13.

[21] The decision to change the yearbook title to the name of the ancient Asia Minor city of Troy reflected a desire to complement the traditional nickname of the Taylor athletic teams, the Trojans.

[22] Interview with Dale M. Jackson, Summer, 1994; interview with Philip Kroeker, Summer, 1994; interview with Richard Parker, Summer, 1994; *TUC*, 1971-73, p. 67, 1984-86, p. 40, and 1994-96, pp. 90-91; interview with Charles B. Kirkpatrick, Spring, 1995; *Taylor Echo*, February 24, 1995, pp. 1-2, and September 1, 1995, p. 3; *Marion Chronicle Tribune*, September 7, 1995, p. A10.

[23] *Taylor Magazine*, Spring/Summer, 1978, pp. 12-13, Winter, 1978, pp. 18-19, Spring/Summer, 1984, p.19; Winter, 1985, p. 21; interview with Joe W. Romine, Summer, 1992. Taylor *Gem*, 1947, p. 110; Taylor *Illium*, 1966, p. 153, 1970, p. 150-52, 1971, pp. 70-71; Taylor *Echo*, March 8, 1974, p. 8.

[24] *Taylor Magazine*, Summer, 1988, p. 5, Spring, 1989, p. 3, and Spring, 1994, p. 6; *Indianapolis Star*, March 6, 1994, p. C4; *Marion Chronicle Tribune*, January 20, 1995, p. B2.

[25] Interview with Joe W. Romine, Summer, 1992; TUTM, May 20, 1983; *Taylor Magazine*, Autumn, 1991, p. 6, Winter, 1994, p. 8.

[26] Interview with Joe W. Romine, Summer, 1992.

[27] *Taylor Magazine*, Fall, 1982, pp. 13-14, 22; TUTM, February 3, 1989; interview with Jack W. King, Summer, 1994.

[28] *Taylor University Fact Book*, October, 1993, Taylor Office of Research and Planning, pp. 6ff.

[29] Annual Fall Semester Registration Reports, 1970-1993, Taylor Records Office.

[30] Student Life Questionnaire, May, 1992, Taylor Student Development Center.

[31] See A. Gregory Schneider, *The Way of the Cross Leads Home: The*

Domestication of American Methodism (Bloomington, Indiana, 1993); and Ringenberg, "Seven Score Years and Beyond: A Personal View of the Taylor Heritage," pp. 11-12.

[32] Interview with Joe Lund, Summer, 1992; *Taylor Magazine*, Fall, 1986, p. 4; Alexander Astin "What Matters Most in College," *Liberal Education*, Fall, 1993, p. 7.

[33] Interview with Joe Lund, Summer, 1992; *Taylor University Fact Book*, October, 1993, p. 11.

Chapter Ten

THE LATE TWENTIETH CENTURY
(PART III): EXPANDING BEYOND THE VILLAGE BORDER

The most recent decade in the institution's history has witnessed an increased effort to reach beyond the limits of the rural, residential campus to embrace an enlarged constituency and a broader world vision. This enhanced emphasis is largely associated with the administration of Jay Kesler (1985-), and featured 1) increasing success in telling the Taylor story nationwide and abroad, 2) new efforts to provide broadening experiences and enlarged perspectives for the traditional students, and **3)** the addition of an urban campus in an effort to serve new student populations.

1. SPREADING THE WORD:

THE MARKETING OF THE UNIVERSITY

While the improvement in the quality of the Taylor program has occurred gradually during the past generation and before, the general public appreciation of the Taylor experience has increased sharply in the past decade. One no longer hears the former oft-repeated claim that "Taylor is the best-kept-secret in higher education." The growing reputation has led to growing prosperity which in turn has provided resources to continue to improve the university even more. This recent prosperity, however, has developed

> *One no longer hears the former oft-repeated claim that "Taylor is the best-kept-secret in higher education."*

only after the downturn of the early 1980s and in large part is the result of the corrective measures introduced in the middle 1980s. The early 1980s was an era which was troublesome for Christian higher education in general. At the meeting of the Christian College Consortium in St. Paul, Minnesota, in 1982, the presidents of the member institutions identified as major problems 1) a volatile economy including high inflationary pressures, 2) government student

241

aid decreases, 3) inadequate enrollments and 4) inadequate marketing efforts in promoting the benefits of Christian higher education. Taylor suffered from all of these conditions plus the leadership instability described in chapter eight. Between 1981 and 1987, government grants as a source of student revenue declined from 32.3% to 20%, while each year from 1980 to 1988 the tuition increase exceeded the growth in the consumer price index. A declining number of students posed the threat of deficit budgets. In the mid-1980s the trustees instituted a hiring freeze and cuts in maintenance and equipment costs. As a long-range solution they called for a major marketing study as a basis for a more effective effort in communicating the value of a Taylor education.[1] "People don't realize what a fine place this is," observed new Dean Richard Stanislaw at his first board meeting in 1982. Concurring with this view was John McDougall, Taylor board chairman and former executive vice-president of the Ford Motor Company, who noted in 1985, "Marketing is certainly a serious problem in this institution." Even with the inadequate visibility of the institution, the trustees were convinced that there were plenty of students who wanted to come to Taylor if they thought that they could afford to do so. The marketing audit led by W. F. Walker Johanson, executive director of the National Institute for Organizational Research and Problem Solving, Ann Arbor, Michigan, confirmed the trustees' assumption that although there was going to be a decline in the number of college-age students through most of the rest of the century, there was not a shortage of students who would consider attending an evangelical college with a quality program. As a result of this study and other institutional planning, the college adopted an aggressive, multifaceted, highly organized and highly personalized admissions effort that marshaled the resources of the entire campus including the Financial Aid Office, the faculty, and the president. Bringing prospective students to campus became an increasing emphasis. "We find that if we can get students on campus they are very impressed with the attractive physical facilities including the campus as a whole and the very friendly environment," noted a university official. The handsomely redesigned Helena Building became the new student visitor center, housing the Offices of Admissions and the President. The Admissions Office carefully recruited and trained a core of student assistants (the "personal touch" staff) who in their work with prospective students communicated the desired image of wholesomeness, vitality, health, and vigor.[2]

The new recruitment effort sought to develop an enlarged appreciation for the Taylor academic environment and to attract higher-ability students.

Accordingly visiting students regularly met with professors in their major area of interest. Even as the minimum admissions standards increased (from 2.5 to 2.8 GPA and from the top 50% to the top 40% of the graduating class), larger numbers of applicants met them, in part attracted by the sharp increase in institutional-based merit scholarship awards which, beginning in 1983-84, Taylor introduced to replace the declining, largely need-based government aid.[3]

Concurrent with the recruitment of increasingly able students was another concern, namely to provide opportunities for students who didn't meet the normal entrance criteria but whose school counselors or ministers believed deserved special consideration. Beginning in 1985, the RAP (Right Approach Program) program led by Billie Manor, director of the learning support center, accepted a limited number of such students (e.g. 25 to 50 per year in the late 1980s) and provided them with special counselling and tutoring services during their first semester. The program especially sought to assist disadvantaged minority and learning disabled students.[4]

The sharp increase in institutional-based merit scholarship awards...[began] to replace the declining, largely need-based government aid.

Symbolic of the enhanced emphasis upon student recruitment was the expansion of the responsibilities of Wynn Lembright, who had been the director of admissions since 1983. In 1986 Lembright added administrative oversight for the Office of Financial Aid (as well as the Offices of Student Development and Athletics). Increasingly the financial aid officials, including Timothy Nace, director since 1991, began to see their office as an important component in the student-recruitment process, and they allocated aid that increasingly came from internal as opposed to external sources. The Taylor proportion of the total student aid funds increased from 21% ($836,620 of $4,031,239) in 1981-82 to 42% ($3,459,896 of $8,297,567) in 1991-92. Earlier Taylor students had received significant aid from the post-World War II era G. I. Bill, the Sputnik period National Defense Education Act, the Lyndon Johnson administration Higher Education Act of 1965, and successive similar legislation; however, the sharp cutback of federal aid since the Reagan administration forced the institution to increase its commitment to financial aid from its own sources. By the early 1990s the most common types of institutional aid were the academic merit awards (i.e., President's, Dean's, Trustees' and Leadership Scholarships) and the Taylor General Grant, a need-based award of up to $7,000 per student per

Wilbur Cleveland

"The hallmark of Will's work was always excellence," commented Milo Rediger in a fitting tribute to Will Cleveland ('49). As editor of the *Taylor Magazine* and other institutional publications for 27 years, Cleveland served as the main information link between Taylor University and her constituents. An able writer and skillful humorist, he was also proficient with the camera, and some of his striking photographs (e.g. of the fire that roared through Wright Hall as well as the demolition of Magee-Campbell-Wisconsin Dormitory) appear in this book.

Cleveland's devotion to Taylor and the Christian faith were evident to all who knew him. His wife Alyce reflected, "If anyone asked me who was the best Christian I'd ever know, it would be Will. . . I lived with him, I saw him in every situation. He was consistent."

year designed to assure each student of coming within $1,000 of meeting the formula definition of financial need. The most attractive awards were the Leadership Scholarships (currently twelve awards annually for 40% to 80% of tuition for four years) which were introduced in 1985 as a part of the High School Leadership Conference requested by the trustees during the mid-1980s enrollment downturn. This conference was designed to parallel the leadership conference for college students (see chapter nine) and, like the high school summer honors program (see chapter eight), to attract high-ability high school students to Taylor.[5]

Meaningful student recruitment efforts, of course, were not new to the 1980s; however, the extent to which Admissions Office officials directly participated in and led those efforts has been without precedent in the recent period. Significant activities, programs, and other endeavors originating before 1985 and having a positive impact in recruiting students and promoting institutional goodwill in general have included the Sammy Morris biographies and films (from Thaddeus Reade's original biography to the recent videos), the Youth Conference (since the 1930s), the gospel teams (especially from the 1920s to the 1960s), the athletic evangelism program (especially in the 1950s and 1960s), the Math and Science Field Days for high school students (since the 1970s), the *Taylor Magazine*, and the summer conference programs. Between the late 1950s and his death in 1985, Wilbur Cleveland produced 85 issues of the *Taylor Magazine*. Milo Rediger stated that officials in other colleges highly regarded Taylor publications, and he believed that their impact contributed significantly to the growth of the university. The summer conference program grew from Don Odle's basketball camp in the 1950s—the first of the many such camps in the basketball-crazed Hoosier state—to an operation with over 9000 registrants, including denominational and missions conferences, athletic, band, and citizenship camps, and $500,000 gross income during a ten-week period in 1990. Before the completion of the chapel-auditorium in 1975, the summer program was largely limited to camps. After 1975, the program expanded to host groups requiring a large assembly hall. These included the World Gospel Mission (WGM), the Oriental Mission Society (now OMS International), and the Evangelical Mennonite Church. Further stimulating the ability of the campus to hold conventions was the completion of Bergwall Hall, an airconditioned motel-like residence hall immediately adjacent to the dining commons. Plans to build a conference center in the same complex did not develop.[6] Thomas Beers served as conference program director from 1970 to 1990 and provided the vision for a greatly enhanced program.

The single most significant factor in the recent success in marketing the institution was the appointment of Jay Kesler as president in 1985. A Taylor alumnus (class of 1958) he, like other Taylor graduates Ted Engstrom and Sam Wolgemuth (see chapter six), served as the leader of the para-church organization, Youth for Christ, (YFC) where his presidential tenure, 1973-1985, was the longest in the history of the youth organization. This position plus his writings (19 books by 1994) and especially his syndicated radio program, Family Forum (which in 1995 was broadcast five days a week

> *The single most significant factor in the recent success in marketing the institution was the appointment of Jay Kesler as president in 1985.... His reputation and visibility allowed Taylor to develop an enhanced and enlarged national and international reputation, the most obvious effects of which were the growth in the number of applications coming into the Admissions Office. As president, Kesler focused upon external relations and internal spiritual development and community morale.*

on 250 American stations that had a listening audience of three million people), meant that he became the most widely recognized president in Taylor's history.[7] Consequently the institution had a president who loved and understood Taylor and attracted a ready hearing with the type of students—and their parents—most likely to be interested in enrolling in a Christian college. Kesler possessed unusual skill as a communicator, and he worked through disciplined study and sensitivity to apply solid content in practical and engaging ways for both the sophisticated and educated members of his audience and also those whose background was more humble. His reputation and visibility allowed Taylor to develop an enhanced and enlarged national and international reputation, the most obvious effects of which were the growth in the number of applications coming into the Admissions Office.

As president, Kesler focused upon external relations and internal spiritual development and community morale. He spoke in chapel more regularly than did any of his modern predecessors, with his speaking dates regularly including the Friday high school visitation days. Popular with students and one of the most engaging platform speakers in the history of the institution, at the outset of his tenure he sometimes found it difficult to adapt his talks to the relatively short chapel period. One clever presiding student recognizing this presented

Jay Kesler

President

Daryl Yost

Daryl Yost came to Taylor in 1983 as the vice-president for development, served a brief term as acting president in 1985, and then with the advent of the Kesler era became the university provost. Except for Christian Stemen, Burt Ayres, and Milo Rediger no other Taylor employee in a non-presidential role has held as much responsibility and/or influence as has Yost.

Kesler to the assembly thus: "President Kesler is a man who needs no introduction; he just needs a conclusion."[8]

One major reason for Kesler's success was the organization of his governing team. At the outset of his tenure the trustees divided the responsibility of the Office of the President to free Kesler to do the things which he did best. Daryl Yost, who briefly had been the Director of Development after serving nine years as the Superintendent of Schools, East Allen County, Indiana (near Fort Wayne), became the manager of internal operations as provost. The division of labor between Kesler and Yost worked well. Each was strong in an area where the other was not. Kesler made it easy for someone to work with him, and Yost was able to adjust his own goals. Also the past decade has witnessed a high degree of stability within the senior level administrative team and a growing ability of the board of trustees to understand and perform its function well. In 1994 Kesler described the trustees as "one of the best behaved boards I know." Noting that the board members understand that their role is to establish policy, he observed, "They don't seek to micromanage." Kesler and Yost encouraged the board to continue to add to their group younger experienced leaders— especially business leaders—with the capability both personally and through their contacts of helping the school financially.[9] Current trustees new to the board since the mid-1980s have included senior executives Roger Beaverson, Theodore Brolund, Kenneth Flanigan, Marta Gabre-Tsadick, Richard Gygi, Jerry Horne, John Horne, Carl Moellering, Arthur Musselman, Paul Robbins, Paul Steiner, and Paul Zurcher; educators Joseph Brain, Beverly Jacobus Brightly, and William Pannell; surgeon James Woods; and Christian laywoman Roselyn Kerlin. Board chairs since Lester Gerig's lengthy tenure (1964-1981, see chapter 8), have included Donald Jacobsen (1981-84), John McDougall (1984-87), Carl Hassell (1987-1990), Theodore Brolund (1990-93), and John Horne (1993-). Current Chair Horne is the president and chief operating officer of Navistar International Transportation. During the 1990-1993 capital campaign the board members personally contributed approximately 30% of the costs of the two new major buildings.[10]

If Kesler's first responsibility was to sell Taylor to prospective students and their families, his second task was to promote the institution to prospective donors. Indeed nearly the whole of the Kesler presidency has been one continuous capital campaign. Fortunately Kesler, because of his Youth for Christ experience, was comfortable with the demanding travel and speaking schedule which this required. Other college presidents with less tolerance for travel and less aptitude for speaking did not enjoy their responsibility as well in an era which called for college presidents to be nearly full-time fund-raisers.[11]

The capital campaign of 1990-1993 was the most successful fund-raising effort in the institution's history. The principal leaders in aiding President Kesler in the campaign were Trustee Carl Moellering, the campaign committee chair; Charles Jaggers and Gene Rupp, successive vice presidents for development; George Glass, associate vice president for alumni relations; and Thomas Beers, campaign coordinator. The campaign relied heavily upon major gifts and fund-raising dinners, and it exceeded its goal of nearly $9 million by the early 1990s. Most of these funds supported the construction and maintenance endowment of the new Communication Arts and Environmental Studies Centers.[12]

Plans for the new Samuel Morris Hall.

The university plans to launch a $60 million sesquicentennial campaign in 1996. The goals of this campaign reflect the designs of the trustees' Long-Range Planning Committee and the President's Council for Assessment and Strategic and Long-Range Planning. Capital construction targets for the near future include the replacement of the Sammy Morris Residence Hall with a new and larger structure (the third Upland residence hall with the Morris name), the construction of the third phase (visual arts) of the fine arts complex, the remodeling of the Ayres Building, the enlargement of Rediger Chapel/ Auditorium, and the building of a student activity center.[13]

Other new vehicles for institutional fund-raising and public relations have included the reactivated William Taylor Foundation and a series of videotapes. In 1988 the new William Taylor Foundation[14] became the planned giving division of the institution's development department. It was directed by Charles Newman until his retirement in 1993, when he was succeeded by Kenneth Smith. Another part of the modern plan for marketing Taylor was the development of videos primarily for use in public-relations efforts including those of the Admissions, Alumni, and Development Offices. Significant among these have been "A Charge to Keep" and "A Purpose to Serve" (produced by Dale Sloat) on the

Jere Truex was seven years old when polio struck leaving him quadriplegic and unable to breathe on his own. When his parents were told that he would live only a few years, they refused to accept the prognosis. A year later, Jere returned to school. "My parents really pushed [my] education," Truex later reflected. When he enrolled at Taylor in 1964, he attended classes via an intercom system with his mother Maxine acting as a secretary. Four years later, Jere graduated and Maxine was awarded an honorary bachelor's degree from Taylor.

Until his death in 1996, Jere was one of the longest surviving post-polio respiratory quadriplegics. "I...believe that God...blessed me through what we would call an 'affliction,'" Jere stated, and then added, " I'm grateful that he gave me a family that helped bring me through all this and that He sees fit to use my weakness in at least some small way to help others."

Taylor heritage, and "Against the Wind" (produced by Barry Pavesi) which tells the inspiring story of Taylor employee Jere Truex, a 1968 magna cum laude graduate of Taylor and a quadriplegic.[15]

By most objective standards of measurement the marketing campaign of the past decade has been very successful. Even with the introduction of the higher admission standards in the mid-1980s, the number of freshman and transfer applications increased from 867 in 1984 to 2011 in 1994.[16] Similarly increasing in this same ten-year period were the number of total students from 1473 to 1831 (see Figure V, chapter 6) and the number of graduates from 309 to 387.[17] The alumni responded especially well to the installation of one of their own as president; the number of their dependents enrolled as students increased from 52 in 1985 to 252 in 1991, and the percentage contributing funds to their alma mater grew from 18% in 1983-84 to 45% in 1993-94.[18] The number of contributors enrolled as President's Associates (those giving $1000 or more per year) enlarged from 151 in 1985 to 383 in 1991, and total giving grew from $1,895,483 in 1983-84 to $5,363,715 in 1993-94. Also increasing was the university endowment (see Figure IX), which since the late 1970s has been managed by Kahn Brothers Investment Firm of New York City.

FIGURE VIII

Degrees Granted
1971-1995

Upland Campus
(A.B., B.S., and B.M.)(A.A.)

	(A.B., B.S., and B.M.)	(A.A.)
1971-72	313	
1972-73	275	
1973-74	298	
1974-75	292	
1975-76	270	0
1976-77	262	2
1977-78	257	11
1978-79	289	10
1979-80	301	22
1980-81	300	9
1981-82	325	12
1982-83	280	18
1983-84	309	18
1984-85	268	13
1985-86	273	9
1986-87	278	10
1987-88	268	8
1988-89	291	8
1989-90	332	9

	Upland Campus		**Fort Wayne Campus**	
	(A.B., B.S., and B.M.)	(A.A.)	(A.B. and B.S.)	(A.A.)
1990-91	344	3		
1991-92	407	6		
1992-93	333	9	55*	17
1993-94	387	5	57	9
1994-95	372	7	34	4
	7324	189	146	30

During the first year following the merger with Summit Christian College, the Fort Wayne graduates could elect to receive a Taylor or a Summit degree.

FIGURE IX

Taylor University Endowment
1970-1995

1970	$ 728,814
1971	764,051
1972	887,636
1973	841,116
1974	1,432,731
1975	1,522,038
1976	1,728,298
1977	1,731,057
1978	1,657,056
1979	1,786,763
1980	1,981,707
1981	2,238,873
1982	2,296,975
1983	3,143,823
1984	3,191,119
1985	4,534,231
1986	5,998,434
1987	6,996,689
1988	7,448,376
1989	8,321,006
1990	8,718,649
1991	9,490,632
1992	10,209,262
1993*	12,702,634
1994	14,784,137
1995	19,234,373

Beginning with 1993 these figures identify the combined endowment of Taylor University Upland and Taylor University Fort Wayne.

During the decade ending in 1993-94 on the Upland campus the physical plant increased from 27 to 33 facilities with its book value growing from $18,601,329 to $35,064,853; however, the institutional debt in this period also expanded, growing from $5,226,819 to $8,367,701. Educational and general expenses (i.e., total costs excluding dining commons, residence halls, and bookstore operations) which had been $8,967,700 in 1983-84 reached $20,853,583 in 1993-94. The total 1994-95 budget was $28,400,000. Of course, a significant part of these financial increases reflected inflationary changes. This is seen also in the doubling of the annual student cost for tuition, room and board, and fees from $7156 in 1983-84 to $14,450 in 1993-94.[19]

With the growing popularity of Taylor with its evangelical Protestant constituency and the college's ability to attract increasingly able students came an enhanced reputation within the educational community. Although the *U.S. News and World Report* in its annual edition of *America's Best Colleges* (based upon its survey of college and university administrators) had cited Taylor as early as 1983, the university regularly made this listing after the mid-1980s (e.g. #10 in 1992, #7 in 1994, and #6 in 1995 among Midwestern liberal arts colleges). Typically this survey and that in the magazine's more recent *Colleges: Best Buys* edition scored Taylor high on student satisfaction, student selectivity, academic reputation, student retention and graduation rates, faculty commitment to teaching, and educational quality-to-cost ratio, and less high on academic and financial resources. Also, beginning in the late 1980s Taylor began to appear on the Templeton Foundation Honor Roll acknowledging colleges "that encourage the development of strong moral character among [their] students." On its 1989 list, Taylor was one of three (with Notre Dame and Wheaton) institutions (out of over 700 suggested) receiving the highest recognition. *Peterson's Competitive Colleges* listed Taylor for the first time in its 1993-94 edition. This guide identifies colleges which traditionally attract the most accomplished high school students.[20]

2. AN ENHANCEMENT OF THE GLOBAL VISION

Especially since the late nineteenth century when the name of William Taylor became associated with the college, Taylor University has sought to promote a globalmindedness on the part of its students. Added to this earlier interest—which was largely motivated by concerns for missionary outreach—is the more recent realization that diplomatically, economically, and in terms of communication and transportation, the earth has become a global village. Furthermore the institution increasingly came to realize that it must define "global" not only in terms of the furthest corners of the earth but also in a way that includes the full range of people groups in its own geographic region.

As the modern institution sought to broaden its sense of mission, it faced two realities: 1) the geographic isolation of its location, and 2) the cultural homogeneity of its students and general constituency. With each of these factors there were obvious advantages. A relatively remote location facilitates concentration on the primary task of study and reflection and aids in the development of community. Also, in an ultimately important sense homogeneity within this community is exactly what the institution seeks, for ideally "A Christian college is a community of Christian believers, both teachers and students, who are dedicated to the search for an understanding of the divine Creator, the universe which he has created, and the role which each creature should fill in His universe."[21] Such similar-minded students can be mutually encouraging in the realization of their noble goals, and their commonness aids in the development of life-long friendships and even the finding of a life-long mate. What the college sought to do then was to retain the advantages of its rural location and homogeneous student body while finding ways to reduce the limitations of each.

> *A Christian college is a community of Christian believers, both teachers and students, who are dedicated to the search for an understanding of the divine Creator, the universe which he has created, and the role which each creature should fill in His universe.*

Chapters eight and nine describe many of the ways in which the institution has sought to develop the global-mindedness of the students (e.g. the many January interterm and semester-long off-campus courses, academic programs, and mission opportunities; the cross-cultural general education requirement; the international studies major; and the Internet computer system). Similar developments of note have included the institutional membership in the Cincinnati Council on World Affairs (CCWA) and the increasing number of students who have lived abroad. Since 1972, under the leadership of faculty representatives Dwight Mikkelson, Janet Loy, and Christopher Bennett, Taylor has been an institutional member of the CCWA, a private agency funded by Cincinnati industries and a consortium of small private colleges in the Ohio-Indiana-Kentucky area. The council brings regional authorities—both academians and public policy practitioners—to Cincinnati for general lectures and then sends them to the campuses of the member institutions for presentations to selected classes and meetings.

The Upland college's greatest recent success in its effort to recruit a more culturally diverse student body has been the growth in enrollment of students from overseas missionary families. After Dale Sloat, a veteran missionary to Brazil, joined the Taylor development staff as a public relations/media specialist in 1982, he and his wife, Bonnie, began a support group (Mu Kappa) for "missionary kids" (MKs) or "third-culture" students. The program grew rapidly and in 1985 inspired James Lauer, a traveling representative for the Wycliffe Bible Translators, to found similar organizations on other campuses. Serving under the Barnabas Mission, an organization devoted specifically to providing support to the missionary community in general, Lauer became the full-time director of the Mu Kappa network which by 1995 numbered 42 chapters in United States colleges. In significant part because of its reputation as the founding campus of Mu Kappa, Taylor increasingly became the college

MuKappa.

of choice for MKs from evangelical missions organizations. The Taylor chapter membership reached 120 by 1994-95. The experiences and perspectives of the MKs enriched the learning environment for the other students, and their work ethic led them as a group to achieve high academic success.

Other developments aiding the recruitment of "third culture" students have been the summer missions conferences and training sessions in the 1980s and 1990s. These include the aforementioned WGM and OMS annual conferences; the "Missionary Kids Personnel Pre-field Experience" (a two-week pre-field orientation for teachers and houseparents in missionary schools), sponsored by Christian Schools International, Interaction Incorporated, Missionary Internship, and Taylor University; and the International Conference on Computing and Missions for missions data processors. Also significant has been the growing number of missionaries-in-residence (e.g. five in 1994-95), mission-supported or self-supporting missionaries living in the larger community and working actively with the MKs and other students.[22]

Taylor has always greatly valued its international students and at least since the Lehman administration has actively sought to increase its American minority population. In the early 1980s the trustees stated as one of their goals for the 1980s "to restore a broader cosmopolitan climate by emphasizing multicultural attitudes and programs for minorities and students from various other cultures." Many missionary alumni, trustees, and faculty have assisted international students in studying at Taylor (e.g. alumnus Bishop Ralph Dodge with William Humbane of Mozambique and Paul Kasambira of Zimbabwe, both of whom earned doctoral degrees after leaving Taylor; trustee Marta Gabre-Tsadick with Hanna and Kidan Alemishat and Mahedere Mulgeta of Ethiopia; trustee LaRita Boren with many Bahamian students; and Don Odle with Pamela Gu of mainland

A Songfest of Spirituals.

China). In recent years the countries with the single largest number of students in the International Students Organization have been Singapore and the Bahamas.[23] The *Taylor Magazine* long has had a "Global Taylor" section in its alumni news, and the feature stories of Editor Cleveland and his successors gave major emphasis to minority and international students and mission activities. Another—and related—major emphasis of the *Taylor Magazine* articles was how handicapped and other students, alumni, and trustees struggled—oftentimes heroically—with traumatic and life-changing experiences.[24]

As the Admissions Office increased its efforts in minority recruitment, the Student Develoment Office created the position of multicultural services coordinator in the mid-1980s, the minority student organization reorganized as AHANA (Africans, Hispanics, Asians, and Native Americans) in 1993, and the minority enrollment grew from 55 in 1990 to 115 (American Indian or Alaskan native, 5; Asian or Pacific islander (Oriental), 47; Black, non-Hispanic, 39; and Hispanic, 24) by 1994. Nevertheless the institutional leaders were becoming increasingly aware that there were real limits to the size of the minority population that they could—or perhaps even should—seek to attract to a rural campus in an area (eastern Grant County) whose population base was nearly 100% Caucasian. Throughout its history, the institution had sent out its alumni as missionaries. Perhaps now, the school leaders thought, it was time for the institution, itself, to go out from Upland to minister to a broader base of students than its recent population of mostly 18-22-year-old, white, residential and increasingly elite students.[25]

From the start of his administration Kesler had identified as one of his goals the strengthening of the institutional financial base so as to make Taylor accessible for qualified, worthy students regardless of family income. "I feel a strong responsibility to the egalitarian roots of Taylor," he said. "Traditionally Taylor had encouraged its students to enter the helping professions (e.g. the ministry, missions, teaching, social work) but," Kesler lamented, "these people now found it difficult to obtain the finances to send their children to an increasingly expensive Taylor." "Diversity" therefore became a key word in Kesler's thinking of whom Taylor should serve; he wanted neither economic nor ethnic factors to limit access to a Taylor education. Increasingly he talked about his "Vision for Taylor University," an exposition which he developed from the Taylor Mission Statement.[26] One of the three major Kesler vision statement goals was "Taylor education and experience should be made accessible to all worthy and qualified students regardless of socioeconomic background."[27] This goal was partially realized through the Singapore program (see chapter eight) and the enlarged commitment to enrolling minority, international, and handicapped students on the Upland campus. In 1991 the trustees adopted resolutions supporting both the Kesler vision statement and a 12-page "Plan for Actualization" of the statement, with the latter prepared by the board's Long-Range Planning Committee. The Plan for Actualization specifically called for acquiring an urban satellite campus,[28] and during the next year Taylor officials considered sites in Indianapolis, Fort Wayne, South Bend, and Gary. While the motivation for adding an urban campus included a sense of mission, it is important to note that no less important was a sense of self-interest. As the trustees looked ahead to the next century they saw fewer traditional 18-22-year-old students and more nontraditional students, and they envisioned a time when the planned-for urban campus would have a larger enrollment than would the Upland campus. Therefore the search for a satellite college represented in part an effort to protect the future viability of the university by diversifying its program offerings and clientele.[29]

The major emphasis upon interacting with the larger world did not mean that the university neglected its relationship with the Upland-Grant County community. Especially significant as local ambassadors were Chancellor Rediger, the Development and University

> *Taylor education and experience should be made accessible to all worthy and qualified students regardless of socioeconomic background.*
> - *Jay Kesler*

Relations Offices, the local service divisions of the Taylor World Outreach programs (see chapter nine), the many faculty and students providing ministry services in area churches, and local trustee LaRita Boren and her husband, Leland. The Borens, the only major entrepreneurs in the Upland area, strongly identified with both the college and the community, and when they built their new Avis Corporation Building, they designed it with a large meeting room for the use of community and campus groups. Also, upon the celebration in 1993 of Taylor's 100th year in Upland, the university worked with the community to purchase and relocate from Muncie the Upland train depot (through which many early twentieth-century students passed when traveling between home and college) to serve as a local museum. The depot together with the new town hall and library were major developments in the downtown renewal project of Our Town Upland, Inc.[30]

Still one more aspect of the university's increasing effort to relate meaningfully with the general culture needs further discussion here. The faculty in general very much enjoy their students, even while also citing a limitation in the academic environment. While applauding the graciousness, intelligence, and work ethic of the students, many faculty lament what political scientist Stephen Hoffmann has called "a poverty of discourse."[31] While constructive debate does take place in the classroom, it is true that it does not exist to a degree commensurate with the ability level of the students. Several factors contribute to this phenomenon: 1) the students possess limited life experience (almost all of them are in the 18-23 age bracket); 2) the evangelical Protestant environment in which most of them developed typically places greater emphasis on listening to authority figures than on pursuing and expressing independent thought; 3) most of the students share not only similar theological views but also similar socioeconomic backgrounds; thus, the same factors which help to facilitate the high level of community spirit can often limit the valuable interactive learning that takes place between students of widely differing backgrounds.

As previously discussed, university officials do seek to broaden the base for campus discourse by the promotion of cross-cultural awareness, the noteworthy travel/study curriculum, the efforts to create a more diverse student body, and the commitment to intellectual openness. Perhaps they could further these efforts and enlarge the institutional witness at the same time by increasing the effort to schedule on-campus dialogues on important controversial issues with careful spokespersons for views not commonly expressed at Taylor.

3. A Fort Wayne Campus Again

In June of 1991 President Donald Gerig of Summit Christian College of Fort Wayne came to Upland to suggest to Daryl Yost—one of his former parishioners when he was the minister of the Grabill, Indiana, Missionary Church—that representatives of Summit and Taylor begin exploratory talks considering the possibility of merging the two institutions. Shortly thereafter President Kesler and Paul Steiner, Summit board chairman and a Taylor graduate, joined the conversations. Subsequently, in July Yost and Kesler received the permission of the Taylor trustee board executive committee to form a task force to consider the Summit proposal. The Summit negotiating team preferred to call the potential linkage a merger; however, as the talks continued it became evident that what was going to happen was more an acquisition than a merger as Taylor would assume the liabilities ($4,000,000) as well as the assets (nearly $8,000,000) of Summit. Eventually the Taylor officials described the transaction as a "merger-acquisition." At its fall meeting the trustees approved the idea of continuing the negotiations with the idea of consummating the merger if all continued to go well in the negotiations. The plan was that the board would decide at its winter meeting whether to approve the merger that would then take place on July 1, 1992.[32]

Summit Christian College, which until 1989 had been known as Fort Wayne Bible College, had long been one of the most respected Bible colleges in North America. Its problem was in part the problem of the Bible college movement in general, namely that the enrollment growth pattern of the period up to the late 1970s did not continue thereafter. The decline in the number of college-age students was one factor in the enrollment decline, but no less significant was the fact that conservative Protestant church communities that traditionally had viewed the Bible college as the preferred type of higher education for their youth increasingly began to favor the Christian liberal arts colleges and other types of institutions with their broader range of vocational preparation options. The 1989 name change for the Fort Wayne school was an attempt to respond to this changing environment, but even then its major field offerings were limited to Biblical studies, Christian education, Christian counselling, elementary education, management, music, pastoral ministries, and world mission.[33]

When the Fort Wayne institution constructed Witmer Hall as its central facility in 1970, it did so on the assumption that the record enrollments of the previous decade would continue. Yet the enrollment declined from a peak of 562 in

1968 and 558 in 1974 to the 350 range in the mid-1980s. Although there was some recovery—especially with the growth of the older, nontraditional student population, still, Gerig thought, it was "too little, too late considering the debt load we were working with." While Summit was not yet in a desperate financial situation, it had experienced deficit budgets for several years, and its leaders projected that this pattern would not become better. Therefore, they sought a solution that they could negotiate quickly while still operating from a position of relative strength. Steiner saw the Summit options as these: 1) they could close the school and find a buyer for the physical plant or 2) they could merge with a compatible institution. The latter was the preferred option, and Taylor was the preferred institution with which to propose merger because of geographic proximity, the historic relationship between the two schools,[34] and the relative strength of the Upland institution.[35]

When the Fort Wayne institution constructed Witmer Hall as its central facility in 1970, it did so on the assumption that the record enrollments of the previous decade would continue.

The Taylor officials immediately were very interested in the Summit proposal because of their recently expressed desire to acquire an urban campus. The problem was that the Upland officials wanted the merger conversations to be deliberate while the Fort Wayne leaders preferred a quick decision. Complicating this difference was the additional preference of Kesler and Yost to involve the Taylor faculty in the decision-making process because if the merger were to be consummated they would want to have meaningful interaction between the faculties of the two campuses. Ultimately the merger took place on a timetable acceptable to the Fort Wayne officials even though many of the Upland faculty believed that 1) the decision-making process had been cut short, 2) the institution did not possess adequate marketing data on which to base a merger decision, and 3) there had been inadequate thought about program development. The merger issue became the greatest controversy on the Upland campus since the decision a generation earlier (see chapter seven) not to move the entire university back to Fort Wayne. Still once the decision was made, there was a general faculty conviction that "even if the decision-making process had been imperfect, nevertheless the decision may turn out to be a good one, and we must work together to assure that it does."[36] Ultimately, the rationale for merging with Summit Christian College, as presented by Charles Jaggers, who headed the Taylor merger task force, was as follows:

1.   The urban setting provides a base for introducing programs and adding

constituent groups that would be very difficult if not impossible to introduce in Upland. Taylor now can more effectively diversify its student mix by 1) socioeconomic status, 2) age, and 3) race.

2. It helps meet the goals of the long-range plan of the institution.

3. Summit Christian College is not in desperate financial straits. It has some good resources. Its problems are economies of scale and declining demand for the traditional Bible college product. Its enrollments have been dwindling, and with an uncertain future it seeks to do something constructive before the situation becomes critical.

The faculty, staff, and students of Summit Christian College...were very grateful for the much better prospects of long-term survival as an institution of Christian higher education. Yet there was also a sense of sadness at the offical closing of their own Bible college.

4. Taylor has taken steps to contain the financial risk of the merger.

5. The merger opens up some new revenue source possibilities that would not be available otherwise.[37]

The faculty, staff, and students of Summit Christian College looked at the merger with mixed sentiments. In many ways they were very grateful for the much better prospects of long-term survival as an institution of Christian higher education. Yet there was also a sense of sadness at the official closing of their own Bible college. These mixed sentiments were apparent at the climactic Alumni Day program at the end of the school year in May, 1992, when the alumni gathered to commemorate in a moving presentation, that seemed part funeral and part wedding, the nearly century-long history of the institution that founder Joseph Ramseyer had called "A vine of God's own planting." The

Students leaving a chapel service in Founder's Hall.

next part of this section is a summary of the history of that one vine that now was to be grafted into another.

Summit Christian College began as Bethany Bible Institute in the oversized house of Mr. and Mrs. B. P. Lugibihl of Bluffton, Ohio, in 1895, two years after Taylor University had relocated from Fort Wayne to Upland. The original teachers in the Bethany school were Joseph P. Ramseyer and Daniel Y. Schultz.

B.P. Lugibihl

Founder and
Business Manager

Joseph
Ramseyer

Founder and
President

Ramseyer served as presiding officer of both the denomination and the school for over three decades, until his death in 1944.

Ramseyer (1869-1944), a Defenseless Mennonite minister, traveled widely in the late nineteenth century among the Mennonite churches proclaiming the major emphases of the new Christian and Missionary Alliance, an evangelistic and missionary movement begun in 1881 by Canadian Presbyterian minister A. B. Simpson. Primary among the teachings of both the Alliance and Ramseyer was the importance of foreign missionary activity. The Lugibihls and Schultz had studied at the Alliance's Nyack Bible Institute near New York City. The Nyack Institute and Moody Bible Institute in Chicago had begun in the 1880s as the first two Bible schools in North America. When in 1904 enrollment in the Bluffton school reached thirty-six, the institution's eighteen-room structure proved inadequate, and the leaders began to explore the possibility of building a larger school on another site. Meanwhile, also in 1904, the leaders changed the name of the school to The Bible School of the Missionary Church Association in recognition of their affiliation with the new denomination which Ramseyer and others had organized in 1898 as a split from the Defenseless Mennonite Church.[38]

Lugibihl, Ramseyer, and Schultz joined with William Egle, a former preacher in the Missionary Church who lived in Fort Wayne, and David and Henry Roth, preacher-farmer brothers from the Grabill Missionary Church north of Fort Wayne, to search for a new city for the school. After examining possible locations in Kansas, Nebraska, and Illinois, the group examined several Fort Wayne sites including the old Taylor University property in the western section of the city and the site of what is now the Lutheran College of Health Professions on Fairfield Avenue. Finally they accepted the offer of a 4 1/2 acre oak and hickory grove on South Wayne Avenue four blocks beyond the southern terminal of the streetcar line, at a price of $1,800.[39]

Plans for the school and its sponsoring denomination developed quickly. Schultz designed the first school building (later called Schultz Hall), and classes began meeting in it during the winter term of 1905. The courses, largely reflecting the standard curriculum of the early twentieth century Bible schools, emphasized the English Bible, evangelism, missions, Christian education, rhetoric, music, English grammar, and—in reflection of the German-speaking background of most of the early students—German grammar. The school enrolled seventy-three students in its first semester, and most of these, like most of the Bluffton students, had German

Mennonite names such as Amstutz, Baumgartner, Bixler, Burkey, Diller, Eicher, Goldsmith, Grabill, Klopfenstein, Lehman, Leightner, Leichty, Moser, Nofzinger, Oyer, Regier, Rupp, Sprunger, Stauffer, Steiner, Stuckey, Wagler, Welty, Yaggy, and Zeigler. In 1904, the Missionary Church Association established its headquarters in Fort Wayne, and a year later the denomination organized the First Missionary Church of Fort Wayne. The new congregation met in the Bible school chapel until 1921 when it moved into its own structure across the street.[40]

The leaders of the Bluffton school continued as the leaders of the new institution in Fort Wayne. Lugibihl served as the business manager for most of the years from the move until 1916. Schultz served as the superintendent, or general administrator, from 1904 to 1911 at which time he became a field representative. The catalog listed Ramseyer as a Bible preacher; however, he always spent much of his time off-campus on preaching and evangelistic tours. Mrs. (Macy) Ramseyer served as a music teacher, and Mrs. (Bertha) Lugibihl managed the dining hall.[41]

The personality of Joseph Ramseyer vitally influenced the Bible school for its first four decades. He served as the spiritual leader from the beginning. Then, with the departure of Schultz in 1911, he became general superintendent (later called president). Since he had also become president of the denomination in 1900, he served as presiding officer of both the denomination and the school for over three decades, until his death in 1944. His function as college leader, however, was symbolic and spiritual rather than practical and administrative. When he was on campus, he spoke at chapel, to some of the Bible classes, and on other special occasions; he gave counsel to individual students; and in general by word and example, he created a tone which characterized the institution throughout its history.

Ramseyer believed that intellectual knowledge should never be valued above spiritual illumination because one can never acquire the most important knowledge apart from instruction by the Spirit of God. Therefore, the Bible institute educational process was designed to produce holy students as well as students who were knowledgeable about holy things. Additionally, Ramseyer taught by example. His humble and gracious personality, dignified manner, serious study of the Bible, and intensely pietistical approach to the Christian

Daniel Y. Schultz

Founder and Superintendent

Ramseyer believed that intellectual knowledge should never be valued above spiritual illumination because one can never acquire the most important knowledge apart from instruction by the Spirit of God.

Safara Witmer

Safara Witmer was the first
graduate of Taylor to serve as
president of the Fort Wayne
school. The other Taylor alumnus
to become president of the Fort
Wayne institution was Witmer's
son-in-law, Timothy Warner.

experience were qualities impressionable students tried to imitate. He was especially effective in teaching by example through the evangelistic tours which consumed much of his adult life; and when he did return to campus, it was primarily to perform for the faculty and students the same preaching and counseling services offered to others on his travels. His speaking engagements were the primary focus of his personal diary. Even when he was talking about the institute, he rarely mentioned any school activity or business other than his sermons and lectures there. Mrs. Ramseyer's claim in her biography of her husband that he "always kept in vital touch with its [the Bible school's] work" suggests that Ramseyer did not participate in day-to-day administrative decisions. In terms of function as opposed to title, he was the school evangelist and public relations agent; if he did not raise large amounts of money, he did attract a large number of students.[42]

One could describe the theological orientation of the early twentieth-century institution as evangelical, pietistical, and moderately Arminian (historically, however, the majority of Bible schools have emphasized a modified Calvinism), with some continuing Mennonite influences. Although the school has always held a doctrinal statement, it has emphasized a desire to "lay as much stress on the Christian character of the messenger as upon the orthodox correctness of his message." Nevertheless, staff members who refused to sign the institution's doctrinal statement—as did two men in 1923—thereby placed in jeopardy their continuing employment. Also, Professor D. H. P. Welton was reappointed in 1912 on the condition that he "refrain from teaching his strong Calvinistic views." The school was not a fundamentalist institution in that it did not participate directly in the twentieth-century struggles between Protestant conservatives and Protestant liberals; however, it shared many of the views of the fundamentalists and at times expressed such an orientation. For example, in the 1930s, the governing board chose not to select a prospective board member because he was associated with Bluffton College (Ohio), "it being felt by our constituency that Bluffton College has the stigma of modernism upon it."[43]

If Ramseyer was the spiritual father of the school, Safara A. Witmer (1899-1962) was its intellectual leader. Witmer was born and raised in the northern part of Allen County approximately fifteen miles from Fort Wayne. His parents were of Defenseless Mennonite heritage and joined those who followed Joseph E. Ramseyer at the turn of the century. Witmer's father was one of the earliest students of the Fort Wayne Bible Training School, and Witmer himself graduated from the school in 1922. He briefly served as a minister in Canada and as an advanced undergraduate student at Taylor University before returning to the Bible school.[44] Witmer spent most of his adult life at the Fort Wayne institution. He served as instructor (1924-32), pastor of the across-the-street First Missionary Church (1932-35), dean (1935-43) and, after a two-year stint as a military chaplain in the Second World War, president of the college (1945-58).[45]

Witmer was a serious scholar. In 1951, he earned his Ph.D. degree from the University of Chicago where he studied under such educators as Norman Burns and Manning Pattilo, whose respect and friendship he earned. As an instructor and an academic leader, Witmer insisted that a Bible education not be a simplistic one that avoided facing difficult questions. As an administrator, he was a diligent worker who expected similar efforts from others.[46]

Given his fertile and expansive mind, it is not surprising that during his administration.... [Witmer] broadened the base of intellectual inquiry at the institution by changing its status from that of a diploma-granting Bible institute to that of a four-year degree-granting Bible college.

Unlike Ramseyer, Witmer had wide-ranging interests and talents. He pursued athletics, horticulture, astronomy, photography, and flying with both participatory and intellectual enthusiasm. Given his fertile and expansive mind, it is not surprising that during his administration he broadened the base of intellectual inquiry at the institution by changing its status from that of a diploma-granting Bible institute to that of a four-year degree-granting Bible college.[47]

In the early years, the institute limited its curriculum to instruction in Bible and such subjects as could be directly useful in evangelistic programs (e.g., music, communication). Gradually, liberal arts graduates such as Witmer replaced less well educated preachers as instructors and administrators and began to emphasize that students could acquire a better education and be more effective in their Christian vocations if they supplemented their Bible knowledge with work in general education. Accordingly, the college slowly broadened its course offerings until, during Witmer's presidency in 1949, it formally adopted a liberal arts core curriculum as a requirement for all students.[48]

As an educational institution, a Bible college is somewhere between a Bible institute and a Christian liberal arts college. Like a Bible institute, its students all earn a major in Biblical literature and theology and all experience as a part of their academic program a significant applied component in practical Christian service. Like the Christian liberal arts college, however, the Bible college enrolls all of its students in a series of general education courses. The Christian liberal arts college student has a wider choice of general education courses and of disciplines to choose for a major; however, the academic experience of a Bible college student is very similar to that of a student who majors in religion in a Christian liberal arts school. The Bible college curriculum is four years long and results in a B.A. degree, whereas the Bible institute program is shorter—frequently three years—and results in a diploma.[49]

In the year after the institute became a college, the newly organized Division of General Education offered fourteen liberal arts courses; by 1975 the school listed sixty courses in the liberal arts and seventeen in education.[50] To some it appeared that in the 1950s the college was moving—however hesitatingly—in the direction of becoming a Christian liberal arts school when it added a few major programs which were not historically associated with a Bible college curriculum: missionary nursing; music; and teacher education programs in elementary education, music, social studies and speech. Soon, however, the school dropped its education programs in social studies and speech, and by the mid-1960s its continuing identification as a Bible college appeared certain. In recent years the most popular of the nontraditional majors has been elementary education which in 1975 enrolled ninety-five of the 605 students; only Christian education (141) and pastoral ministries (117) attracted more majors that year.[51] One significant part of the late twentieth-century curriculum has been the department of correspondence studies. Dean Witmer and Professor Loyal R. Ringenberg had introduced a limited number of correspondence courses as early as the 1930s; however, the correspondence department did not begin to operate on a large scale (e.g. 2050 students in 1978) until the school purchased the correspondence program of Judson College (Illinois) in 1970.[52]

It was during the Witmer administration that the college became especially concerned about improving the quality of the academic program. Witmer worked actively as one of the original leaders of the American Association of Bible Institutes and Bible Colleges (AABIBC), which was founded in 1947 to be an accrediting agency as well as a source of communication for Bible schools. Fort Wayne was one of the first eighteen schools in the collegiate division to be accredited by the association, and by 1976 the organization claimed in its membership 61 of the 250 Bible schools in North America. By that time, the United States Office of Education had recognized it as the single accrediting agency in the field of Bible or undergraduate theological education. Shortly after the Bible college received AABIBC accreditation, Indiana University and similar institutions began to announce that they would accept transfer credit on a regular basis from the school. Also during this period, the college had become the first Bible institution to have its teacher training program fully accredited by a state department of education.[53]

Just as Witmer worked diligently to upgrade the quality of education at the Fort Wayne school, he also became increasingly interested in efforts to improve the quality of education at Bible institutes and colleges throughout the

In the late 1950s and early 1960s Witmer generally was recognized as the leading authority on Bible institututes and Bible colleges; some even referred to him as "Mr. Bible College."

continent. In his doctoral dissertation research he had studied higher educational accreditation, and when he resigned from the presidency of the Fort Wayne school, it was to serve as the first full-time executive secretary of the AABIBC. He made this career change in part on the advice of John Dale Russell, director of the Commission of Higher Education of the U.S. Office of Education, who suggested that he could do more for the Fort Wayne institution as executive secretary of the national association than by remaining at the school.[54]

In his new position, Witmer traveled widely to visit many of the Bible institutes and Bible colleges in North America. He both criticized freely what he saw as major weaknesses in the schools and also served as their leading spokesperson to the general public which he felt too little appreciated the significance of what they were achieving.[55] While Witmer acknowledged that the schools were understaffed, undersupported, inadequate in their ability to integrate the general education disciplines with Biblical values, and lacking in academic respectability and creativity, he also argued with logic and passion that higher education in general should be increasingly accepting of the Bible college philosophy of education as a viable option.[56] He lamented, "While Bible College education ranks first in values...it is frequently regarded as inferior and only partially evolved as an acceptable type of college education." Additionally, he argued that since the Bible college offers both a Bible education and a college education, it provides an integrated world view in contrast to much of modern education which, because of its compartmentalized approach to education, gives no overarching meaning to the sum of its curricular parts. In the late 1950s and early 1960s Witmer generally was recognized as the leading authority on Bible institutes and Bible colleges; some even referred to him as "Mr. Bible College."[57]

Perhaps emboldened by the reputation of both the institution and Witmer in the Bible college movement, the college leaders decided to apply for regional accreditation—a step without precedent for a Bible school. The North Central Association first reviewed the school in the 1950s but did not give it membership; however, the accrediting organization granted the school candidacy status in the spring of 1964, marking the first time that it had thus acknowledged a Bible school. Consequently, other Bible colleges within the geographical boundaries

Schultz Hall.

of the North Central Association viewed the Fort Wayne application as a test case, the results of which would significantly influence their future decisions on whether to seek regional accreditation. On each review the North Central Association agreed to examine the Fort Wayne school as a Bible college and not as a liberal arts college. The Association report granting candidate status commented favorably on the physical plant, the faculty and student morale, and the ability of the alumni to perform well in graduate studies at Indiana University. On the other hand, the North Central visitors called for improvements in the general education program, increases in the library holdings and faculty salaries, and reductions in the teaching loads. After due deliberation the association in 1969 chose not to grant accreditation to the Bible college. Ultimately the Fort Wayne school was to await sixteen more years to receive this coveted recognition.[58]

The campus plant expanded as enrollment needs dictated and the economic conditions of the institute allowed. The large original building, Schultz Hall, housed the entire school until the appearance of Bethany Hall in 1930. Located immediately west of Schultz Hall on the original five-acre tract, the new building took its name from the predecessor institution, Bethany Bible Institute of Bluffton, Ohio. Bethany Hall is a 40' X 120' three-story brick and sandstone structure and to this day remains one of the most stately buildings on the campus. As was the case with Schultz Hall, Bethany Hall at the outset was a multipurpose building housing classrooms, music practice rooms, the laundry, a reception room, faculty offices and student residence rooms.[59]

The next major campus building was constructed in 1942. The original plan for the Founders Memorial Building called for it to be only a small music hall, but when actually built, the $110,000 structure contained a gymnasium and dining hall as well as music practice rooms and a 500-seat auditorium.[60]

FIGURE X

Resident Enrollment at Fort Wayne Bible College/ Summit Christian College[61]

1904	66	1934	135	1964	468
1905	82	1935	159	1965	520
1906	69	1936	155	1966	505
1907	50	1937	158	1967	526
1908	46	1938	160	1968	562
1909	52	1939	162	1969	502
1910	45	1940	176	1970	499
1911	43	1941	206	1971	490
1912	50	1942	209	1972	533
1913	65	1943	231	1973	545
1914	62	1944	242	1974	558
1915	71	1945	306	1975	547
1916	61	1946	314	1976	554
1917	77	1947	279	1977	520
1918	80	1948	308	1978	510
1919	75	1949	288	1979	473
1920	65	1950	268	1980	484
1921	93	1951	328	1981	450
1922	75	1952	321	1982	463
1923	95	1953	315	1983	433
1924	132	1954	321	1984	405
1925	112	1955	327	1985	356
1926	118	1956	342	1986	355
1927	104	1957	306	1987	377
1928	118	1958	312	1988	384
1929	132	1959	325	1989	406
1930	111	1960	362	1990	385
1931	118	1961	379	1991	425
1932	118	1962	353		
1933	106	1963	408		

The 1960s was a decade of growth for much of higher education, and the experience of Fort Wayne Bible College followed that pattern. Its student body grew from 325 students in 1959 to 562 students just nine years later, and growth in the size of the physical plant kept pace. The president of the school during this period was Jared F. Gerig (1907-). Gerig had served as dean of the school from 1945 to 1950, and as president of the sponsoring denomination from 1952 to 1958. During much of the post-World War II period, people with Gerig

Witmer Hall.

names (see footnote 74 to this chapter) or family connections provided much of the leadership for the college. Such extensive familial relationships can exist only in a family-operated school or in a small denominational college such as this one.[62]

With the completion of the Founders Memorial Building, the school had no remaining space for plant expansion. By mid-century, the campus, which originally had been located in a rural-like setting at the edge of the city, found itself almost totally surrounded by one of the most exclusive of Fort Wayne's residential areas. Just southwest of the campus, however, lay an undeveloped twenty-two acre section of land, a remnant of what once had been a Miami Indian Reserve granted by the United States government to Chief Jean Baptiste Richardville in 1818. The college completed the purchase of this tract in 1959, and this south campus became the site for the expansion that took place during the Gerig administration.[63]

The development of the south campus included the Lehman Memorial Library (1961), the Lexington Hall for women (1964) and the Witmer Administration/ Classroom Building (1970). The college, which had always adopted a conservative policy toward financing new construction, refused to accept loans or grants from the government even during the educationally generous years of the Johnson Administration. In explaining the refusal of the college to seek federal funds, Gerig stated—in a manner suggestive of the independence and separateness of his denomination forebears, "America's strength was molded from the tough fibers of its private and voluntarily supported educational institutions, and we believe in upholding this tradition."[64]

The construction of the $1.2 million Witmer Administration/Classroom Building in 1970 was a significant achievement. This well-furnished, four-story facility contained administrative offices, sixteen classrooms, laboratories and, beginning in 1976, a studio for the 50,000-watt college radio station, WBCL. Furthermore, the appearance of Witmer Hall allowed the school to convert what had been administrative offices and academic rooms in Schultz Hall and Bethany Hall to residence rooms for an additional one hundred students.[65]

The cocurricular activities have complemented the academic program to a greater extent at the Fort Wayne school than has been the case in most institutions. For example, during the years of the Bible training school and the Bible institute, when religious studies dominated the curriculum, the most important activities were religious in nature. The Student Mission Band began during the first year in Fort Wayne, and involved the entire student body. By the 1920s, gospel teams and similar Christian service activities had become very popular. Guest speakers included missionaries, evangelists and ministers.[66]

After the school became a Bible college in 1950, it gradually began to add some of the activities normally associated with liberal arts institutions. By the 1960s the college program included dramatic productions, student publications, a student education association, a college-community artist series, a Greek language club, social organizations, and intercollegiate debating competition. Additionally, the college continued the several musical groups and the student government organization which it had begun earlier.[67] Intercollegiate athletics began cautiously in the 1950s. The executive committee of the board of trustees urged school officials to schedule contests primarily with "definitely Christian colleges (preferably Bible colleges) and local schools." Above all, the board was anxious to keep the school's involvement in athletics limited to avoid "interfering with the spiritual and educational objectives of the students and the college." The institution joined the National Christian College Athletic Association in 1971. By the 1980s intercollegiate sports included soccer and basketball for men and volleyball and basketball for women.[68]

Throughout its history the college operated from a very meager financial base. As late as the middle 1930s the annual operating budget was in the $20,000 to $25,000 range; however, by the early 1960s this figure had increased to nearly $500,000.[69] Faculty salaries grew from bare subsistence payments in the early years to more moderate levels in the modern period. Originally the school did not guarantee salaries for its workers. It stated maximum salaries and then paid them to the extent possible from the revenues that remained after paying the fixed expenses. Thus the faculty and staff members sometimes did not receive their stated salaries, but later the school tried to meet the deficiency. A typical salary for a major professor in 1912 was $35 per month plus housing. By 1939 a major professor received $1140 a year. At the same time President Ramseyer received an allowance of only one-fourth that amount; such a minimal figure reflected the fact that he spent most of his time away from campus pursuing evangelistic work. When college income was enough to pay more than a minimum salary, the institution might supplement the salaries with end-of-the-year bonus payments of 5 to 45 percent. The Fort Wayne school moved to a system of comprehensive annual contracts in 1951. A major professor in 1963-64 earned $5100; faculty members of similar rank at the time earned $6400 at Taylor University, $6900 at Valparaiso University, and $7400 at Franklin College. By the 1960s the institution provided the faculty with the fringe benefits usually enjoyed by professors in liberal arts colleges.[70]

The increase in student fees closely paralleled the changes in faculty remuneration. During the school's first year in Fort Wayne a student paid $3.50 per week and contributed one hour of work per day. The work requirement continued through World War II while the comprehensive weekly charge increased to $5.50 in 1917 and $9 in 1931. Since 1933, students have paid by the semester, and the comprehensive charge per term has increased from $104 in 1933 to $238 in 1951, $503 in 1960, $1,367 in 1975, and $2,610 in 1989. In 1980 students paid approximately 85% of the cost of their education. While the college has hesitated to accept government aid for itself, it regularly has participated in state and federal student aid programs. Thus the college enrolled in the GI Bill program beginning in the post-World War II years, its students received National Student Defense Loan payments beginning in the late 1950s, and the school participated in the Indiana State Scholarship Commission program and the federal Educational Opportunity Grants Program.[71]

By the 1970s only approximately thirty percent of the students came from the Missionary Church Association; nevertheless, events within the denomination in the 1960s and 1970s significantly influenced the college. The Missionary Church Association nearly merged with the much larger Christian and Missionary Alliance in 1962. The two groups had worked closely throughout the century, and President Ramseyer for many years had been an honorary vice-president of the Alliance. President Gerig and Registrar Herald J. Welty both believed that the proposed merger would have had a distinctly positive effect upon the college enrollment. A sizeable percentage of the Alliance constituency lived in the Midwest, but the denomination did not operate an institution of higher education in the region. The Missionary Church Association membership, however, rejected the proposed merger by a very narrow margin.[72] In 1969 the Missionary Church Association did join with the Mennonite Brethren in Christ denomination, which since 1947 had been known as the United Missionary Church. Unfortunately, this church body had its own college in northern Indiana. As a result, the Bible college and Bethel College of Mishawaka found themselves competing for students from a denomination that scarcely was large enough to support one such institution. In 1973 the new denomination,

Veteran Bible Professor Wesley Gerig in the classroom.

which took the name of the Missionary Church, avoided the difficult decision of selecting one of the institutions as the denominational school and closing the other by changing its relationship with both of them. The Bible college governing board became self-perpetuating; however, in return for designation as an approved denominational college with continued financial support from the denominational budget, the college agreed to elect the president and at least fifty percent of its board members from the membership of the Missionary Church. The relationship between the denomination and the college, therefore, remained close, even if technically unofficial. In the late 1970s the Bible college and Bethel College considered merging but decided against the idea in part because of the desire of the Fort Wayne officials to continue the Bible college mode of operation.[73]

The major developments of the 1980s included 1) the achievement in 1985 of the long-sought regional accreditation by the North Central Association; 2) the 1991 acceptance into membership of the nearly 100-member Christian College Coalition of primarily liberal arts institutions; 3) the 1989 construction—

nearly debt-free—of the Gerig Activities Center,[74] a 23,000-square-foot combination gymnasium and convocation center on the South Campus; 4) the continually increasing popularity of the campus radio station, WBCL; 5) a decline in the relationship between the college and the denomination as some of the Missionary Church members looked with dismay upon both the 1980 hiring of a non-Missionary Church member (Harvey Bostrom, director of development at Trinity College in Illinois) as college president, and also the 1989 replacement of the traditional college name with its clear identification of the Bible college nature of the institution[75]; and 6) the aforementioned decline in enrollment and the budget deficits which led to the decision to propose merger with Taylor.[76]

The ceremonial opening of the Taylor Fort Wayne campus.

Following the July 1, 1992, merger with Summit Christian College, the Taylor officials worked with the Marcon marketing consulting firm of Anderson, Indiana, to determine how the Taylor goals might best blend with the needs and opportunities of the Fort Wayne environment. The resultant 1993 report recommended these functions for the Taylor Fort Wayne campus:

1) Serve a diverse student population, providing a balance of both traditional and nontraditional programs for students of differing age and ethnic groups.

2) Offer a curriculum which emphasizes major programs in directly career-related areas such as business, computer science, criminal justice, elementary and secondary education, nursing, public relations, religion and Bible, social work, and degree completion.

3) Offer courses in the evenings and on weekends to accommodate the non-traditional students.

4) Seek to compete with less expensive institutions such as Indiana-Purdue University at Fort Wayne by offering an appealing combination of academic reputation, religious orientation, friendliness, and job placement.

5) Work to overcome the perception of a quality differential between the Upland and the Fort Wayne campus.[77]

During the first three years in Fort Wayne, the Taylor officials emphasized program development and planning. New majors included psychology (1992, replacing Christian counseling), business (1992, replacing management), criminal justice (1993), public relations (1993), and journalism (1995), with plans for adding approximately one new program per year. Especially noteworthy were these changes and plans: the new criminal justice program initiated by Dean Pitts and developed under the direction of Ronald Powell, former commissioner of corrections for the State of New Hampshire; the hiring of several new African-American faculty and staff members; and the desire to find funds to add a low-cost, one-year, open-enrollment branch (perhaps to be named the Samuel Morris Institute) to serve the needs of academically and economically disadvantaged students. Programs being considered for future introduction include computer science, English, nursing, social work, accounting, and history majors, and a limited graduate curriculum (the institution offered graduate work in education and criminal justice beginning in the summer of 1995). To accommodate the anticipated program growth, the sesquicentennial campaign plan calls for the construction of an academic building linking Witmer Hall with Lehman Library.[78]

Char Binkley

Station Manager
WBCL

On-air studio at WBCL.

The two major programs serving primarily the external public, the correspondence school and the radio station, continued to grow following the merger. The Institute of Correspondence Studies, which underwent extensive revision and updating of its curricular materials after the merger, enrolled approximately 2200 students in 66 courses in 1993, and 2500 students in 73 courses in 1995. WBCL ("We Broadcast Christ's Love") was already a well-developed FM station at the time of the merger. Its estimated 1994 audience of 100,000 gave it, according to the Arbitron ratings, the largest listenership in proportion to its area population (northeastern Indiana, northwestern Ohio, and southeastern Michigan) among non-commerical Christian stations in the United States. Its community-orientation and personalized style have contributed much to its popularity among its primarily Christian adult audience. Beginning broadcasting in 1976, the station came into existence because of the efforts of Fort Wayne Bible College President Timothy Warner and Vice-President for Development Robert Weyeneth. An early station manager was James Schweikart, a Taylor graduate and a former broadcaster with KDKA, Pittsburgh, and WOWO, Fort Wayne. In 1992 WBCL added a 20,000-watt satellite station,

WBCL Fort Wayne 90.3 fm
Northwest Ohio 89.5 fm
Your Christian Music Station

WBCY of Archbold, Ohio. Current general manager, Char Binkley, leads a staff of sixteen full-time and eight part-time employees and envisions a continued enlargement—especially to the south—of the station's broadcast area.[79]

The merger process has not escaped a normal degree of transition pain. Some of the Fort Wayne faculty were not retained. At the time of the merger some of the Upland faculty and students wondered if the Fort Wayne campus was sufficiently academic, and some of the Fort Wayne faculty and students wondered whether the Upland campus was unduly elitist in spirit. By 1995 these attitudes were softening, however, as by then the new Fort Wayne faculty and most of the students had no remembrance of the Summit period. In May of 1993 the Fort Wayne and Upland faculties sharply disagreed on the wisdom of offering a degree completion program at Fort Wayne. Also, in 1994 the Religion department of the two schools resolved their philosophical differences on whether their programs should be academic or professionally-oriented by separating into two departments (Upland's department of Biblical studies, Christian education, and philosophy, and Fort Wayne's department of Christian ministries).[80]

Ultimately, the long-term continuance of the Fort Wayne campus will depend upon the enrollment and budget figures. What has changed in the past three years is seen not so much in the figures as in the development of an infrastructure that hopefully will provide for long-term growth. The fall semester residence enrollment data (i.e., exclusive of the correspondence school registration which in full-time equivalency exceeds the residence enrollment) for the early 1990s (the two years before the merger and the first four years following it) is as follows:

	Head Count	Full Time Equivalency	Full Time Freshman	Full Time Sophomores	Full Time Juniors	Full Time. Seniors
1990-91	385	339				
1991-92	425	363				
1992-93	410	327	135	52	61	47
1993-94	388	311	149	57	42	40
1994-95	423	328	154	58	52	35
1995-96	426	348	160	68	55	42

It is noteworthy that the enrollment remained stable despite a sharp drop in Missionary Church students following the merger. The number of such students which had been approximately 30% of the enrollment during the two decades before the merger dropped to less than 10% in 1995. By 1994 fewer Missionary Church students were studying in Fort Wayne than in Upland. After the merger the denomination declared that Bethel was again its college, and it increasingly encouraged its young people to enroll in the Mishawaka institution. That official support plus the introduction of a nursing program and a degree completion program led to a sharp increase in the enrollment and financial stability at Bethel.

The Fort Wayne campus maintained its enrollment in the first years after merger only by recruiting deferred applicants to the Upland campus with the assurance that they could transfer to the Upland campus if they would first enroll at Fort Wayne. In the fall of 1992 there were 82 Upland applicants enrolled in Fort Wayne. By 1995 the number of applicants to and the retention rate at the Fort Wayne campus had increased sufficiently that the Admissions Offices no longer felt a need to offer the transfer promise as an enrollment incentive.[81]

The annual budget deficits in the years before the merger (i.e., the late 1980s and early 1990s) typically had been approximately $350,000. Financial officer Al Smith expects that the annual deficits on the Fort Wayne campus will be eliminated altogether by 1997. The accumulative $4-million deficit at the merger is being paid by a twenty-year loan from the Taylor Upland endowment.[82]

The addition of the Fort Wayne campus was merely the most dramatic example of the general institutional effort in recent years to broaden the Taylor influence, visibility, and vision. This thrust, of course, was built upon the less rapid but solid progress in the development of the academic and cocurricular programs during the past generation and longer. Despite these changes, both rapid and gradual, the university retains basic elements of continuity with its past. The identification of the college as an evangelical Christian institution of higher education and the determination of its graduates to use their educational experience as a means to serve God and humanity characterizes the Taylor of the mid-1990s just as it had described the institution in earlier times.

[1] TUTM, January 30, 1982, May 21, 1982, October 15, 1982, February 8, 1985, April 19, 1985, June 28, 1985, February 6, 1988.

[2] TUTM, October 15, 1982, February 8, 1985, May 17, 1985, October 25, 1985, February 14, 1986, May 22, 1986; *Taylor Magazine*, Spring, 1986, pp. 14-15, Summer, 1988, p. 9, Fall, 1988, p. 3.

[3] Interview with Wynn A. Lembright, Summer, 1992; interview with Herbert W. Frye, Summer, 1992; interview with Joe W. Lund, Summer, 1992; interview with Timothy A. Nace, Summer, 1992.

[4] Letter, Wynn A. Lembright to author, Fall, 1995; interview with Billie J. Manor, Fall, 1994.

[5] Interview with Joe W. Lund, Summer, 1992; interview with Timothy A. Nace, Summer, 1992; Annual Report of the Office of Student Financial Aid, 1992, p. 6; TUTM, May 17, 1985; *Taylor Magazine*, Summer, 1987, p. 27.

[6] *Taylor Magazine*, Winter, 1985, pp. 3-5, Summer, 1990, p. 9; interview with Thomas G. Beers, Summer, 1992.

[7] Kesler was in high demand as a speaker and participant at evangelical Protestant conferences and meetings. He was less well known outside of the evangelical community and in the academic community in general.

[8] Interview with Jay L. Kesler, Summer, 1995; letter, author to Jay L. Kesler, February 15, 1990.

[9] One model for this type of board member was John McDougall (trustee, 1978-1989, and board chair for three years), who worked for the Ford Motor Company for 47 years, eventually serving as executive vice-president and director. Of him Henry Ford II wrote, "I do not know anyone who has more willingly taken on challenges at home and overseas. I do not know anybody who has given more encouragement to his people on the floor....leadership, after all, comes from the heart." See *Taylor Magazine*, Spring, 1988, pp. 28-31.

[10] TUFM, June 27, 1980, June 28, 1985, February 10, 1994; interview with

Daryl Yost, Summer, 1992; *Taylor Magazine*, Summer, 1983, p. 21; Taylor University Board of Trustees Roster, 1994-95, Taylor University President's Office; Taylor University Board of Trustees Membership Roster History, Taylor University President's Office.

[11] See "The Terrible Toll on College Presidents," *U.S. News and World Report*, December 12, 1994, p. 82.

[12] TUTM, October 21, 1993, January 27, 1994; *Taylor Magazine*, Winter, 1995, pp. 18ff.; interview with Jay L. Kesler, Fall, 1995.

[13] Interview with Jay L. Kesler, Spring, 1995; memo, Daryl R. Yost to the Taylor Faculty and Staff, March 9, 1994.

[14] On the earlier form of the William Taylor Foundation, see chapter five.

[15] TUTM, February 3, 1989, February 14, 1991; *Taylor Magazine*, Summer, 1989, pp. 6-7, December, 1992, p. 6, Summer, 1995.

[16] Unless otherwise noted the data in this section refers to the Upland campus only.

[17] The number of degree recipients in the 1971-1994 period numbered 8844 (8662 bachelors degrees and 182 A.A. degrees), a figure more than double the number of degrees awarded during the first 75 years in the Upland location (see Figure VIII, chapter 10 and Figure VI, chapter 6).

[18] The Taylor alumni (the definition of an alumnus is one earning 25 or more credit hours) numbered 15,000 by 1995, and were very active through their geographic area organizations and otherwise in recruiting students and promoting financial support during the Jay Kesler—George Glass era.

[19] TUTM, May 18, 1979, May 23, 1991; Taylor University Office of Admissions Statistical Report, 1984; *Taylor University Fact Book*, October, 1994, p. 4; Al Smith, Ten Year Statistical Report, President's Office Information Meeting, October 27, 1994; interview with Al Smith, Fall, 1994; interview with Robert C. Gilkison, Fall, 1994; Annual Statistical Reports, Taylor University Records Office.

[20] *U. S. News and World Report*, September 28, 1992, p.125, September 26, 1994, p. 114, October 3, 1994, p. 80, September 18, 1995, p. 140-41, September 25, 1995, p. 98; *Taylor Magazine*, Summer, 1989, p. 3, Winter, 1991, p. 7, December 1992, p. 4; Autumn, 1993, p. 7, Summer, 1990, p. 48, Spring, 1991, p. 3, Summer, 1992, p. 3, TUTM, December 9, 1983, October 20, 1988, May 18, 1989; *Peterson's Competitive Colleges*, 1995-96 (Princeton, 1995), p. 270; *Taylor Echo*, September 23, 1994, p. 1.

[21] Ringenberg, *The Christian College,* p. 215.

[22] *Taylor Echo*, March 3, 1972, p. 1; letter, Dwight L. Mikkelson to author, May 8, 1995; interview with Dale Sloat, Summer, 1992, Summer, 1994; interview with Charles Moore, Fall 1992; *Taylor Magazine*, Winter, 1995, p. 3.

[23] TUTM, October 15, 1982; February 11, 1984, May 25, 1984 *Taylor Magazine*, Fall, 1974, pp. 20-21; Fall/Winter, 1982, pp. 16-17; Spring/Summer, 1984, pp. 4-5; Summer, 1991, p. 5; Fall, 1991, p. 8.

[24] See, for example, *Taylor Magazine*, Spring, 1973, pp. 11-13, Winter, 1975, pp. 3-5, Spring, 1975, pp. 10-13, Winter, 1976, pp. 6-9; Spring, 1980, pp. 14-16. Some of these stories have been expanded into books (e.g. Marta Gabre-Tsadick, *Sheltered By the King*, (Lincoln,Virginia, 1983); Janet Sonnenberg, *Race for Life: The Joel Sonnenberg Story*, (Grand Rapids, 1983); and Becki Conway Sanders and Jim and Sally Conway, *What God Gives When Life Takes: The Story of a Family in Crisis* (Downers Grove, Illinois, 1989).

[25] TUTM, May 23, 1986, *Taylor Magazine*, Fall, 1993, p. 6; *Taylor University Fact Book*, October, 1994, p. 11-12, interview with Jay L. Kesler, Summer, 1995.

[26] The Taylor Mission Statement in its most recent form as amended by the trustees at their meeting of January 27, 1994, reads:

Taylor University is an interdenominational evangelical Christian institution educating men and women for lifelong learning and for ministering the redemptive love of Jesus Christ to a world in need. As a Christian community of students, faculty, staff, and administration committed to the Lordship of Jesus Christ, Taylor University offers postsecondary liberal arts and professional education based upon the conviction that all truth has its source in God.

27 The two other major concerns of the "Vision for Taylor University" were 1) "that Taylor University actualize the intent of the mission statement to the greatest possible degree, given our limited resources," and 2) "that the word 'Christian' as used in 'Christian college' mean more not less to a watching world." See TUTM, October 18, 1991.

28 Other major parts of the Plan for Actualization called for 1) minority, international, and handicapped recruitment programs for employees as well as students, 2) improved assessment programs, 3) additional income to increase faculty salaries and to provide an endowment base to aid the less affluent students, and 4) new campus facilities including a student activity center and a visual arts building. See letter, John Horne to the Board of Trustees, October 7, 1991, and TUTM, October 18, 1991.

29 *Taylor Magazine*, Fall, 1986, pp. 3-6; TUTM, May 23, 1991, October 18, 1991, January 30, 1992; interview with Jay Kesler, Summer, 1995.

30 *Taylor Magazine*, Winter, 1994, p. 6; interview with Leland and LaRita Boren, Summer, 1993.

31 See Stephen P. Hoffmann, "Reflections on the Relationship Between General Education and Civic Education at Taylor," June 29, 1994, Taylor University Archives.

32 Letter, Donald Gerig to author, December 14, 1994; interview with Paul A. Steiner, Fall, 1994; interview with Daryl R. Yost, Summer, 1993; interview with Robert C. Gilkison, Fall, 1994; interview with Al Smith, Fall, 1994; TUTM, July 3, 1991, October 17, 1991.

33 Ringenberg, *Christian College*, pp. 172-73; interview with Wesley L. Gerig, Fall, 1995; *Summit Christian College Catalog*, 1989-91, p. 24; Fort Wayne Bible College, Minutes of the Meetings of the Governing Board, January 26-27, 1989.

34 Traditionally the two institutions reflected an Arminian theological

orientation. Also, especially before the Fort Wayne school offered a baccalaureate degree, many of its graduates transferred to Taylor. The two institutions share 86 mutual alumni with 67 of those holding Taylor baccalaurate degrees. These graduates of the Upland campus include Fort Wayne Bible College presidents Safara Witmer (1929) and Timothy Warner (1950). Letter, William D. Gerig to author, August 29, 1995.

[35] Letter, Donald Gerig to author. December 14, 1994; interview with Paul Steiner, Fall, 1994; Summit Christian College, Minutes of the Meetings of the Governing Board, September 27, 1991.

[36] TUFM, February 13, 1992; "Merger Agreement Between Taylor University and Summit Christian College," June 1, 1992 (to take effect July 1, 1992), Taylor University President's Office; interview with Jay L. Kesler, Summer, 1995; interview with Robert V. Gortner, Summer, 1994; interview with William A. Fry, Summer, 1994; interview with Kenneth D. Swan, Summer, 1993.

[37] The larger text of this case for the merger-acquisition appears in *Taylor Magazine*, Spring, 1992, p. 4.

[38] In 1948, the Defenseless Mennonite Church assumed its present name, the Evangelical Mennonite Church.

[39] Walter H. Lugibihl and Jared F. Gerig, *The Missionary Church Association* (Berne, Indiana, 1950), pp. 19-55; Ringenberg, *The Christian College*, p. 158; MS Missionary Church Association, Minutes of the Meetings of the Governing Committee, August 29, 1898 (Missionary Church archives, Fort Wayne, Indiana); Joseph E. Ramseyer, "Diary," July 5, 11-12, 1904 (Taylor University Fort Wayne archives); Macy Garth Ramseyer, *Yet Speaking: Joseph E. Ramseyer* (Fort Wayne, 1945), pp. 86-91, 93; William C. Ringenberg, "Development and Division in the Mennonite Community in Allen County, Indiana," *Mennonite Quarterly Review*, April, 1976, pp. 129-30. Also see Harry M. Shuman, et. al., *After Fifty Years: A Record of God's Working Through the Christian and Missionary Alliance* (Harrisburg, Pennsylvania, 1939). Two of the best accounts of the early Bible college movement are Safara A. Witmer, *The Bible College Story: Education with Dimension* (New York, 1962), and Virginia Lieson Brereton, *Training God's Army: The American Bible School, 1880-1940* (Bloomington, Indiana, 1990).

[40] Ringenberg, "Development and Division in the Mennonite Community in Allen County, Indiana," pp. 129-30; William C. Ringenberg, "A Brief History of Fort Wayne Bible College," *Mennonite Quarterly Review*, April, 1980, p. 138.

[41] Ramseyer, *Yet Speaking*, pp. 96, 100; Lugibihl and Gerig, *Missionary Church Association*, pp. 44-49; Missionary Church Association, Minutes of the meetings of the Governing Committee, May 4 and August 9, 1915; Ramseyer, "Diary," January 2-5, 24, 26, 1905.

[42] Lugibihl and Gerig, *Missionary Church Association*, pp. 52-53; S. A. Witmer, "If J. E. Ramseyer Had Lived in Times Like These," *The Missionary Worker*, June 15, 1962, pp. 6-7; Ramseyer, *Yet Speaking*, p. 12; Ramseyer, "Diary," 1893-1935.

[43] *Fort Wayne Bible Institute Catalog*, 1942-43, p. 5; Ramseyer, "Diary," May 25-26, 1923; Missionary Church Association Governing Committee Meetings, March 6, 1912, and May 28, 1935.

[44] Timothy M. Warner, ed., *S. A. Witmer: Beloved Educator* (Wheaton, Illinois, 1970), pp. 7-17; *Vision Magazine*, June-July 1957, p. 1.

[45] *Ibid.*

[46] Warner, Witmer, pp. 7-13.

[47] *Ibid.*, pp. 14-17.

[48] *Fort Wayne Bible Training School Catalog*, 1905-06, pp. 6-10; *Fort Wayne Bible Training School Catalog*, 1926-27, pp. 18-24; *Fort Wayne Bible Institute Catalog*, 1942-43, pp. 15-37; *Fort Wayne Bible Institute Catalog*, 1948-49, pp. 29-35; Fort Wayne Bible Institute, MS Minutes of the Meetings of the Board of Trustees, March 31, 1949 (Taylor University Fort Wayne archives).

[49] Safara A. Witmer, "A New Form of American Education," in Frank E. Gaebelein, ed. *Christian Education in a Democracy* (New York, 1951), pp. 158-62, 176; S. A. Witmer, "Bible College Education," *School and Society*, Oct. 16, 1954, pp. 113-15.

[50] *Fort Wayne Bible College Catalog*, 1951-52, pp. 23-40; *Fort Wayne Bible College Catalog*, 1975-76, pp. 44-88.

[51] Given the curricular emphases of the Bible college, it is not surprising that a majority of the graduates became Christian workers, educators, or nurses. A comprehensive survey conducted in 1963 showed the following vocational distribution: ministers, 20 percent; missionaries, 14 percent; other Christian workers, 8 percent; elementary teachers, 13 percent; secondary teachers, 3 percent; college instructors, 3 percent; other educators, 2 percent; and nurses, 6 percent. See "Fort Wayne Bible College Alumni Survey, 1963." Office of the Director of Research.

[52] *Fort Wayne Bible College Catalog*, 1956-57, 32-34; *Fort Wayne Bible College Catalog*, 1975-76, p. 36; Correspondence Department Enrollment Report, Feb. 1978.

[53] Fort Wayne Bible Institute Trustees Meeting, March 8, 1949; Warner, *Witmer*, p. 14; S. A. Witmer, *Report: Preparing Bible College Students for Ministries in Christian Education* (Fort Wayne, 1962), p. 13; *Bible Vision*, Dec. 1952, 3; *American Association of Bible Colleges Directory*, 1976-77, pp. 2, 4-12; Kenneth O. Gangel, "A Study of the Evolution of College Accreditation in the North Central Association and its Effect on Bible Colleges" (unpublished Ph.D. dissertation, University of Missouri at Kansas City, 1969), pp. 130-31.

[54] *Vision Magazine*, June-July 1957, p. 1; Annual Report of Fort Wayne Bible College, 1950-51; letter, S. A. Witmer to Fort Wayne Bible College Governing Board, July 10, 1957.

[55] For an explanation of the Bible college philosophy by another leader at the Fort Wayne institution, see Herbert W. Byrne, *The Christian Approach to Education* (Grand Rapids, 1961).

[56] "The Changing Scene on the Christian Campus," *Moody Monthly*, September, 1961, p. 15; S. A. Witmer, "The Paradox in Bible College Education," in Warner, Witmer, pp. 31-33; Witmer, "Bible College Education," pp. 115-16.

[57] Witmer, "Paradox in Bible College Education," pp. 33-35; *The Missionary*

Worker, June 15, 1962, p. 2; Warner, *Witmer*, p. 5.

⁵⁸ *Vision Magazine*, June-July 1957, p. 1 and May-June 1964, p. 1; Gangel, "Accreditation and Bible Colleges," pp. 129-31; Fort Wayne Bible College, Minutes of the Meetings of the Governing Board Executive Committee, June 21, 1985.

⁵⁹ Missionary Church Association General Conference Meeting, Aug. 19, 1930.

⁶⁰ Ramseyer, *Yet Speaking*, p. 201; Fort Wayne Bible Institute Trustees Meeting, Sept. 22, 1942; *Fort Wayne Bible Institute Catalog*, 1942-43, p. 7; *Vision Magazine*, Fall 1965, p. 1.

⁶¹ Reports of the Registrar of Fort Wayne Bible College and Summit Christian College, 1944-45, 1956-57, 1965-66, 1975-76, 1976-77, 1985-86, and 1991-92; *Fort Wayne Bible College Catalog*, 1945-46, p. 59; *Fort Wayne Bible College Catalog*, 1946-47, p. 7.

⁶² *Vision Magazine*, Sept. 1957, p. 1; *The Missionary Worker*, June 15, 1962, p. 2; Lugibihl and Gerig, p. 64.

⁶³ Fort Wayne Bible Institute Trustees Meetings, Sept. 27, 1945, Aug. 15, 1946, and April 29, 1947; *Vision Magazine*, Jan. 1953, pp. 5, 6, 14 and July-Aug., 1958, p. 1; Jared F. Gerig, *A Vine of God's Own Planting: A History of Fort Wayne Bible College* (Fort Wayne, 1980), p. 23.

⁶⁴ *Vision Magazine*, July-Aug. 1958, p. 1 and Fall 1966, p. 1.

⁶⁵ *Vision Magazine*, Fall 1966, p. 1 and Summer 1970, p. 1.

⁶⁶ *Fort Wayne Bible Training School Catalog*, 1906-07, p. 10; *Fort Wayne Bible Institute Light Tower*, 1928, p. 42; Missionary Church Association General Conference Meeting, Aug. 24, 1937.

⁶⁷ *Fort Wayne Bible College Light Tower*, 1960, pp. 23-28; *Fort Wayne Bible College Light Tower*, 1967, pp. 62-63; *Fort Wayne Bible Institute Catalog*, 1942-43, p. 12; *Fort Wayne Bible College Catalog*, 1975-76, pp. 24-28.

[68] Fort Wayne Bible College Trustees Meetings, Nov. 24, 1952, Dec. 5, 1953, and Dec. 19, 1960; Jeff Raymond, "Taylor University Fort Wayne Athletic History, 1952-1993."

[69] Missionary Church Association General Conference Meeting, Aug 24, 1936; Fort Wayne Bible College Trustees Meeting, May 27, 1963.

[70] Missionary Church Association General Conference Meeting, Aug. 22, 1938; Fort Wayne Bible Institute Trustees Meetings, March 21, 1939, Sept. 22, 1942, and Sept. 27, 1945; Missionary Church Association Governing Committee Meeting, Aug. 10, 1911; Fort Wayne Bible College Trustees Meeting, March 19, 1963; *American Association of University Professors Bulletin*, Summer 1964, p. 163; *Fort Wayne Bible College Faculty Manual*, 1967-69, pp. 14-17.

[71] *Fort Wayne Bible Training School Catalog*, 1905-06, p. 8; *Fort Wayne Bible Training School Catalog*, 1917-18, pp. 11-12; *Fort Wayne Bible Institute Catalog*, 1931-32, pp. 32-33; *Fort Wayne Bible Institute Catalog*, 1951-52, p. 45; *Fort Wayne Bible College Catalog*, 1960-61, p. 11; *Fort Wayne Bible College Catalog*, 1975-76, pp. 18, 20-21; *Summit Christian College Catalog*, 1989-90, p. 9; Fort Wayne Bible Institute Trustees Meeting, March 14, 1946; Fort Wayne Bible College Trustees Meetings, March 3, 1959, and Sept. 30, 1960.

[72] *The Missionary Worker*, June 15, 1962, p. 4 and Sept. 1, 1962, p. 2; *Vision Magazine*, Nov.-Dec. 1962, p. 1; Lugibihl and Gerig, *Missionary Church Association*, p. 52.

[73] Interview with Timothy M. Warner, Aug., 1977; Eileen Lageer, *Merging Streams: Story of the Missionary Church* (Elkhart, Indiana, 1979), pp. 138, 163, 319; Gerig, *Fort Wayne Bible College*, pp. 174-75.

[74] A year after the merger, the trustees named the activities center in honor of the many Gerigs who had served as long-term leaders of the Fort Wayne institution — Jared, the dean and president; Donald, the president; Joy, the director of the Christian service program; Ira (music) and Wesley (Bible and theology), the best recognized professors of the past generation; and William, the alumni and church relations director.

[75] This branch of the denomination, which included some of the faculty and staff members at the college, also held the strongest doubts about the need to seek merger with Taylor.

[76] Interview with James A. Saddington, Summer, 1995; interview with Richard P. Dugan, Summer, 1995; interview with David D. Biberstein, Summer, 1995; interview with Roger W. Ringenberg, Summer, 1995; *Summit Christian College Catalog*, 1989-91, p. iv.

[77] "Findings and Recommendations: Marcon Marketing Survey for Taylor University Fort Wayne," 1993, Office of the President, Taylor University.

[78] *Taylor Magazine*, Autumn, 1993, p. 8; Minutes of the meeting of the Taylor Academic Policies Committee, March 16, 1995; interview with Jay L. Kesler, Summer, 1995; interview with Al Smith, Fall, 1994; *Summit Christian College Catalog*, 1989-91, p. 24; interview with Stephen S. Bedi, Summer, 1995; interview with Robert W. Nienhuis, Fall, 1995; interview with Robert D. Pitts, Fall, 1995; *Taylor Times*, October 6, 1995, p. 1; memorandum, Office of the President to Taylor University employees, November 28, 1995.

[79] Taylor University Academic Affairs Annual Report, 1994-95, p. 9; interview with Heather Zenk St. Peters, Fall, 1995. Gerig, *Fort Wayne Bible College*, pp. 152-55; TUTM, May 20-21, 1993, p. 4; *Marion Chronicle Tribune*, June 5, 1994, p. C1; interview with Char Binkley, Fall, 1995; interview with Timothy M. Warner, Fall, 1995.

[80] TUFM, May 13, 1993; interview with Paul R. House, Fall, 1995; interview with Robert W. Nienhuis, Fall, 1995.

[81] Annual Statistical Reports, Taylor University Upland and Fort Wayne Records Offices; interview with William D. Gerig, Summer, 1995; interview with Jay L. Kesler, Summer, 1995; TUTM, January 28-29, 1993.

[82] Interview with Al Smith, Fall, 1994, and Fall, 1995.

EPILOGUE

*A*merican society needed schools such as Taylor much less in the last century than it does today. In fact, it is difficult to see any need for the school during the Fort Wayne period. Indiana Asbury College offered excellent academic and spiritual training for the Methodist youth of the state. It is true that Asbury did not admit female students until after the Civil War; however, the Indiana Methodists could have placed greater pressure upon the Asbury officials in the antebellum period to make their institution coeducational. Such an arrangement would have been advantageous economically to the Indiana Methodists and educationally to the students who would have attended the Greencastle school rather than the nineteenth-century one in Fort Wayne. Fort Wayne Female College was only one of the hundreds of church-related educational institutions that began in the middle part of the last century. Unfortunately, the intensely individualistic spirit of the period encouraged the beginning of dozens of church colleges as each new frontier area opened. The church leaders would have better served their own interests if they had concentrated on establishing a few good, well-financed institutions instead of encouraging the endless proliferation of "log colleges."

> *American society needed schools such as Taylor much less in the last century than it does today.*

One might even ask the question of whether the mid-nineteenth-century Protestant colleges needed to exist at all. Not only was evangelical Protestantism the prevailing world view at the church colleges, but it was also the dominant faith at almost all American colleges and universities, including the state universities. Although such a relationship between religion and a state institution may not gain the approval of twentieth-century interpreters of the Constitution, the fact remains that most early state universities indeed operated as Christian schools. For example, the University of Michigan by virtually all criteria of measurement was a Protestant college. The faculty professed their belief in the Christian faith, and they thought that most of the students were devout Christians. The president and the faculty frequently sought to instill Christian teaching in the minds of the students. A similar situation existed at Indiana University. The Bloomington school held daily and Sunday chapel exercises through most of the nineteenth century, and usually required attendance at these services. Until 1885 the Bloomington school always chose a Protestant minister for its president. Given this religious orientation of the state universities, the early denominational colleges had little reason for existence.[1]

A need for the evangelical Christian schools soon became apparent, however, when in the late nineteenth century relativistic philosophy increasingly began to dominate the teaching in the state universities and even in some of the traditionally Christian colleges.[2] The turn-of-the-century intellectual revolution in this country showed that laws established by men in earlier periods were not necessarily the best principles to guide society in a different era. The evangelical colleges did not object because the new learning was changing economics, sociology, and jurisprudence into ways that hopefully could better serve humanity; rather they reacted against the implication of relativism that no fixed body of truth existed in any area of human experience and knowledge. These schools argued that there are certain eternal spiritual verities that remain constant through the continuous changes in the nature of society, a view increasingly challenged in the state schools.

Orthodox Christians could not legitimately complain when their world view lost its place of dominance in the state universities because it was losing its position of supremacy in society in general, but they had proper cause to protest when their ideas lost nearly all influence in these schools. A public university has a responsibility to serve as a sounding board for all points of view, but while the state schools began to give a fair audience to the new non-Christian philosophies, they gradually ended their practice of giving the case for Christian orthodoxy a hearing commensurate to its still relatively prominent position in the nation. The evangelicals complained of growing discrimination against their position, but they lacked the power to change the situation. Accordingly, the need for the Christian college became greater than it had ever been before.

The secular nature of the state universities has continued largely unabated throughout this century.[3] Not only did many of the early twentieth-century state schools assume the position that the Christian faith should not receive a fair opportunity to answer its rival philosophies (they welcomed divergent points of view on controversial subjects in other areas, however), but they also made the strange judgment that religion as an academic discipline should not appear in nonparochial educational institutions. Imagine the incongruity of the position of institutions that pretended to teach the whole of human knowledge and experience and yet avoided the serious study of an area that has exerted such a profound influence in shaping the course of human lives and civilizations. Most of the public universities gradually recognized the error of this earlier position, and many of them in varying degrees reintroduced religion courses and departments. One should not exaggerate the significance of this positive note, however. In the public universities that offer religion courses, the great majority of students do not enroll in even one such subject. Often the instructors of these courses teach them solely from historical and sociological viewpoints and do not appreciate the fact that they could teach the courses in a manner that would aid the student in the selection and development of his or her personal world view and life commitment.

The Christian college believes that acceptance of the Christian faith is an integral part of true knowledge and that lack of this faith often leads the seeker of truth to a philosophical vacuum.

The major reason then for the continued existence at the end of the twentieth century for schools such as Taylor is to provide a liberal arts education within a Christian frame of reference. The Christian college urges its students to seek knowledge and truth wherever it may be found. This does not mean that objectivity in the search demands that the seeker abstain from any philosophical commitment. On the contrary, the Christian college believes that acceptance of the Christian faith is an integral part of true knowledge and that lack of this faith often leads the seeker of truth to a philosophical vacuum.

Even though secularization continues to dominate higher education and much of society in general in America, by contrast, it is less of a threat to Christian higher education now than it was during the early and middle 1900s. Not many traditionally Christian colleges have begun to secularize since 1965. Furthermore in recent years even while the surviving Christian colleges have achieved a greater public respect, there has occurred a growing sense of disillusionment within the American academy in general over the intellectual barrenness in its traditional centers of power.[4]

If secularization has been a declining threat to the Christian colleges, one of the greatest needs of Christian higher education as we move into the next millennium is the continuing development of intellectual integrity. The Christian colleges have readily recognized the lack of such integrity in the secular institutions and would concur, for example, with the observation of George Buttrick that "Secularism at its best is naive and at its worst is a refusal to confront life's dimensions of depth." But the religious community, including the evangelicals who according to Mark Noll have now become "the largest and most active component of religious life in North America," also often fall short of being intellectually open in their search for truth.[5] In fact some careful scholars, including devout Christians, have argued that the evangelical community has a special problem in this area. Charles Malik in his dedicatory address at the opening of the Billy Graham Center at Wheaton College in 1980 noted, "The greatest danger besetting American Evangelical Christianity is the danger of antiintellectualism." A few years earlier N. K. Clifford observed, "The Evangelical Protestant mind has never relished complexity. Indeed its crusading genius, whether in religion or politics, has always tended toward an over-simplification of issues and the substitution of inspiration and zeal for critical analysis and serious reflection." More recently and more sharply, Os Guinness has charged, "Evangelicals have been deeply sinful in being anti-intellectual ever since the 1820s and 1830s. ...most evangelicals simply don't think.... It has always been a sin not to love the Lord our God with our minds as well as our hearts and souls...."[6] While one might dismiss part of these critiques as the tendency of many intellectuals (and perhaps most other people as well) to wish that others were like them or at least appreciated their thinking, still there is enough truth to them to be convicting.

Probably no type of institution is better positioned than is the Christian college to assist the evangelical community in more fully loving God with their minds; and the assumption of this role may be easier for Taylor than for many Christian colleges. For one thing the university has a long tradition of emphasizing loving

> *One of the greatest needs of Christian higher education as we move into the next millennium is the continuing development of intellectual integrity.*

God in general. One recalls the explicit desire of the school leaders in the 1890s to develop an institution "distinguished for the piety and religious fervor of her students and faculty," (see chapter four) and while this emphasis obviously was much more on heart love than on mind love, the one can naturally lead to the other. Also during the first half of the twentieth century the then Methodist-oriented university avoided much of the antiintellectualism more frequently found in institutions which more directly experienced the fundamentalist movement. Gradually with the growth in the quality of the academic program the institution increasingly came to value the spiritual potential in the life of the mind. Furthermore the university's long-standing freedom from the control of a religious denomination made it easier for it to seek to integrate the academic disciplines with the Christian faith apart from the concerns of a specific theological system. Finally, the vigorous commitment to intellectual openness by longtime institutional leaders Burt Ayers, Milo Rediger, and Jay Kesler has been a vital factor in this pattern.

Still Taylor can and must do even more in its promotion of intellectual integrity.[7] Essentially it needs to more clearly communicate the message that the pursuit of intellectual integrity is inherently a spiritual task. Thinking Christianly is the condition of being intellectually honest before God, and while this condition may begin at conversion with a deep general realization of one's hopelessness apart from God, it doesn't end there but rather must be practiced and developed continuously throughout this earthly pilgrimage. Thinking Christianly means that one wants to hear and know God more than anything else; therefore, one's intellectual orientation is inherently open, eager to receive new truth. One may and should fear bad science, bad philosophy, or bad theology, but one doesn't fear science, philosophy, or theology. Indeed one fears missing the truth. Truth is a friend because it leads to God.

> *Probably no type of institution is better positioned than is the Christian college to assist the evangelical community in more fully loving God with their minds.*

Sometimes this openness is very painful for it demands that one be willing to examine and possibly change one's pet theories and practices. Intellectual integrity means that one be ruthlessly honest in examining both or all sides of an issue. Thoughtful Christianity requires that one determine to see how other sincere Christians of different ages, places, and traditions have held different understandings even while sharing the conviction that the incarnation is the central act of all human history, revealing a personal loving creator God who offers His grace and truth to all who freely seek Him. Indeed so precious is this conviction to the discerning Christian, providing fulfillment, joy, and confidence, that it allows one to practice charity, grace, and elasticity of mind on the host of secondary issues (e.g. political and economic philosophy, social policy, theological systems) on which sincere Christians differ.[8] How wonderful it would be if a generation from now Taylor

> *The pursuit of intellectual integrity is inherently a spiritual task....Thinking Christianly is the condition of being intellectually honest before God....Thinking Christianly means that one wants to hear and know God more than anything else; therefore, one's intellectual orientation is inherently open, eager to receive new truth....Truth is a friend because it leads to God.*

is known not only for its friendly supportive environment and attractive physical plant but also for the exemplary degree to which it realizes its goal of inspiring its students to love God with all of their minds as well as all of their hearts.

[1] *University of Michigan Regents' Proceedings,* 1837-1864 (Ann Arbor, 1915), pp. 720-22; *University of Michigan Catalog,* 1852-53 (Detroit, 1853), p. 25; Erastus O. Haven, *Autobiography* (New York, 1883), pp. 144, 150; Woodburn, *Indiana University,* pp. 299-300.

[2] On the secularization of higher education in America—and beyond, see "The Movement Toward Secularization," chapter four in Ringenberg, *The Christian College;* Marsden and Longfield, eds., *The Secularization of the Academy*; and Marsden *The Soul of the American University.*

[3] The early twentieth-century Christian community probably contributed to this problem by inadequately promoting the importance of scholarly learning in general and by encouraging the scholars that it did have to teach in Christian schools instead of the state universities. Both of these practices began to change for the better after World War II.

[4] See, for example, Allan Bloom, *The Closing of the American Mind: How Higher Education Has Failed Democracy and Impoverished the Souls of Today's Students* (New York, 1991).

[5] George A. Buttrick, *Biblical Faith and the Secular University* (Batan Rouge, 1960), p. 7; Mark A. Noll, *The Scandal of the Evangelical Mind* (Grand Rapids, 1994) p. 9.

[6] These three quotations appear in Noll, *Scandal of the Evangelical Mind* (pp. 12, 23, 25-26), a noteworthy even if overstated indictment that laments not only the underappreciation of the life of the mind by the evangelical community but also the inability of the latter to significantly impact the larger intellectual community in America. Also see Nathan O. Hatch, "Evangelical Colleges and the Challenge of Christian Thinking" in Joel A. Carpenter and Kenneth W. Shipps eds., *Making Higher Education Christian: The History and Mission of Evangelical Colleges in America* (Grand Rapids, 1987), pp. 155-71.

[7] As recently as fifteen years ago D. Elton Trueblood, the Quaker theologian and, with C. S. Lewis, a modern apostle of rational Christianity, while expressing to the author his sincere appreciation for the state of spirituality that he observed at Taylor, added his perception that the intellectual component of that spirituality was not yet commensurate with its experiential element (i.e., Taylor religion, he observed, was more heart religion than mind religion).

[8] See Herbert Butterfield, *Christianity and History* (New York, 1950), especially pp. 145-46; and M. Scott Peck, *The Different Drum: Community Making and Peace* (New York, 1987), pp. 234ff.

APPENDIX A

TAYLOR UNIVERSITY, UPLAND FACULTY

1970-1995

Abbott, Judith W.	1971 - 1973	Music
Adkison, H. Leon	1974 -	Systems
Anglin, A. J.	1969 - 1982	Chemistry and Administration
Antonian, Robert	1975 - 1978	Music
Aycock, David W.	1983 - 1988	Counseling Center
Baker, Beulah P.	1979 -	English
Bakerink, Denise A.	1988 -	Student Development
Banker, E. Stanley	1964 - 1974	Administration
Baptista, Robert C.	1975 - 1979	Administration
Barr, Robert A.	1973 - 1978	Student Development
Barrick, Eleanor A.	1990 -	Modern Languages
Bassett, Sheldon J.	1970 - 1979	Physical Education
Bauer, William L.	1986 - 1992	Physical Education
Bedford, Clark W.	1973 -1976	Music
Bedi, Stephen S.	1991 -	Education and Administration
Beers, Stephen	1992 -	Student Ministries
Beers, Thomas G.	1969 - 1994	Administration and Student Development
Bemis, Cynthia J.	1986 - 1987	Student Development
Benbow, Ronald M.	1987 -	Education and Mathematics
Benjamin, Robert P.	1979 -	Accounting
Bennett, Christopher P.	1989 -	Business
Bicksler, Marith R.	1982 - 1983	English

Bird, Steven P.	1993 -	Sociology
Blume, Robert K.	1967 - 1973	Physical Education
Boyd, Robert L.	1967 - 1973	Music
Braden, Anna Rose	1966 - 1976	Student Development
Brane, John R.	1970 - 1973	Music
Breuninger, Ruth Ann	1964 - 1975	Religion
Bromley, Charles D.	1961 - 1971	Education
Brooks, Steven G.	1993 -	Physical Education
Brown, Sonya K.	1993 - 1994	Political Science
Buck, H. Michael	1986 - 1989	English
Bullock, Ray E.	1966 - 1991	Art
Burden, Stanley L.	1966 -	Chemistry
Burkholder, Timothy J.	1970 -	Biology
Burnworth, Joe	1969 -	Education
Burr, Kenneth W.	1971 - 1974	Business
Button, Rose Ann	1972 - 1974	Student Development
Cameron, Lorraine M.	1974 - 1975	Physical Education
Campbell, Harvey F.	1971 - 1974	Speech and Drama
Campbell, Jean	1967 - 1974	Student Development
Campbell, Walter E.	1969 -	Student Development and Administration
Carlson, Dale R.	1990 - 1994	Physical Education
Carlson, Tom	1974 - 1977	Physical Education
Carruth, Hazel E. Butz	1946 - 1978	English
Carter, Charles W.	1959 - 1971	Philosophy and Religion
Case, Kimberly F.	1988 -	Student Development
Chambers, Timothy	1976 - 1980	Student Development and Psychology
Chapin, M. Michelle	1990 - 1992	Psychology

Chapman, Mildred Stratton	1956 - 1961 1975 - 1991	English and Education
Choe, Sunki	1970 - 1978	Political Science
Chechowich, Faye E.	1989 -	Religion
Christy, Brian G.	1978 - 1986	Student Development and Administration
Cicero, Nancy J.	1976 - 1983	Student Development
Codding, Eric S.	1993 -	Student Development
Coe, James G.	1983 -	Business
Colgan, Mark O.	1992 -	Mathematics
Collins, Dana L.	1992 -	Music
Collymore, Ronald S.	1991 -	Biblical Studies
Conn, David	1985 - 1987	Student Development
Corduan, Winfried	1977 -	Philosophy and Religion
Cosgrove, Mark P.	1976 -	Psychology
Cotner, Robert A.	1963 - 1965 1977 - 1980	English and Administration
Cox, L. Angela	1992 -	Physical Education
Craig, Daniel R.	1980 - 1984	Business
Craig, Sue Herbster	1980 - 1984	Physical Education
Crawford, R. Kevin	1977 - 1980	Business
Crouch, Willard J.	1975 - 1976	Development
Crouse, Gilbert L.	1981 - 1983	Administration
Crouse, Janice Shaw	1984 - 1990	Administration
Daniel, Elbert P.	1978 - 1980	Education
Davenport, Barbara	1993 -	Administration
Davenport, Robert W.	1958 - 1990	Physical Education and Development
Davin, Amy	1982 - 1983	Student Development
Davis, Charles M.	1962 -1974	English

Davis, Jamma	1988 - 1990	Student Development
Davis, Tara E.	1980 - 1986	English and Administration
Davis, Thomas A.	1976 - 1982	Student Development
Dayton, Nancy C. Klinger	1988 -	English
Dean, William M.	1966 - 1973	Religion
Delcamp, Samuel L.	1965 - 1978	Student Development and Administration
Del Vecchio, Benjamin	1970 - 1975	Music
Demmitt, Kevin P.	1991 - 1994	Sociology
DeSanto, Charles P.	1990 - 1991, 1993	Sociology
Dicken, Susan K.	1976 - 1980	Student Development
Dickey, Barbara Carruth	1961 -	Music
Dickey, David C.	1972 -	Library
Diller, Timothy C.	1981 -	Computing and Systems Sciences
Di Menna, Linda	1983 - 1987	Student Development
Dinse, Edward E.	1970 - 1992	English
Dixon, Norman W.	1991 - 1992	Christian Education
Dixon, Richard	1982 -	Spanish
Dodge, Randall	1984 - 1988	Student Development
Dorman, Theodore M.	1988 -	Religion
Dowden, G. Blair	1977 - 1980	Administration
Downs, Donna J.	1993 - 1994	Communication Arts
Drake, Corlyle	1968 - 1974	Music
Ellis, Malcolm E.	1971 - 1977	Philosophy and Religion
Erickson, Lee E.	1979 -	Economics
Evans, Jan M.	1972 - 1974	Student Development
Ewbank, Frances W.	1964 - 1982	English

Ewbank, William A.	1964 - 1987	Mathematics
Faul, George E.	1970 - 1978	French
Figueroa, Samuel	1994 -	Computing and Systems Sciences
Freese, Robert J.	1971 - 1992	Education
Fritzsche, Joseph L.	1970 - 1978	Administration
Fry, William A.	1978 -	English
Frye, Herbert	1981 - 1993	Administration
Gasiorowski, Colleen	1979 - 1980	Student Development
Gates, Jeryl	1973 - 1976	Student Development
Gates, Richard W.	1969 - 1991	Physical Education
Gaw, Ka Tong S.	1976 - 1977	Sociology
Geivett, R. Douglas	1991 - 1993	Philosophy
Gifford, Charles D.	1990 -	Student Ministries
Giger, Jerry E.	1988 - 1994	Music
Girton, Marcia D.	1986 - 1989	Physical Education
Glass, George A.	1960 -	Physical Education and Administration
Glover, Mary Edna	1973 - 1981	Physical Education
Goetcheus, Allen A.	1968 - 1974	Speech and Drama
Gongwer, Carl E.	1966 - 1988	Spanish
Gould, Nelson F.	1969 - 1974	Physical Education
Gortner, Robert V.	1980 - 1995	Business
Gorton, Beatrice A.	1976 - 1980	Physical Education
Greathouse, Gladys M.	1960 - 1973	Speech and Drama
Greve, Amerentia	1975 - 1976	Physical Education
Griffin, Charles D.	1966 - 1974	Student Development, Counselling Center and Administration
Griffin, Robert R.	1981 - 1990	Student Ministries

Grizzle, Raymond	1994 -	Environmental Science
Groeneweg, Thomas C.	1968 - 1973	Business and Economics
Hafemann, Scott	1985 - 1987	Religion
Haines, George S.	1961 - 1978	Education
Haines, Paul Lowell	1977 - 1987	Student Development and Administration
Halteman, James	1974 - 1979	Economics
Hammond, Daniel G.	1981 -	Chemistry
Harbin, Michael A.	1993 -	Religion
Harms, Paul M.	1971 -	Mathematics
Harner, Cathy J.	1992 -	Social Work
Harrison, Albert D.	1977 -	Music
Harrison, George W.	1963 - 1994	Biology
Hart, Nelson H.	1970 - 1973	Sociology
Haubold, Robert L.	1971 - 1983	Psychology and Counselling Center
Heath, Dale E.	1961 - 1988	Ancient Language and History
Heavilin, Barbara A.	1991 -	English
Hedin, Eric R.	1993 -	Physics
Heller, Karl H.	1972 - 1974	History
Helyer, Larry R.	1979 -	Religion
Hendrix, James C.	1980 - 1982	Student Development
Hermanson, Edward H.	1966 - 1974	Music and Development
Herrmann, Timothy W.	1978 -	Student Development
Hess, David D.	1967 -	Education
Hess, Vickie L.	1980 - 1981	Chemistry
Heth, William A.	1987 -	Religion
Hill, Richard A.	1993 -	English

Hill, William J.	1970 - 1981	Student Ministries
Hoagland, Joann E.	1971 - 1974	Student Development
Hodson, Gerald L.	1967 -	Education, Art, and Learning Resources
Hodson, M. Jane Vanzant	1966 -	Education
Hoffman, Cathryn	1979 - 1980	Business
Hoffmann, Stephen P.	1976 - 1977 1981 -	Political Science
Holcombe, Alice K.	1946 - 1950 1952 - 1983	Library
House, Cornelius G.	1968 - 1976	German
House, Paul R.	1986 -	Religion
Houser, Bonnie J.	1993 -	Archives and Library
Hruska, Thomas J., Jr.	1978 - 1981	Political Science
Hubbard, Oliver F., Jr.	1976 -	Communication Arts
Huffman, Terry	1994 -	Sociology
Jackson, Alice A.	1985 - 1992	Social Work
Jackson, Dale M.	1966 -	Communication Arts
Jackson, Martha	1970 - 1971	Student Development
Jaggers, Charles R.	1972 -	Student Development and Administration
Jantzen, John B.	1959 - 1973	French
Jarman, Thomas S.	1969 - 1980	Physical Education
Jenkinson, Roger L.	1965 -	Geography and History
Jeran, Daniel	1980 - 1991	Education
Jessup, Dwight	1993 -	Administration
Johnson, Kimberly K.	1987 - 1991	Student Development
Johnson, Ronald D.	1986 - 1988	Student Development
Jones, Aletha A.	1980 - 1983	Art
Jones, Diana L.	1980 - 1986	Physical Education

Jones, Philip B.	1978 - 1982	Spanish
Jones, Thomas G.	1977 - 1978 1988 -	History
Kastelein, John E.	1974 - 1984	Computing and Systems Sciences and Administration
Kaufmann, Lon D.	1992 -	Art
Kauth, William A.	1990 - 1994	Physical Education
Keiser, Jane	1990 - 1992	Mathematics
Keller, Ronald L.	1966 - 1984	Student Development and Administration
Kenline, Bruce W.	1971 - 1972	Ancient Language
Kern, Elwood Lee, Jr.	1971 - 1976	Psychology
Kern, Melba L.	1970 - 1974	Physical Education
Kesler, Jay L.	1985 -	Administration and Christian Education
King, Jack W.	1961 - 1971 1988 -	Physical Education and Development
Kirkpatrick, Charles B.	1979 -	Communication Arts
Kirkpatrick, Patricia E.	1982 -	Learning Skills
Kirms, Frederick O.	1975 - 1979	Business
Kitterman, Joan	1994 -	Education
Kitzmann, Kathleen A.	1978 - 1980	Chemistry
Kleist, James H.	1990 -	Learning Resources
Kline, Lynda S.	1991 -	Student Development
Klinger, William R.	1989 -	Mathematics
Klopfenstein, David E.	1967 - 1974	Student Development and Psychology
Knox, Charlotte G.	1969 - 1973	Physical Education
Knudsen, Donald	1994 -	Business
Koons, Wendy	1984 - 1991	Student Development

Krause, Tena M.	1989 -	Physical Education
Krause, Scot N.	1971 - 1974	Physical Education
Kroeker, Philip K.	1963 -	Music
Kroll, Leroy O.	1979 -	Chemistry
Krueger, Gordon M.	1955 - 1979	Chemistry
Kukuk, Linda S.	1974 - 1976	Speech and Drama
Landon, John	1973 - 1974	Sociology and Social Work
Landrum, Judith	1987 - 1988	English
Langat, Robert	1988 - 1991	Religion
Larson, Steven	1977 - 1979	Student Development
Law, James B.	1982 -	Physical Education
Lee, Herbert G.	1955 - 1975	English
Lee, Janet C.	1978 - 1980	Physical Education
Lee, Jennie Andrews	1951 - 1975	Elementary Education
Lee, Twyla F.	1993 -	Social Work
Lehman, Gregg O.	1973 - 1974 1976 - 1985	Business and Economics Administration
Lembright, Wynn A.	1983 -	Administration
Lightfoot, Connie D.	1982 - 1993	Information Sciences and Administration
Lloyd, Mark L.	1977 - 1979	Communication Arts
Lottes, Charlotte	1977 - 1978	Physical Education
Loy, Janet C.	1971 -	Modern Languages
Loy, R. Philip	1964 -	Political Science
Lund, Joe W.	1973 -	Psychology
Lusk, Franklin L.	1973 - 1975	Music
Luthy, Fred H.	1955 - 1987	Religion
Maloney, Vance E.	1981 -	Psychology
Manor, Billie J.	1980 -	Learning Skills

Mansfield, Lynn A.	1970 - 1974	Student Development
Marsee, Jeffrey W.	1987 - 1990 1994 -	Physical Education
Mathis, James J.	1968 - 1974	Student Development
Matthew, John A.	1984 - 1985	English
McGee-Wallace, Nellie	1982 - 1984	Student Development
McQueen, Marilyn	1974 - 1988	Sociology and Social Work
Mealy, Betty	1982 - 1984	English
Mealy, J. Lawrence	1988 -	Student Development
Messer, Elizabeth B.	1988 -	Modern Languages
Messer, Stephen C.	1990 -	History
Meyer, Allen D.	1979 - 1989	Psychology
Meyer, Diane A.	1980 - 1989	Student Development and Student Ministries
Mikkelson, Dwight L.	1968 - 1993	History
Miller, Darvin L.	1963 - 1971	Psychology
Miller, D. Larry	1973 - 1975	Sociology
Miller, Rodney	1977 - 1978	Music
Millspaugh, Grace M.	1968 - 1972	Library
Mitchell, Hadley T.	1993 -	Economics
Mitchell, Judith A.	1989 -	English
Moller, Nancy	1994 -	Education
Montgomery, T. Alexander	1975 - 1977	Music
Montgomery, William	1985 - 1990	Social Work
Moore, Craig W.	1979 -	Art
Moore, John M.	1992 -	Biology
Moore, Rebecca S.	1990 -	Administration
Moore-Jumonville, Kimberly	1992 -	English
Mott, Carol	1994 -	Counselling Center

Mowery, Erick B.	1991 - 1994	Student Development
Muenzer, Timothy A.	1988 - 1989	Computing and Systems Sciences
Muthiah, Richard	1994 -	Student Development
Muzik, Richard C.	1975 - 1979	Religion
Nace, Timothy A.	1987 -	Student Development and Administration
Neuhouser, David L.	1971 -	Mathematics
Neuroth, Joann	1971 - 1973	Student Development
Newton, Gary C.	1985 - 1995	Religion
Nies, Charles M.	1972 - 1982	Psychology and Counselling Center
Nordquist, John P.	1976 - 1981	Music
Nussbaum, Elmer N.	1949 - 1953 1957 - 1962 1963 - 1985	Physics
Nygren, E. Herbert	1969 - 1991	Philosophy and Religion
Oakley, Berford S., Jr.	1968 - 1971	Business and Economics
O'Brien, Roger Lee	1968 - 1971	Mathematics
Odle, Don J.	1947 - 1979	Physical Education
Oliver, Gerald D.	1981 - 1984	Advancement
Olson, Grace D.	1945 - 1971	History and Administration
Oosting, James E.	1974 - 1976	Speech and drama
Ozmun, Ruth Warner	1981 - 1984	Physical Education
Parker, Richard A.	1974 -	Music
Patterson, Paul W.	1979 -	Physical Education
Patton, Jack D.	1952 - 1979	Art
Peppard, Joanne E.	1972 - 1974	Physical Education
Phillips, Roger W.	1982 -	Library
Pitts, Robert D.	1973 -	Administration and Religion

Pletcher, Janice L.	1992 -	Communication Arts
Poe, Elisabeth	1953 - 1983	Biology
Polsgrove, Scott	1989 - 1992	Student Development and Physical Education
Pontius, Bradley D.	1988 - 1992	Student Ministries
Prell, Michael	1988 - 1990	Student Development
Randall, Walter C.	1987 - 1993	Natural Sciences
Rapp, Doris J.	1988 - 1992	Counseling Center
Rayburn, Mary G.	1991 -	Student Ministries
Reber, Jan	1994 -	Biology
Rediger, Milo A.	1943 - 1950 1952 - 1981	Philosophy, Religion, and Administration
Rice, Carl W.	1969 - 1985	Education
Rich, Laura	1994 -	Psychology
Ringenberg, William C.	1968 -	History and Administration
Rogers, Helen E.	1976 -	Education
Rohrman, Douglas H.	1986 - 1992	Social Work
Romine, Joe W.	1972 - 1976 1981 -	Student Development and Physical Education
Rosario, Pedro	1994 -	Student Development
Roth, R. Waldo	1967 -	Computing and Systems Sciences and Mathematics
Roth, Roger W.	1965 -	Physics
Rothrock, Paul E.	1981 -	Biology and Environmental Science
Rotruck, E. Stanley	1979 - 1992	Business
Rottmeyer, Larry W.	1992 - 1994	Business
Rousselow, Jessica L.	1967 -	Communication Arts
Roycroft, Gordon	1983 - 1985	Student Development
Roye, Frank H.	1955 - 1982	Sociology
Ruberg, Rodney C.	1974 - 1978	Administration

Sample, Samuel W.	1977 - 1982	Physical Education and Development
Sather, Jerome L.	1971 - 1972	Speech and Drama
Schemmer, Beverly A. S.	1992 -	Education
Seaman, Richard A.	1989 -	Business
Sharp, Timothy W.	1981 - 1988	Music
Sheeley, Scott	1993 - 1994	Environmental Science
Shigley, R. Lavon	1973 - 1980	Library
Shulze, Frederick B.	1970 -	Music
Sigworth, Susan L. Winger	1986 -	English
Sims, Charles K.	1962 - 1973	Music
Sisson, Robert M.	1987 -	Student Development
Slabaugh, Walter R.	1973 - 1976	Biology
Sloan, Ronald M.	1981 -	Music and Administration
Smith, Daniel P.	1992 -	Science Laboratories
Smith, Eleanor A.	1970 - 1972	English
Smith, W. Doug	1990 - 1993	Student Development
Snyder, Ellen E.	1968 - 1974	Learning Skills
Snyder, Harold Z.	1962 - 1985	Biology
Snyder, Stephen J.	1982 -	Psychology
Sorenson, Dana K.	1980 - 1986	Physical Education
Spicuzza, Paul J.	1966 - 1971	Music
Spiegel, James S.	1993 -	Philosophy and Religion
Squiers, Edwin R.	1976 -	Biology and Environmental Science
Stafford, Katherine R.	1979 - 1982	Student Development
Stanislaw, Richard J.	1982 - 1992	Administration
Steiner, Richard	1962 - 1967 1970 - 1971	French

Stewart, Robert H.	1968 - 1974	Student Development and Administration
Steyer, Hilda L.	1954 - 1984	Music
Sutherland, Timothy L.	1980 - 1982	Library
Swan, Kenneth D.	1968 -	English and Administration
Talley, David L.	1989 - 1994	Student Development and Psychology
Talley, Kirk A.	1992 -	Physical Education
Tarry, Rebecca	1973 - 1976	Student Development
Taylor, Donald L.	1991 -	Physical Education
Taylor, Howard E.	1975 - 1978	Administration
Taylor, John W.	1982 - 1983	Music
Taylor, Melanie A.	1984 - 1988	Resident Hall Director; instructor
Toll, William E.	1990 -	Computing and System Sciences
Town, Stephen J.	1978 - 1981	Music
Sloat, Dale L.	1982 - 1994	Administration and Communication Arts
Traut, Karen K.	1988 - 1992	Physical Education
Valutis, Ernest W.	1965 - 1976	Psychology, Counselling Center, and Administration
Voss, Henry	1994 -	Research
Walker, Marilyn A.	1966 -	Communication Arts
Wallace, John M.	1977 -	Social Work
Warren, Colleen A.	1992 -	English
Webb, Jan	1971 - 1975	Student Development
Weed, Lois A.	1953 -	Library
Welch, R. Edwin	1992 -	Academic Support Services
Wenger, Dale E.	1963 - 1989	Mathematics

Westerfelt, Herbert	1982 - 1985	Social Work
Westerfield, Jane	1987 - 1988	Music
Wheeler, John W.	1984 - 1988	Business
Whipple, Andrew P.	1984 -	Biology
White, Arthur J.	1984 -	Computing and Systems Sciences
White, Deborah J.	1982 - 1984	Student Development
White, Lori	1994 -	Music
Williams, Mozelle I.	1973 - 1983	Student Development
Wiley, J. William	1989 -	Computing and Systems Sciences
Wilson, Charles R.	1965 - 1983	Religion and Philosophy
Wilson, Patricia M.	1992 - 1994	Education
Wilt, Stephen	1994 -	Physical Education
Winquist, Alan H.	1974 -	History
Winterholter, Larry C.	1979 -	Physical Education
Wolcott, Laurie J.	1983 -	Library
Wolfe, Robert C.	1962 - 1993	Chemistry and Physics
Wood, Theodore N.	1975 - 1979	Business and Economics
Wyant, Jill A.	1984 - 1988	Physical Education
Yost, Daryl R.	1983 -	Administration
Young, Julie D.	1984 - 1987	Student Development
Yutzy, Daniel	1976 - 1993	Sociology
Zimmerman, Gordon G.	1965 - 1973	Administration
Zielke, Sigurd H.	1979 - 1985	Religion

APPENDIX B
TAYLOR UNIVERSITY, FORT WAYNE FACULTY
1992-1995

Arthur, Carolyn L.	1992 - 1995	Student Development and Administration
Barcalow, Douglas A.	1992 -	Christian Education
Bard, Gary G.	1994 -	Mathematics
Barnes, Marc W.	1992 -	Psychology
Barrantes, Kim	1993 -	Student Development
Baxter, Richard H.	1992 -	Student Ministries and Student Development
Biberstein, David D.	1992 -	Pastoral Ministries
Birkey, Arlan J.	1992 -	Greek
Brown, Joel	1993 - 1995	Student Development
Bueschlen, Wava M.	1992 -	Library
Cavanaugh, Claire	1992 - 1993	Student Development
Conrad, Eunice, J.	1992 - 1995	English
Coon, Barbara L.	1992 - 1993	Administration
Dugan, Richard P.	1992 - 1994	Administration
Gerig, Wesley L.	1992 -	Bible and Theology
Gerig, William D.	1992 -	Alumni and Church Relations
Gray, Richard L.	1994 -	Christian Ministries
Hamilton, Marvin (Bud)	1992 -	Chaplain and Athletic Director
Hendrix, James C.	1993 -	Administration
Jordan, Pamela L.	1992 -	English
Koch, Rita	1992 -	Spanish
Martin, C. Joseph	1992 -	Counselling and Psychology
Miller, Etta B.	1992 - 1995	Education

Mitchell, Hadley L.	1993 -	Economics
Nienhuis, Robert W.	1993 -	Administration
Platte, Jay D.	1992 -	Music
Pletcher, Janice	1992 - 1993	Communication
Powell, Ronald L.	1993 -	Criminal Justice and Criminology
Pratt, Bruce A.	1992 -	Physical Education
Resch, Stephen J.	1992 -	Business
Ringenberg, Roger W.	1992 -	Bible and World Mission
Saddington, James A.	1992 -	History
Schutt, John R.	1992 -	Biology
Silvers, Ruth E.	1992 -	Library
St. Peters, Heather Zenk	1994 -	Correspondence Studies
Stepnoski, Marilyn B.	1993 -	Education
Strahm, Sonja S.	1992 -	Learning Resources
Swan, Kenneth D.	1992 - 1993	Administration
Van Huisen, Michael D.	1992 -	Library
Vermillion, Mark	1993 -	Communication Arts and Public Relations
Weddle, Alice J.	1992 - 1993	Education

APPENDIX C
TAYLOR UNIVERSITY BOARD OF TRUSTEES
1970-1995

Member	Years of Trusteeship
Robert C. Baptista	1975 - 1979
James H. Barnes, Jr.	1971 - 1989
Norman A. Baxter	1978 - 1982
Roger E. Beaverson	1994 -
John L. Bell, Jr.	1976 - 1981
Ella Mae Berdahl	1966 - 1971
LaRita R. Boren	1975 -
R. David Boyer	1979 -
Joseph D. Brain	1985 -
William R. Bright	1973 - 1975
Beverly Jacobus Brightly	1983 -
Theodore F. Brolund	1983 -
Maurice W. Coburn	1963 - 1973
J. Robert Coughenour	1972 - 1983
J. Thomas Crutchfield	1987 - 1993
Thomas A. Dillon	1985 - 1990
G. Harlowe Evans	1951 - 1973
Kenneth Flanigan	1987 -
Gerald Foster	1967 - 1972
Larry R. Fuhrer	1971 - 1973
Marta Gabre-Tsadick	1988 -
J. Paul Gentile	1962 -
Lester C. Gerig	1955 - 1989

Robert C. Gilkison	1976 - 1995
Richard W. Gygi	1991 -
D. L. Haffner	1963 - 1971
Richard W. Halfast	1956 - 1980
E. Earl Hartman	1979 - 1984
Carl W. Hassel	1964 -
Harold L. Herber	1972 - 1973
Edward H. Hermanson	1980 - 1987
John O. Hershey	1975 - 1989
Jerry Horne	1990 -
John R. Horne	1987 -
V. Donald Jacobsen	1975 -
Gerald H. Jones	1966 - 1972
Charles L. Keller	1973 - 1979
G. Roselyn Kerlin	1984 -
Jay L. Kesler	1985 -
Willard L. Ketner	1968 - 1978
Leroy King	1971 - 1981
Gregg O. Lehman	1981 - 1985
John R. Maddox	1968 - 1978
Allen W. Mathis, Jr.	1972 - 1977
John McDougall	1978 - 1989
Carl W. Moellering	1988 -
Grafton Moore	1971 - 1980
Nancy R. Moore	1982 - 1984
Arthur K. Muselman	1987 -
Jane Carson Myre	1973 - 1978
William E. Pannell	1990 -

Robert L. Pieschke	1980 - 1984
Robert J. Piros	1971 - 1976
Walter Randall	1969 - 1987
Milo A. Rediger	1959 - 1960 1965 - 1988
Paul D. Robbins	1992 -
Merle N. Rocke	1963 - 1973
Henry C. Ruegg	1965 - 1979
Richard Russell	1973 -
Milton V. Schubert, Jr.	1962 - 1974
Elmer G. Seagly	1966 - 1971
Charles W. Shilling	1948 - 1951 1957 - 1972
Charles T. Smith	1983 - 1985
Norman A. Sonju	1982 - 1986
Paul A. Steiner	1992 -
Paul B. Stephenson	1972 - 1976
Fred S. Stockinger	1980 -
Carl J. Suedhoff	1964 - 1971
Clarence H. Varns	1953 - 1972
L. Marshall Welch	1967 - 1989
Paul W. Wills	1973 - 1986
Samuel F. Wolgemuth	1970 - 1989
James H. Woods	1988 -
Paul Zurcher	1990 -

APPENDIX D
THE MARKS OF A CHRISTIAN COLLEGE*
WILLIAM C. RINGENBERG

The founding of private colleges in America has been primarily a Christian endeavor. This was true of the creation and early operation of nearly all colleges, private and public, before the Civil War, and in the great majority of private institutions since. Yet only a few remain avowedly Christian today. Most state universities had become secularized by 1900; however, not until this century did the Christian religion lose its dominant intellectual position in the institutions that began as private Protestant colleges.

> *To measure the Christian orientation of colleges accurately and fairly is not easy, but it can be done.*

The secular character of liberal arts colleges has increased steadily since 1900, so that by 1966 the authors of a major study on small, private colleges in America could conclude that "the intellectual presuppositions which actually guide the activities of most church colleges are heavily weighted in the secular direction." (Manning M. Pattillo and Donald M. MacKenzie, *Church-Sponsored Higher Education in the United States*).

Analysts are now using terms like "non-affirming colleges," "Protestant-change colleges," and "post-Protestant colleges" to describe institutions that either have become or are becoming nonreligious. Frequently these institutions have held an historic connection with mainline denominations. By contrast, clearly Christian institutions most often are aligned with conservative Protestant denominations (e.g. Assemblies of God, most Baptists, Brethren, Christian Reformed, Church of God, Churches of Christ, Evangelical Friends, Free Methodist, Lutheran, Mennonite, Nazarene, Wesleyan), or are transdenominational in nature.

While one can distinguish a decidedly Christian college from an obviously secular one, it is difficult to separate it from one that has recently begun to change.

Despite this difficulty, many high school students, their parents, youth counselors, and pastors, want to know how to evaluate the Christian character of the institutions where they might study. Are there signs they can look for? Yes, but

* *This essay originally appeared in the November 2, 1979, issue of <u>Christianity Today</u>. It is reprinted here by permission.*

they must realize that the completely Christian college does not exist. And the practice of institutions where all members are clearly orthodox Christians in their beliefs will still fall short of the Christian ideal. No completely Christian college exists; so also probably no secular college in America totally lacks at least some Christian influence. This may take the form of chapters of Inter-Varsity Christian Fellowship, Campus Crusade for Christ, or denominational foundations. Is it then inappropriate to identify certain institutions as Christian and others as non-Christian? The answer is that we can do this—but so long as we recognize that our judgments cannot be precise with neat unambiguous lines drawn between various institutions.

While one can distinguish a decidedly Christian college from an obviously secular one, it is difficult to separate it from one that has recently begun to change.

What are the marks of the decidedly Christian college?

1. A clear statement of faith and/or Christian purpose in the college catalogue or other publication.

2. A clear faculty-hiring policy that upholds the twin necessities of Christian faith and intellectual ability.

3. A faculty who operate from a vocational sense of mission and who actively seek to integrate the Christian faith with their professional disciplines.

4. A general education requirement in Bible and/or Christian thought.

5. A regular, well-attended, dynamic chapel program.

6. A campus that displays a positive attitude toward the sponsoring church or religious constituency, and an above average spirit of friendliness and general decorum.

7. A program that gives major emphasis to evangelism.

But the college in transition from primarily Christian to primarily secular has its marks, too.

1. The public statements about its Christian nature begin to include equivocal rather than explicit phrases; these statements often describe Christian goals in sociological but not theological terms.

2. The faculty-hiring policy begins to reduce its emphasis on the importance of the scholar being a committed Christian.

3. The importance of the Bible and the Christian religion in the general education curriculum declines.

4. Chapel is a dying institution to which the students do not respond well.

5. The college reduces and then perhaps drops its church affiliation; if it is an independent institution, it identifies less with interdenominational and parachurch organizations.

6. Budget decisions reflect a drop in emphasis on Christian programs.

7. Students and faculty increasingly come to the college in spite of rather than because of the remaining Christian influences, and the deeply committed Christian students begin to feel isolated and lonely.

How can we apply these tests?

Decidedly Christian Statement of Faith. We can tell much about the religious orientation of a college by examining its catalogue. A college with decidedly Christian purposes will usually say so unmistakably. On the other hand, colleges drifting toward secularity often describe themselves as "church-related" because they fear that "Christian" suggests they are narrow or sectarian. Some colleges proclaim a continuing connection with the Christian religion by identifying with its broad social principles as opposed to its specific theological ones. For example, one college notes that it retains a

The marks of a Christian college: Seven checkpoints.

"basic Christian outlook in the values it espouses," and another states that its "focus of...church relatedness is the enhancement of human dignity and purpose in the world." Still other colleges frankly describe their relationship to the Christian faith as historic, but not current.

Hiring policy. On what terms can a college warrant calling itself Christian? Two commitments must characterize the decisive majority ("the critical mass") of its trustee, staff, and faculty decision-makers and instructors. First, they must confess Jesus Christ as Savior and Lord; second, they must be dedicated to the search for an understanding of God and the universe he created. (I would argue that a Christian college should, in fact, restrict its trustee, administrative, and full-time faculty appointments to confessing Christians, though it might reasonably identify itself as a Christian institution if only a clear majority of its personnel are Christian.)

A problem arises here. A surprisingly wide-spread belief holds that the hiring policy of Christian colleges restricts the academic freedom of professors, and makes it impossible to give students the breadth or perspective necessary for a liberal education.

But does this hiring policy limit intellectual freedom? Such a view misunderstands the essential difference between public and private institutions. The Constitution that prohibits public institutions from discriminating against a professor because of his religious views also protects religious institutions from being forced to support—under the name of academic freedom—philosophical views contrary to their religious convictions. It is no more inappropriate for a college to hold a religious test for membership than for a church to do the same. The college, however, must carefully distinguish between an institutional test for membership and one for truth. It must never attempt to create the latter. The college, like a church, must be a voluntary association of those who share similar views on the basic issues of life. There must be no pressure applied for anyone to subscribe to these views initially or to continue to hold them. Each professor must be uninhibited in his continuing search for truth. He must realize, however, that should his search ever lead him to the point where he can no longer hold the views that originally made him a part of the Christian community, then his choice to withdraw from the group intellectually carries with it the moral obligation to withdraw from the college physically.

> *It is no more inappropriate for a college to hold a religious test for membership than for a church to do the same. The college, however, must carefully distinguish it from a test for truth.*

If a Christian college hires only Christian faculty members, is it then able to expose its students to varying opinions on major issues? Those who say no assume Christian faculty are automatically too provincial to see and fairly explain alternate value systems. But surely such a narrow instructor, though he may be a devout Christian, is unsatisfactory as an educator; he is no better than the secular professor who cannot communicate fairly the case for religious interpretations. His college probably should not have hired him in the first place. One of the criteria for a Christian college in hiring a faculty member must be his ability to be open and fair with alternate world views, while at the same time holding deep convictions about the Christian faith.

Integration. The Christian college faculty member is dedicated primarily to fulfilling the call of God in his life and only secondarily to his academic discipline; however, he strives to apply biblical teaching to his specialty. An example of the concept of a faculty member as a divinely called minister appears in the following statement by a college administrator in Michigan:

"[At our college] all of us are considered as ministers for the church,

and we consider ourselves as servants of God—not merely employees."

In the last 10 or 15 years evangelical colleges have emphasized the need to integrate faith and learning. Christian professors have always sought this, but the unique element of the last decade is the conscious, overt effort of many colleges—such as the members of the Christian College Consortium—to inspire their faculty members to work even harder to realize this goal.

The Bible in General Education. It is difficult to imagine that an institution would claim to be a Christian college and yet not have a general education requirement in biblical Christianity. It is not a satisfactory substitute for a college to allow students to meet an "area" requirement by choosing between a Bible course and a wide range of other religious and metaphysical subjects (e.g., "Living Religions of Asia," "Patterns of Religious Experience," and "Religion as Story"). When a curricular pattern suggests that any one theological/philosophical subject is as worthy of investigation as another, a sense of values disappears. Students quickly understand that the college no longer believes the Judeo-Christian is uniquely important in understanding the meaning of the universe.

Campus Worship. The decline of required chapel frequently is one of the more visible symptoms of decay in the Christian orientation of a school. It often follows gradually after the frequent appointment of faculty who are not committed Christians. A college may say it has eliminated chapel because "we don't want to force religion on anyone," as though a chapel requirement is more akin to the medieval state-church system than to the college's other requirements for graduation. What such a college is really saying, however, is, "We don't think Christian worship is very important anymore—certainly not as important as other requirements in, say, English composition or physical education."

In most colleges where chapel is a dying institution, the students complain that the programs lack meaning. The charge is often valid. As colleges place less emphasis on the importance of the Christian religion, it naturally follows that their officials will appropriate a lot fewer resources to assure high quality religious programming. Also as students and faculty members see an institution reducing its commitment to the uniqueness of the Christian religion, they see less reason to continue participating in religious services whose theology is increasingly relativistic.

Required chapel attendance makes sense only when the message proclaimed in the chapel is considered essential and authoritative.

College chapel is the recurring event the greatest number of students are required to attend. Does it not follow, then, that the college must make certain that the quality of chapel is exceeded by no other campus activity?

The Sponsoring Group. A close correlation exists between two factors: the campus attitude toward the sponsoring denomination, and the denomination's degree of theological orthodoxy. For example, college-church relations tend to be much more positive with denominations that have held faithfully to their evangelical origins, as with new evangelical and fundamentalist groups. Colleges related to churches or denominations that have drifted from their heritage are often even more liberal theologically than their denominations, and as the gap between college and church widens, frequently the two reduce and then end their relationship. When this official divorce takes place, often it is merely the culminating step in a secularizing process active for many years.

Evangelism. Both the vocational plans of Christian college students and the evangelistic programs of Christian colleges have changed over the years. However, Christian colleges must not allow these shifting patterns to alter the practice of giving major emphasis to evangelism. A much smaller percentage of Christian college graduates now enter the ministry or go to the mission field than formerly. This is partly because the rapidly growing Bible institute and Bible college movement now prepares so many Christian workers. Also, young people attend Christian colleges for a broader range of purposes than training for professional Christian ministries.

The Christian college, however, must never forget that evangelism is a responsibility of all Christians, regardless of whether they are preparing for "full-time Christian work" or some other profession. One means of stimulating evangelistic interest—revivals—has become less popular on the Christian college campuses in recent years. This is not necessarily bad, however, if the colleges are able to replace them with other equally effective methods.

Central Issue. What then is the ultimate question in determining the extent to which a college is Christian? We must ask how completely do a college's trustees, faculty, and staff believe that the supreme revelation of God to man through Christ is the central act of history, and therefore is the key to ultimate meaning in the universe.

When doubt begins to grow on this primary issue, many of the later stages in the process of secularization follow quite normally. For example, if the Christian religion is merely one of many good systems of thought, and if Jesus is only a good man, then there is no reason to hire only Christian scholars rather than good and knowledgeable men of all persuasions. Nor is there reason to maintain a Bible requirement for all students instead of, say, a course in religion or values in general. Nor does it make sense to commit precious college resources to maintaining a carefully planned program for campus-wide Christian worship.

The character of an institution, then, develops from its theological foundation; that foundation, however, can be eroded. It is a critical task of Christian college leaders to prevent this. Also, it is the responsibility of Christian ministers, youth leaders, and parents to assist these high school young people looking for a Christian college to identify those intellectually anchored to the Rock of Ages.

To measure the Christian orientation of colleges accurately and fairly is not easy, but it can be done. Moreover, it must be done if Christian young people are to have the best possible information in making the critical decision of where to spend what may be the last major developmental period of their lives.

INDEX OF NAMES

330

INDEX OF SUBJECTS

INDEX OF EDUCATIONAL INSTITUTIONS